Adobe
Photoshop CS/CS2
Breakthroughs

Adobe
Photoshop CS/CS2
Breakthroughs

David Blatner
Conrad Chavez

David: For Don and Thirzalyn, who have been so supportive and loving for all these years

Conrad: To Laura and Thierry

ADOBE PHOTOSHOP CS/CS2 BREAKTHROUGHS
David Blatner and Conrad Chavez

Copyright © 2006 by David Blatner and Conrad Chavez

Blatner Books are published in association with
PEACHPIT PRESS
1249 Eighth Street
Berkeley, California 94710
(800) 283-9444
(510) 524-2178
(510) 524-2221 (fax)

Find us on the World Wide Web at: http://www.peachpit.com
Peachpit Press is a division of Pearson Education

Editor: Nancy Davis
Production Editor Extraordinaire: Lisa Brazieal
Indexer: Patti Schiendelman
Cover design: Charlene Charles-Will, David Blatner
Cover photograph courtesy Getty Images
Interior design and production: David Blatner (moo.com) and Conrad Chavez

NOTICE OF RIGHTS
All rights reserved. No part of this book may be reproduced or transmitted in any form by any means, electronic, mechanical, photocopying, recording, or otherwise, without the prior written permission of the publisher. For information on getting permission for reprints and excerpts, contact permissions@peachpit.com.

DISCLAIMER
The information in this book is distributed on an "As Is" basis, without warranty. While every precaution has been taken in the preparation of the book, neither the authors nor Peachpit Press shall have any liability to any person or entity with respect to any loss or damage caused or alleged to be caused directly or indirectly by the instructions contained in this book or by the computer software and hardware products described in it.

TRADEMARKS
Throughout this book trademarked names are used. Rather than put a trademark symbol in every occurrence of a trademarked name, we state we are using the names only in an editorial fashion and to the benefit of the trademark owner with no intention of infringement of the trademark. All trademarks or service marks are the property of their respective owners.

ISBN 0-321-33410-8
9 8 7 6 5 4 3 2 1

Printed and bound in the United States of America

Overview

Contents

Introduction

*H*EY BUDDY, WHAT'S YOUR PROBLEM? No, wait, we're not trying to be obnoxious; we really do want to know what your problem is—well, as long as it involves Adobe Photoshop. After all, that is our job: listening to problems and coming up with breakthrough solutions.

In fact, we've spent much of the past couple of years listening to seminar attendees about their problems, teaching new and advanced users, working with clients, reading online Photoshop forums, and talking with other Photoshop trainers. We discovered that there are certain questions that are asked over and over again—questions about resolution, opening Camera Raw files, adjusting tone and color, saving files to disk. . .

This book is a compendium of those commonly encountered problems, and—more importantly—their solutions! Some solutions are simple, such as pointing out a feature that you might never have known about. Other solutions are complex, requiring multi-step procedures and waving witchbane around your head while standing on one foot.

A few solutions involve problems with Photoshop CS which were fixed in Photoshop CS2, while some are more concerned with new problems that popped up in this most recent version. Most of the solutions in this book are applicable to both CS and CS2.

Of course, with all this talk about problems and solutions, you might get the feeling that we think Photoshop is buggy or causes headaches. No way: We love Photoshop and it is among the most stable, functional pieces of software we own. But we've been around long enough to know that *all* software has bugs—and they usually bite you just before a big deadline. And *every* major application can cause you to reach for the Ibuprofen at the end of a long day.

Photoshop is the best image-editing software we've ever used (and we've used a lot of them), but if you don't encounter any frustrations with it, then you're just not working hard enough.

How to Read This Book

As much as we'd love to fly out to [insert name of your city here] and sit by your side as you work, we just can't right now. That's where this book comes in: Each chapter of this book covers an area we know people have problems with—organizing myriad images, for instance, or keeping color consistent. We don't expect you to read the whole thing cover to cover. Rather, skip around the book, gathering what you need when you need it.

You might strategically leave this book wherever you go when you have a major problem: For David, it's next to the refrigerator. Conrad prefers a nook at his local coffee house.

For More Information

Note that we have no intention of this book covering every feature in Photoshop. Sure, we cover a lot of ground, and we take an in-depth look at some areas that often cause confusion with users. But we expect that you'll use this book in conjunction with other resources on Photoshop. For example, we don't cover how to script Photoshop or create cool effects that look like fire or ice or whatever else you're in the mood to add to your images. Fortunately, there are other resources out there. Here's a few places you can go for more information.

- ■ ***Real World Adobe Photoshop CS2.*** While we are a bit biased (this book was written by David Blatner and our friend Bruce Fraser), this is also the book recommended by members of the Photoshop development team at Adobe.

- ■ ***Adobe Photoshop CS2 Visual QuickStart Guide.*** This big step-by-step instruction book by Elaine Weinmann and Peter Lourekas offers a great introduction to Photoshop. We tend to like this better than the *Adobe Photoshop Classroom in a Book*, though that one is good, too.

- ■ **Adobe Photoshop Web Site.** Most corporate Web sites are filled with marketing materials. You'll find plenty of that at Adobe, but it's alongside excellent useful information, too. It's definitely worth a trip to *www.adobe.com/products/photoshop*. Also, the answers to many of your most puzzling Photoshop questions can often be answered by the knowledgeable and helpful volunteers in the Photoshop User to User Forums at *www.adobe.com/support/forums/main.html*

- **Web sites.** Besides the Adobe Web site, there are literally thousands of Photoshop resources on the Internet. For keeping up to date, check out *www.photoshopnews.com*. For tips and tricks, see *www.photoshoptechniques.com* or just go to Google, type in "photoshop tips," and have your mind blown.

- *Magazines.* There are an ever-growing number of magazines that cover cool Photoshop techniques. Some of our favorites are *DG Magazine* (formerly *Digital Graphics*, from Australia), *PhotoshopUser* (from the NAPP), and *Layers Magazine.*

Acknowledgements

Any undertaking that involves Adobe Photoshop necessarily taps into the rich and deep web that surrounds this amazing program. We wrote the words, but we couldn't have done it without that infrastructure!

Thanks to Peachpit publisher Nancy Ruenzel, who liked the idea of Blatner Books. To our editor, Nancy Davis, for her extraordinary patience and suggestions. And to our production editor Lisa Brazieal for her happy, reassuring voice on the end of the telephone. To Pamela Pfiffner, our champion embedded inside the Peachpit fortress. And to Don Sellers, for his excellent copyediting.

Our sincere appreciation goes to Bruce Fraser, Anne-Marie Concepción, Deke McClelland, Greg Vander Houwen, and participants in the Photoshop User to User Forums.

David: "I am so thankful to my wife, Debbie, and our two boys, Gabriel and Daniel, who have supported me and this project in so many ways. Thanks, too, to my mom and step-dad, who loaned me the money to buy a laser printer back in the 1980s, even though they thought it was a crazy thing for me to do. And a huge round of applause to my co-author Conrad, who was instrumental in making this book a reality."

Conrad: "My thanks go out to my parents, who from the beginning gave me the kind of support that allowed me to learn, and then to teach. Many thanks also to my friends and family and my co-author David, for their encouragement and patience during those intensive final weeks of writing and editing. Finally, thanks to the entire Photoshop community of developers and users who have turned dry lines of code into a spectacular creative universe."

1

Photoshop Essentials

Photoshop Essentials

WHEN YOU FIRST MOVE INTO A NEW HOME, it's easy to find the basics, such as the kitchen and the shower. But you never quite feel at home until you've got all your stuff arranged just the way you like it: the TV in the best corner of the living room for watching movies, the kitchen utensils stored right where you'd reach for them when you cook, and the alarm clock at just the right position on the nightstand for when your arm swings over to crush the snooze button every morning.

Anyone who spends a lot of time in any software program typically starts treating it like a home, positioning windows, customizing controls, and otherwise tweaking its behavior. Each person uses Photoshop in a slightly different way, and combined with the fact that Photoshop is a very deep program, there is value in bringing forward the parts of the program that you most want to use so that the areas where you spend the most time are most easily accessible to you. This chapter is about personalizing Photoshop until you feel quite comfortable moving around in it.

First Things First

Getting To Know You

? **Each time I launch Photoshop I'm overwhelmed by all the palettes and menus. What's the best way to get familiar with what I see on screen?**

☑ Becoming familiar with Photoshop's work area is a wise first step. The entire work area is designed not only to provide you with the tools you need, but also to surround the document window with useful information about the status of the image, the current tool, and Photoshop itself. Because Photoshop is used in many different and specialized ways, it's possible to customize the work area to a great extent. We show you how in "Making Arrangements for Your Palettes," later in this chapter.

Here is an overview of the Photoshop work area (**Figure 1.1**):

- **Menu bar.** As in other programs, the menu bar contains commands you can apply to alter an image or Photoshop's behavior.

- **Options bar.** Located just below the menu bar, the Options bar presents controls for the tool you've selected in the Tools palette.

- **Palettes.** The Tools palette appears along the left edge of the work area, while other palettes appear along the right edge. You can arrange palettes by dragging the tab at the top of a palette, and you can show or hide palettes using the commands under the Window menu. We give you more palette-arranging tips

TIP: Because the controls on the Options bar change when you change tools, the Options bar isn't like those unchanging horizontal toolbars found in other programs. Note that you can always jump to the first editable field of the Options bar (when there is one) by pressing the Return/Enter key. If there is more than one field, you can Tab or Shift-Tab from one to the next.

in "Windows and Palettes," later in this chapter.

- **Document window.** Photoshop makes good use of the space around the document window. Along the top of the window you see the normal title bar. To the left of the title is a preview icon that's dimmed (on the Mac OS) if recent changes aren't saved. To the right of the title are the zoom percentage, the color mode, and the bit depth—plus the preview mode, if View > Proof Colors is turned on (not shown in Figure 1.1).

  Along the bottom edge of the document window, at the left edge, you'll find a numerical field you can use to control the view magnification. To the right of that is a Version Cue indicator icon (it won't do anything if Version Cue is disabled), and to the right of that is a status bar you can customize by clicking the triangle.

Figure 1.1: In the default Photoshop work area, you see the Tools palette on the far left, the menu bar across the top, and the Options bar under the menu bar. At the far right of the Options bar is the palette well, and to the left of the palette well is the Go to Bridge button that switches to Adobe Bridge (or File Browser in Photoshop CS).

Teaching Yourself Photoshop

? Okay, I've bought your book. But other than your sage wisdom, what might I do when I have a question that isn't answered in this particular book?

☑ While there's been much grumbling about the increasing rarity of printed manuals, information about Photoshop is much faster and easier to find online—both on your own computer, and over the Internet.

The online help system contains all of the topics in the printed manual along with additional topics, so you're more likely to find and answer there. Open the help system by choosing Help > Photoshop Help (**Figure 1.2**).

If you need a quick description of a tool or control that you can see in front

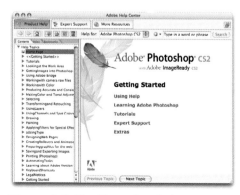

Figure 1.2: The Photoshop help system

of you, a tool tip might help (**Figure 1.3**). If tool tips don't appear when you hover your cursor over a tool or palette, you might need to turn them on; choose Photoshop > Preferences (Mac OS X) or Edit > Preferences (Windows) and turn on Show Tool Tips.

In Photoshop CS2, Adobe uses the bottom of the Info palette to provide a little more information than they could fit in the tool tips (**Figure 1.4**). The Info palette goes beyond simply telling you about the currently selected tool. It reminds you how modifier keys can change the tool's behavior.

In addition to the training resources that come with Photoshop, don't forget about the wealth of educational materials available online. Adobe keeps a vast storehouse of tips and techniques on its Adobe Studio site (*studio.adobe.com*). We also like the Web sites *photoshopnews.com* and *photoshoptechniques.com.* You can discover countless other tips by typing "Photoshop tips" or "Photoshop tutorials" into your favorite online search engine. And, of course, there are always books on the subject, such as this one, David's *Real World Photoshop* (which he co-authored with Bruce Fraser) and others.

Figure 1.3: Tool tips appear in a yellow rectangle

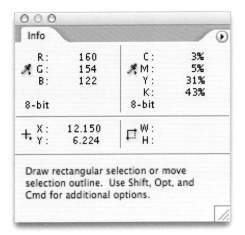 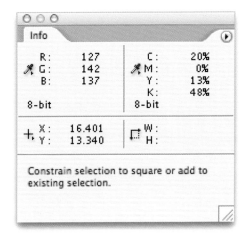

Figure 1.4: The bottom of the Info palette for the Marquee tool with no keys pressed (left) and with Shift key pressed (right)

Upgrading Smoothly

Because Photoshop is upgraded every 18 months or so, you may experience the upgrade process a few times before you've even accumulated five years of experience with the program. But upgrading can lose files and settings that your workflow may depend on. Therefore, we want to include a few topics that help you upgrade Photoshop without throwing your workflow into a tailspin.

Migrating Your Plug-ins

? I upgraded to Photoshop CS2 and none of my non-Adobe plug-ins came along for the ride. Do I have to buy them all over again?

✓ Photoshop plug-ins are installed into the Plug-ins folder inside each Photoshop version's application folder. This means that plug-ins don't automatically appear in a newer version of Photoshop—you have to move them manually. Before you delete your old Photoshop folder, locate each non-Adobe plug-in and drag it to the corresponding folder in the Photoshop CS2 Plug-ins folder (**Figure 1.5**).

If you move a plug-in to a newer version of Photoshop and it isn't compatible,

Photoshop displays an alert (when you launch the program) telling you that the plug-in wasn't loaded. At that point, you know that it's time to get a newer version of that plug-in.

Migrating Actions

? OK, so I've got my plug-ins working in the upgrade. But now I don't see all of my carefully crafted Photoshop actions. What's the answer this time?

✓ Before you upgrade, save your actions from the Actions palette to a file on disk. (This is also a good way to back up your actions at any time.) Here's how:

1. In the Actions palette, click the Create New Set button.

Figure 1.5: The Plug-ins folder inside the Photoshop CS2 folder

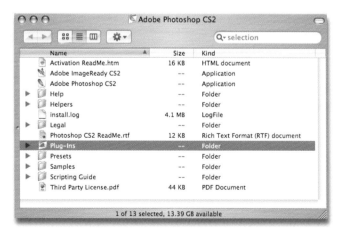

2. Name the folder and click OK. Now you've got a folder where you can store just the actions you create (**Figure 1.6**).

3. If you're storing any custom actions in Photoshop's default actions folder, drag your actions into the folder you created.

4. In the Actions palette menu, choose Save Actions.

5. Specify a name and location, and click Save.

Once your old actions are saved to disk, you can import them into Adobe Photoshop CS2 by choosing Load Actions from the Actions palette menu, locating your saved actions file, and clicking Load.

You'll probably want to test any actions you migrate between versions. Some actions might not work correctly if they depend on commands, palettes, dialog boxes, and file locations that have changed.

TIP: If you have any plug-ins that didn't come with Photoshop, keep them in a folder that's independent of the folders containing the plug-ins that do come with Photoshop. For example, if your name is John, create a folder named John and drag your non-Adobe plug-ins into that folder only. When you upgrade to a new version, just move or copy that whole folder to your new Photoshop's Plug-ins folder. This works because Photoshop finds any plug-in in any subfolder of the Plug-ins folder.

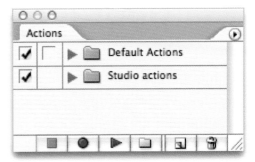

Figure 1.6: A design studio's custom actions kept in their own folder, separately from Photoshop CS2's Default Actions.

Migrating Your Preferences

Can I transfer my Preferences dialog box settings to a new version? The settings I use are quite different than the defaults.

☑ Alas, there's no way to directly transfer your current set of preferences from one version to another, or from one person to another. However, you can make a record of the settings in your Preferences dialog box and enter them into the new version.

Instead of having to write down all of your settings, we like to take a screen capture of each pane and refer to them as we set up our new version of Photoshop. Note that if you put your set of Preferences screen shots into their own folder, you can use File Browser (in CS) or Adobe Bridge (in CS2) to browse to that folder so that you can easily cycle through the screen shots as you adjust each one in the new version of Photoshop (**Figure 1.7**).

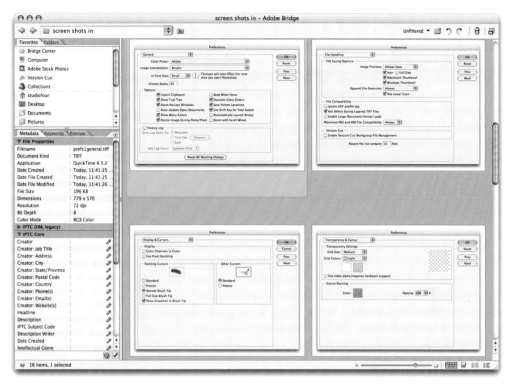

Figure 1.7: Screen shots of Photoshop CS preferences viewed in Adobe Bridge for reference

Migrating Workspaces

? **I've painstakingly arranged Photoshop workspaces. How can I transfer these to a new version of Photoshop?**

☑ Because the number and shape of palettes can change between Photoshop releases, workspaces aren't always carried over to new versions.

You can try to move the old workspace files to the new version. On Mac OS X, workspaces are stored here:

```
Computer/username/Library/
Preferences/Adobe Photoshop CS2
Settings/WorkSpaces
```

In Windows, workspaces are stored here:

```
C:\Program Files\Adobe\Adobe
Photoshop CS2\Presets\Workspaces
```

However, Photoshop is very sensitive to changes in the window environment. Photoshop may reset to the default workspace if there is anything even slightly incompatible about the old workspace, such as if a workspace uses a palette that's changed. If transferring old workspaces doesn't work, you'll need to create new workspaces in Photoshop CS2.

> **TIP:** We hope you've noticed that one of the most important upgrade tips is to keep a backup of your old Photoshop installation until you're sure that you've migrated all of your Photoshop customizations to your new version of Photoshop.

Controls and Menus

Make UI Text More Readable

? My new monitor has such high resolution that it's hard to read text in dialog boxes and palettes. Is there a way to adjust the size of text in those locations?

☑ On large monitors or on monitors set to a very high resolution, the pixels get so small that text in windows and dialog boxes can become hard to read. In Photoshop CS2, you can change the user interface (UI) font size in the Preferences dialog box. Simply open the Preferences dialog box, and in the General pane, choose a size from the UI Font Size popup menu.

Your Keyboard, Your Way

? Is it just me, or does it seem like Adobe is always changing keyboard shortcuts? Why do they do that, and is there any way to stop it? Old habits die hard, and all that.

☑ Well, it's not easy to come up with a single set of keyboard shortcuts that works for everybody. In addition, Photoshop doesn't exist in a vacuum. Over the years, Photoshop has changed shortcuts to be consistent with the other Adobe products that people like to use together; also, the Mac and Windows operating systems have added shortcuts that sometimes clash with Photoshop shortcuts.

Fortunately, Adobe has implemented the right solution: If you can't please each person, let each person do what they want. Photoshop does this by letting you customize keyboard shortcuts (**Figure 1.8**).

1. Choose Edit > Keyboard Shortcuts.

2. Choose a category from the Shortcuts For popup menu.

3. In the commands list, locate the command you want to customize by scrolling and clicking the disclosure triangles as needed.

4. Select the command, and type the shortcut you want to use. Photoshop warns you if the shortcut is already in use or not available for use, so that you can try again.

5. Click Accept.

> **TIP:** Do you often mistakenly press a shortcut that's one key off from the actual shortcut? Photoshop allows more than one shortcut per feature, so you can add your "mistake" shortcut to the same feature. Just click the Add Shortcut button in the Keyboard Shortcuts tab of the Keyboard Shortcuts and Menus dialog box. Now you get what you want whether you press the "right" shortcut or the "wrong" one.

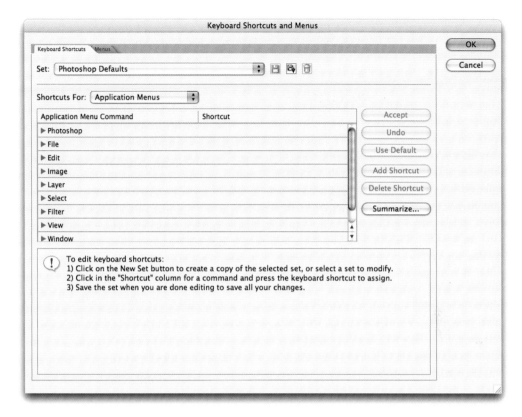

Figure 1.8: The Keyboard Shortcuts tab of the Keyboard Shortcuts and Menus dialog box lets you assign any shortcut to any menu item.

Search for the Missing Shortcut Card

? **I miss the Quick Reference card that used to be included with Photoshop for keyboard shortcuts. How do they expect me to learn the shortcuts now? After all, not all shortcuts appear in the menus.**

☑ It no longer makes much sense to print a card when the shortcuts are so easy to change. What you now have instead is the ability to generate a list of the current shortcut set. In the Keyboard Shortcuts pane of the Keyboard Shortcuts and Menus dialog box, click Summarize. You'll quickly get a reference list in HTML format. You can save the HTML document in any folder and make a convenient bookmark to it in any web browser, or you can print it out if you want to tack it up on the wall with your other shortcut cards. The great advantage of the Summarize button, of course, is that you can always keep your shortcut reference up to date if you change shortcuts.

Roll Your Own Menus

? **Every time I upgrade, the menus in Photoshop get longer and longer. I don't even use half of the commands that**

are available. Can't Adobe make Photoshop modular so that we don't have to see the features we don't use?

✓ There isn't a way to turn features off (unless they're plug-ins), but you shouldn't have to worry about that anyway—while all features are made available at startup, they don't actually load into memory unless you start using them. (That's why it often takes longer to use a feature the first time.)

On the other hand, there is a way to simplify the menus. Starting with Photoshop CS2, Adobe makes it possible for you to hide menu items. You can make Photoshop display only the commands that are useful to you or your workgroup. In addition, you can highlight menu commands with a color. This feature can be useful for emphasizing preferred workflows, or if you want to associate certain commands with each other.

The controls to customize the menus are in a different tab in the same dialog box as the one to customize keyboard shortcuts. To customize menus:

1. Choose Edit > Menus.

2. In the Menus tab of the Keyboard Shortcuts and Menus dialog box, choose a menu set from the Menu For popup menu.

3. Scroll to locate the menu command you want to edit.

4. For the command you're editing, click the Visibility column to hide or show the command, or click the Color column to apply a color to the command.

5. Click the Save icon (the first one to the right of the Set popup menu) to save your changes to the current set.

6. Click the Save New Set icon (second from the left) to create a new set based on the current settings. After you create a new set, you can choose it from the Window > Workspace submenu. Photoshop comes with several custom menu workspaces already installed; to try them, choose one from the Window > Workspace submenu.

Windows and Palettes

Making Arrangements for Your Palettes

❓ I often see other people with interesting palette arrangements, including different ways to attaching palettes to each other. Can you let me in on some of these secrets?

✓ Let us open the book of palette secrets. The three main ideas with palette arrangement are grouping, docking, and workspaces.

When you group palettes, they occupy the same space, so only one of the palettes in a group can be in front at a time. You can group or ungroup palettes by dragging palette tabs to or from other palette tabs.

When you dock palettes, they're attached to each other vertically, so they're all visible at once. You can combine grouping and docking (**Figure 1.9**). To dock a palette, drag its palette tab to the bottom of another palette—you can let go when you see the dark black line appear at the bottom of the palette. Grouped palettes always appear and disappear at the same time. For example, David always docks his Character and Paragraph palettes together.

You can hide or show all palettes at once by pressing the Tab key (as long as the Text tool isn't typing, of course). You can control all palettes from the Window menu, but if you want a palette to be clickable yet still take up no screen space, drag its tab to the palette well, the dark area at the right side of the Options bar (**Figure 1.10**).

Individual palettes have their own tricks. The minimize/zoom button in a palette's title bar alternates between collapsing a palette into its title bar, and showing all of its options. If a palette is touching the bottom of the screen when you collapse it, the palette conveniently collapses at the bottom of the screen.

To save different palette arrangements, choose Window > Workspace > Save Workspace, name it, make sure Palette Locations is checked, and click OK. Workspaces are great for saving different palette arrangements for specific tasks or situations. For example, when Conrad plugs his calibrated monitor into his laptop, he chooses a workspace that fills the laptop monitor with palettes.

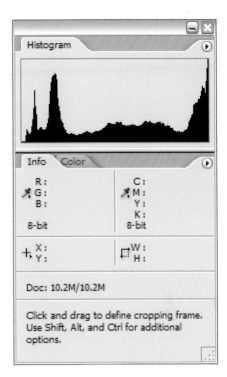

Figure 1.9: Here, the Histogram and Info palettes are docked, and the Info and Color palettes are grouped. Dragging the title bar moves all three palettes.

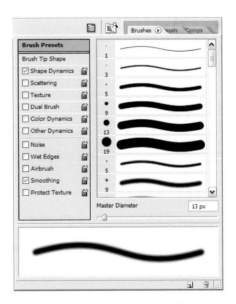

Figure 1.10: Clicking the Brushes palette tab in the palette well reveals the entire palette.

Customize the Status Bar

? I see two numbers at the bottom of my document window, and I've never known what those numbers stand for. How can I find out?

☑ What you're seeing is the status bar. By default, it displays the document size, or rather, sizes. The first number is the size of the document if you flatten it, and the second number is the size of the document as saved (uncompressed) on disk with all of its layers (**Figure 1.11**). If the document doesn't have any layers, the first and second numbers are probably the same.

If you click-and-hold on that information, you can see how the image will print on the current page size. If you Option/Alt-click, you get info about the image size and dimensions.

How can you tell that they're document sizes? Because it says so: Click the black triangle to the right of the status bar to see a popup menu of the different kinds of information you can display in the status bar. You can choose a different status bar display from the popup menu, such as the document dimensions or the document's color profile.

Navigate the Seas of Photoshop

? Dragging the scroll bars all day long sure makes my arms tired. Are there better ways to move around a document?

☑ You're going to get tired of us saying this, but it's always good to hear: Photoshop provides many ways to accomplish the same thing. You can get around quite well in a document without any scroll bars at all. You can:

- Use the Navigator palette to zoom and scroll around a document window.

- Use the Hand tool to push the document around in its window.

- Press Page Up and Page Down to scroll vertically. To scroll horizontally, add the Command/Ctrl key. These shortcuts are like clicking the scroll bars. To scroll in smaller increments, add the Shift key; it's like clicking the scroll bar arrows.

- Press Home to scroll to the top left corner of a document, or press End to scroll to the bottom right corner of a document.

Figure 1.11: The status bar at the bottom of a document window can display different kinds of document information, such as the disk usage information shown at right.

Organize Multiple Windows

? **Are there some quick ways to organize multiple windows on screen? When I work with many images at a time for my publication, the document windows get out of control pretty quickly.**

☑ Why, you can practically turn yourself into a window-managing drill sergeant with the options that Photoshop provides.

- To offset windows across the screen while keeping them large, choose Window > Arrange > Cascade (**Figure 1.12**).

- To see all open document windows evenly spaced across the screen, choose Window > Arrange > Tile Horizontally or Tile Vertically.

- To cycle through each window, press Ctrl-Tab (or Shift-Ctrl-Tab to cycle backward; yes, that's the Control key, even on the Macintosh). This is useful for flipping through a stack of large windows, particularly when your windows are in Full Screen mode.

TIP: You probably already know that palette edges snap to each other. But you can also snap a palette to the nearest edge of the screen by Shift-dragging a palette's title bar.

- On Mac OS X, press F10 to use the Exposé window-selection feature on the current application's windows only (in this case, Photoshop). You can't edit documents in this mode, so it's useful mostly for comparing documents.

- To close all open image windows, press Option (Mac OS) or Shift (Windows) while clicking any image window's close button. If any open images have unsaved changes, you'll be asked whether you want to save them before closing the document.

Figure 1.12: Multiple document windows cascaded (left) and tiled (above).

Preserve Windows when Zooming

? I arranged my document windows on the screen just the way I like them, but when I use the keyboard shortcut to zoom in or out, the size of a window changes, and I have to arrange the windows again. This is driving me nuts… please, make it stop!

✓ Don't worry, there is a way out of this. By default, Photoshop resizes the image window when you zoom a window using the keyboard shortcuts, such as Command-+ (plus sign) (Mac OS) or Ctrl-+ (Windows) (**Figure 1.13**). This can sometimes be inconvenient, such as when you have a carefully tiled window arrangement that you want to preserve.

You can prevent Photoshop from resizing windows when keyboard zooming, and you can set which behavior is the default. Choose Preferences > General (Mac OS) or Edit > Preferences > General (Windows), deselect Zoom Resizes Windows, and click OK.

TIP: There's no built-in shortcut for closing all open documents without saving changes. However, you can use the Actions palette to create an action that closes a document without saving, and then run that as a batch action on all open documents. Of course, you have to be sure you want to discard all changes—that's why there's no built-in shortcut for this inherently risky operation.

To reverse the default window resizing behavior, add the Option (Mac OS) or Alt (Windows) key. For example, if you set the Zoom Resizes Windows default to be on but you'd like to override it this one time, press Command-Option-+ (plus key) instead of Command-+.

The Big Screen Experience

? Is there a way to fill the screen with an image, similar to when you view a slide show?

✓ Photoshop provides two full screen modes—with or without the menu bar. Either way, you'll hide all of the window trimmings and have an unobstructed view of the current document. To change the screen mode, click one of the three screen mode icons on the toolbox. To cycle through the three screen modes when the toolbox is hidden, press F repeatedly.

Of course, you do lose some features in full screen view. For example, you don't have scroll bars, the title bar, or the status bar, or even the menu bar if you hid that. However, there are plenty of ways to be productive and flexible in full screen mode:

- To hide and show the menu bar, press Shift-F.

- To hide and show all palettes, use the Tab key.

- If you're addicted to the status bar, you can display the same information in the Info palette (choose Palette Options from the palette's menu) and leave the palette open.

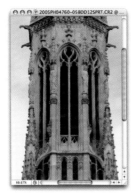

Figure 1.13: Original (left), zoomed in without window resizing (middle), and zoomed in with window resizing (right).

- You can still switch tools and open palettes using keyboard shortcuts. Remember, you can customize Photoshop's keyboard shortcuts!

- To zoom and scroll, use the Navigator palette. If you prefer to hide the Navigator palette, use keyboard shortcuts or a mouse wheel to zoom and scroll. See the topic "Navigating the Seas of Photoshop," earlier in this chapter.

- If you move the document window to another monitor before entering full screen mode, the document displays in full screen mode on that monitor without affecting other monitors.

Change the Window Background Color

? When an image is zoomed out to a size smaller than the window, there's a gray background behind the image. Is there a way to change that window background color? I would prefer to work against a black background, not the default gray one.

✓ Yes, there is a way. First, set the foreground color using the toolbox, the Swatches palette, or the Color palette. In your case, set the foreground color to black. In a document window, zoom out until you can see the background area outside of an image. Then select the Paint Bucket tool, and Shift-click the window background. Voilà, now black is the new gray!

TIP: Full screen mode is a great way to make the most of a laptop monitor or a relatively small desktop monitor. It's also a great way to present an image to a client when you happen to have it open in Photoshop.

One Document, Two Views

? Can I see two views of the same document? What I'd like to do is see the same document at two zoom levels—a close-up of the area I'm editing in the document, and a big-picture view I can keep an eye on.

☑ We've got the perfect solution: the New Window command. With your document open, choose Window > Arrange > New Window For <document name>. You can certainly set one window to a different zoom level than the other window (**Figure 1.14**). But you can also use the New Window command for other useful purposes, such as having one window show the normal view, and another window that previews the same document as a CMYK or sRGB soft-proof.

You don't even have to limit yourself to two views. You can open as many new windows as you want, and set each of them to different view settings.

Synchronize Multiple Windows

? I'm having fun with the multiple view feature, but when I move around in one window, I have to go to the other window and change its view too. Can I avoid this tedious shuffling between windows?

☑ You're in luck—there's an easy answer. First, activate the window that you want the other windows to match. Then choose one of the following commands from the Window > Arrange submenu: Match Zoom, Match Location, or Match Zoom and Location.

The commands are pretty self-explanatory. Match Zoom sets all other windows to the same zoom level, and Match Location sets them all to the same scroll position (of course, Match Location is most predictable if the windows are the same size).

Match Zoom and Match Location commands affect all open windows, whether they're views of the same document or different documents. When you use these commands, you might want to make sure that the only windows you have open are windows that you want to be affected by these commands.

> **TIP:** For a clean preview of your document, you can instantly hide all non-printing objects like the grid, guides, annotations, current selections, and slices. Just press Command/Ctrl-H, which is the keyboard shortcut for enabling or disabling the View > Extras command.

> **TIP:** Photoshop has a nasty habit of resetting palettes to their default locations every time you connect or disconnect monitors, or change monitor settings. Once you have a palette arrangement you like, be sure to save the arrangement as a workspace (see the topic "Making Arrangements for Your Palettes," earlier in this chapter). This is especially important on a laptop, where you may be connecting and disconnecting monitors often.

Figure 1.14: Two windows on the same document. In each window's title bar and status bar, you can see that each window is set to a different zoom percentage.

When Print Size... Isn't

? Here's something that's been bugging me for years: If I choose **View > Print Size**, and hold a print of that same document up to the screen, it isn't the same size! Not only that, but the on-screen ruler doesn't match up to a real ruler. What exactly does Print Size mean, then, and can I make it work right?

☑ This is a tricky answer, but stick with us. To display an image at its real-world size, an application must know both the resolution and the physical size of the monitor it's displaying on. While it isn't too hard to obtain the monitor dimensions in pixels, it's usu-

ally impossible to automatically detect the size of the screen in inches. However, there is a manual way.

First, find out the pixel dimensions of your monitor. On Mac OS X, this information is in the Display tab of the Displays system preference. On Windows, right-click the desktop, choose Properties from the popup menu, and

> **TIP:** A scroll wheel mouse is extremely useful in Photoshop. Obviously you can spin the scroll wheel to pan a window vertically, but such a mouse can do other tricks. too. To pan horizontally, press Command/Ctrl as you spin the mouse wheel. To zoom in and out, Option/Alt-scroll. To scroll or zoom in larger increments, press Shift as you spin the mouse wheel.

click the Settings tab. For example, Conrad's laptop screen is at its native setting of 1280 × 854 pixels.

Next, get the physical dimensions of your monitor's display area. Conrad's laptop screen is $12^{11}/_{16}$ inches (12.6875 inches) wide. Now divide the width in pixels by the width in inches, and you'll get the actual resolution of the screen in pixels per inch. Conrad's monitor works out to about 100 pixels per inch.

Now open up the Photoshop Preferences dialog box and switch to the Units & Rulers pane. For Screen Resolution, enter the resolution that you worked out in the previous paragraph.

To verify that you've got it right, turn on the rulers (View > Rulers) and hold an actual ruler up to the screen. One inch on screen should now match one inch on your real-world ruler. And the next time you choose View > Print Size, the image should display at an accurate size.

Monitors

Fun with Multiple Monitors

? **I've heard of people using multiple monitors with Photoshop. What makes multiple monitors so useful? I usually only look at one image at a time.**

☑ In an application like Photoshop, you're usually not just looking at an image. You also need space for palettes and dialog boxes. Multiple monitors are useful whenever more screen real estate would come in handy. Here are some ways to use multiple monitors:

- Keep your palettes on a less expensive monitor, so you can dedicate your best calibrated and profiled monitor to image display. A monitor used only for palettes doesn't have to be of high quality.

- Spread out palettes that you want to have visible all the time. For example, if you often use the History and Actions palettes, drag them apart. It'll take a lot of space, but that's what the second monitor is for.

- Keep Photoshop on one monitor and other applications on another monitor. For example, on your second monitor you can keep Adobe Bridge nearby for easy image access, or watch for incoming messages in your e-mail application.

- When a dialog box opens, drag it to the monitor that doesn't contain the image, so you can see the entire image.

- Take advantage of multiple-window views. If you choose Window > Arrange > New Window, you get a second window on the same image. For example, one window can show the entire image while another window shows a zoomed-in detail of the same image.

Match Color Across Monitors

? I connected a second monitor, but when I look at the same image on both monitors simultaneously, they don't look the same. How can I fix this?

☑ To match image tone and color across multiple monitors, you pretty much have to use a hardware monitor calibrator (such as the Gretag Macbeth Eye-One device) to create a monitor profile for each monitor. However, even calibrated monitors may not match completely if their basic characteristics are different, such as comparing the same image on a CRT monitor and an LCD monitor.

Note that doing this is usually easier to do on the Macintosh than on Windows. On Windows, you may need to do a little research before attempting to calibrated multiple monitors connected to the same video card. Many video cards that have multiple video ports are unable to assign specific profiles to each connected monitor under Windows. If you have a video card with this limitation, you'll have to use one monitor for accurate color and another just for palettes. Just calibrate the monitor that you're using for good color, and don't worry about accurate color on your palette monitor. Just be aware that you don't want to preview image colors on the palette monitor.

Tools

Reveal the Multiple Personalities of a Tool

? I'm really getting into using the keyboard so I don't have to mouse around so much. But I'd like to find a way to select the tools that are in the popup menus in the toolbox. Any shortcuts for that?

☑ The key to achieving your goal is the Shift key. First, make sure you're familiar with the single-letter keyboard shortcuts for your favorite tools, such as M for the Marquee tool or V for the Move tool.

Next, open the Preferences dialog box, switch to the General pane, and enable the Use Shift Key for Tool Switch checkbox. After you click OK, you'll be able to use the Shift key to cycle through the tools in each of the popup tool menus. For example, press J to switch to the Spot Healing Brush tool, and press Shift-J to cycle through the other tools in the same popup menu (the Healing Brush, Patch, and Red Eye tools).

If you don't select the Shift key preference mentioned above, you can cycle through tools without adding the Shift key. For example, to cycle through the marquee tools, you would simply press M repeatedly. However, we prefer to use the Shift key to cycle, because it's a safer way to work, especially if you like to hide the toolbox. If the Shift key preference is on, you always know that pressing a tool's shortcut selects the last-used variation of that tool. If Shift-switching is off and you can't see the toolbox, you might not realize that pressing the tool shortcut key switched you to a tool you weren't expecting.

Keep Your Options Open

? **I once saw an option that lets me scroll all windows simultaneously. I want to do this when I'm comparing different views of the same document. I looked in Window > Arrange submenu, but the Match commands there aren't real-time.**

☑ An often overlooked area of available options is the Options bar. In your example, select the Hand tool and you'll see that this is where the Scroll All Windows option appears (**Figure 1.15**). (The Options bar for the Zoom tool contains a similar Zoom All Windows option.)

Even more experienced users can miss the Options bar, because it only appears when a tool is actually selected in the toolbar. For example, if you're in the habit of pressing the spacebar to use the Hand tool, as many advanced users

do, you might not select the Hand tool in the toolbox very often. As a result, you might not see the other options that are available for the Hand tool.

Give Tools a Memory

? **I have a few crop sizes that I always use, but I'm getting tired of entering each set of dimensions over and over again. Is there a way to save the settings?**

☑ If you haven't yet clicked the button at the left end of the Options bar, now would be a good time. That button manages tool presets, which are saved settings for the current tool. When you have tool settings that you want to save, click the tool presets button and then click the Create New Tool Preset button. Name the preset and click OK, and from now on you can use that preset by clicking the Tool Preset button and selecting your preset from the list.

Adobe must really want you to use tool presets, because the Options bar isn't the only way to use them. You can more easily manage tool presets by using the Tool Presets palette (**Figure 1.16**), especially when the Options bar isn't visible. If you disable the Current Tool Only checkbox, tool presets for all tools are listed. Then, clicking a preset in the Tool Presets palette both switches tools and selects a preset in one step.

Figure 1.15: Even though the Options bar is usually at the top of the screen, most people don't look closely at the cool tool options and buttons it contains.

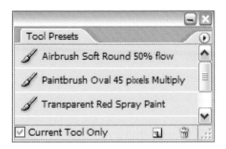

Figure 1.16: The Tool Presets palette is a central location for applying and managing tool presets.

A More Precise Cursor

? When I do detailed retouching, the tool icons seem a bit clumsy and imprecise. Is there a way to make the cursor show the size of the brush I'm using?

✔️ You've got lots of options here. Open the Preferences dialog box, and then open the Display & Cursors pane. In the middle of the dialog box, you'll see a number of cursor options.

Photoshop ships with the cursors set to the Standard option you see in the Display & Cursors pane. You can set any cursor to Precise, which displays a little crosshair so that you can tell exactly where you're clicking.

For painting cursors, which have a brush size, you can choose the Normal Brush Tip or Full Size Brush Tip. The Full Size Brush Tip is a little more intuitive; it's the outer edge of the brush size you're using. Normal Brush Tip is a little trickier—the circle it draws is where the brush opacity is at 50%, based on how much feathering you've applied. Knowing where 50% falls can be handy because it is a common threshold value for things like magic wand selections.

You can see both the precise click point and the brush size if you enable the Show Crosshair in Brush Tip option.

> **TIP:** For a temporary crosshair cursor, press the Caps Lock key. (And a caveat: If your cursor seems to be stuck on a crosshair and editing preferences has no effect, make sure Caps Lock is turned off!)

Editing Objects

Adjust Numbers Easily

? I've seen people use shortcuts for nudging numbers in palettes and dialog boxes. How exactly does that work?

✔️ There are several handy shortcuts you can use when you just want to tweak a number up or down a little. These shortcuts work in number fields in both palettes and dialog boxes.

- Press the up arrow or down arrow key to increase or decrease a value by 1 increment. The increment varies depending on the option.

- Press Shift-Up Arrow key or Shift-Down Arrow key to increase an increment by ten times the normal arrow key increment.

- Position the cursor over a numeric field and Command/Ctrl-drag left to increase a value, or right to increase a value (**Figure 1.17**). You can add the Shift key here too, if you want to change the numbers more quickly.

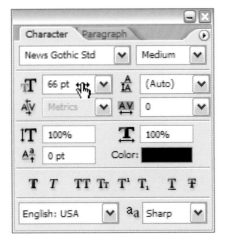

Figure 1.17: Adjusting font size by Command/Ctrl-dragging horizontally in the font size field.

Take the Fast Lane through Dialog Boxes

In other programs, I've used the keyboard to move around in dialog boxes. Can I do the same thing in Photoshop?

You can do more than you possibly imagined. In Photoshop, there are several cool shortcuts that can make dialog boxes much more pleasant to use:

- As in palettes and many other applications, you can press Tab and Shift-Tab to highlight the next and previous text or number fields.

- In many dialog boxes, such as Curves, Levels, and filter dialog

boxes, you can actually zoom and pan the window with keyboard shortcuts while the dialog box is still open. For example, you can press the spacebar to use the Hand tool, and you can press the Zoom tool shortcuts to zoom in and out.

- Instead of clicking OK to close the dialog box and apply changes, you can press Return or Enter. Instead of clicking Cancel, you can press Esc. Instead of clicking Don't Save, you can press the D key.

Context Menus are Your Friend

I am a long-time Mac user and am used to the single mouse button. What's so special about having a right mouse button bring up a context menu, when I can do the same thing from menu bar commands and keyboard shortcuts?

The beauty of context menus is that you don't have to remember where a command is on a menu, and you don't have to remember the command's keyboard shortcut either. As the feature's name suggests, context menus show you commands that relate directly to whatever you clicked, automatically excluding a whole lot of commands that don't apply to what you're trying to do.

Context menus can be so useful that many Mac power users like them too. You don't need a two-button mouse to enjoy context menus. On the Mac, Control-click to see an object's context menu. If you use a graphics stylus or other non-mouse pointing device on Mac OS X or Windows, you can usually program one of its buttons to bring up context menus.

Handling Documents

Open Multiple Documents at Once

? Is there a good way to open many images at the same time? It would help me when I have to process large numbers of images from my camera or scanner.

☑ There are actually several ways to open multiple documents in Photoshop.

From a Mac Finder or Windows desktop folder window, select the files and drag them to the Photoshop icon in the Dock (Mac OS) or to the Photoshop application window (Windows).

In Adobe Bridge, you can select multiple files and choose File > Open or just press Return or Enter. Dragging and dropping to Photoshop works too. If the images open in a program other than Photoshop, from Bridge choose File > Open With > Adobe Photoshop CS2.

Or, in Photoshop, choose File > Open, locate a folder containing multiple files you want to open, and select them. As on the desktop, you can use the Shift key to select a continuous range, and

you can use the Command (Mac OS) or Ctrl (Windows) to select a discontinuous range.

Reducing File Size

? I have a file that takes up way too much disk space. How can I make it smaller?

☑ How you make it smaller depends on what it's for. If you're making a copy for the Web or e-mail, choose File > Save for Web and use the optimization controls there to lower the file size.

If you're trying to reduce the size of a file that you want to archive or use on press, you need to be more careful in order to preserve high resolution and quality. Here are a few ideas:

- If you no longer need to use layers, choose Layer > Flatten Image. If you don't want to flatten, look for unneeded layers you can delete.

- If you've been working in 16-bit mode but you no longer need to, choose Image > Mode > 8 Bits/ Channel.

- If the image dimensions are currently larger than the largest size at which you anticipate using the graphic, you can choose Image > Image Size, turn on the checkbox labeled Resample Image, and reduce the image dimensions.

All of those methods are irreversible once you save and close the document, so be sure you want to do them.

TIP: On Mac OS X, Command-click the filename in the title bar of the document window to see the file's path on disk. On Windows, if a document window is not minimized, hold the cursor over the title bar and the path appears in a tool tip.

Renaming Many Files at Once

? **I don't like the way my digital camera names photos. Does Photoshop provide a way to rename many files at once?**

✓ In CS2, you can easily take care of this using the Adobe Bridge application, which includes a powerful batch renaming feature.

1. In Adobe Bridge, select the images you want to rename. If no images in the current folder are selected, they'll all get renamed, so be sure to move or delete images you don't want to rename.

2. Arrange images in the order you want to number them during renaming. You can drag images

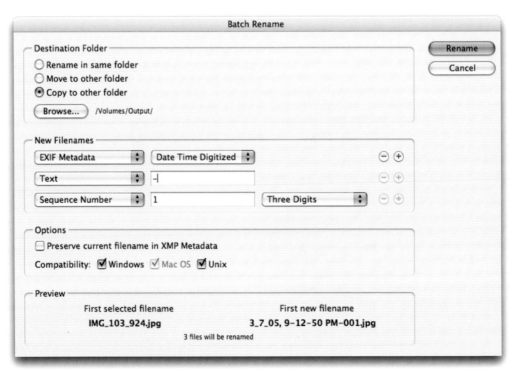

Figure 1.18: The Batch Rename dialog box

into the order you want, or you can choose View > Sort and choose a sort order.

3. Choose Tools > Batch Rename. In the Batch Rename dialog box (**Figure 1.18**), select a Destination Folder. It's always safest to use the Copy to Other Folder option so that your originals are intact in case you make a mistake.

4. In the New Filenames section, set up options for renaming. To build a name out of the naming option such as date, sequence number, or metadata, click a plus button. The Preview section shows you what you'll get.

5. In the Options section, change the options if needed, and click Rename.

TIP: On Mac OS X, you can drag the title bar icon of a document as if it was the file icon in the Finder (but only after saving the document). For example, dragging the title bar icon to a Finder folder window moves the document to that folder.

TIP: Here's a quick way to manually reset Photoshop preferences to their default settings. Immediately after you start up Photoshop, hold down the Shift, Option, and Command keys on Mac OS X, or Shift, Alt and Ctrl keys on Windows. An alert appears, asking you if you want to delete the Adobe Photoshop Settings file. Click Yes to throw out the existing Preferences file and continue with default preferences.

Backing Up Your Preferences File

? A little while back, Photoshop was acting strangely, and the next time I started Photoshop, my preferences were somehow reset to their default settings, so I had to enter all my customized preference settings again. Is there a way to restore preference settings?

✓ It is a fact of life that the preference file of any application can become corrupted at any moment. If that happens, Photoshop may revert back to its default preferences. Photoshop has no mechanism for backing up its preferences file, but it's a good idea to do it yourself. Once you've got the Photoshop preferences just the way you like them, make a copy of the preferences file wherever you keep backup copies of other valuable documents. The file you're looking for is called Adobe Photoshop CS Prefs.psp or Adobe Photoshop CS2 Prefs.psp. It's located in Mac OS X at:

```
Computer/Users/[username]/Library/
Preferences/Adobe Photoshop CS2
Settings
```

In Windows, it's located at:

```
C:\[username]\Application Data\
Adobe\Photoshop\9.0\Adobe Photoshop CS2
Settings
```

If you ever find that your Photoshop preferences are reset, you can easily copy your backup preferences file into the Settings folder and continue on your merry way.

Observe and Control Memory Usage

? Photoshop seems a little sluggish. How can I tell if I need to install more memory in my computer?

✓ At the bottom of a Photoshop document window, click the black triangle to the right of the status bar, and choose Efficiency (or Show > Efficiency if Version Cue is installed). If Efficiency falls below 100%, you may want to install more RAM in your computer.

You can also switch the status bar to display Scratch Sizes. The number on the left tells you how much RAM your open documents are using; it goes up and down depending on what's open and how much work you're doing. The number on the left tells you how much unused RAM you have available. If the number on the left becomes more than the number on the right, Photoshop starts using disk space to store temporary working files. If you find that your hard disk space is running low when you use Photoshop, connect another hard disk and assign it as a scratch disk in the Plug-Ins and Scratch Disks pane of the Preferences dialog box.

If you don't run many other programs at the same time as Photoshop, you can try increasing the percentage of RAM that you allow Photoshop to use. Open the Memory & Image Cache pane in the Preferences dialog box (**Figure 1.19**) and increase the Maximum Used by Photoshop value. It's usually a good idea to set a value no higher than 75% unless you have several gigabytes of RAM installed, because you must leave a few hundred megabytes for the system to use. If you plan to use Photoshop alongside other programs, such as those in the Adobe Creative Suite, you may want to lower Photoshop memory usage to leave RAM for those other programs.

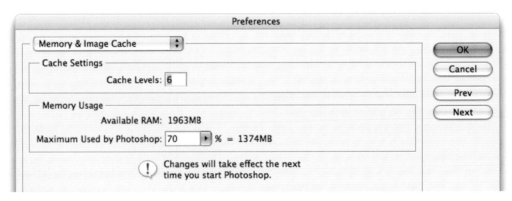

Figure 1.19: The Memory & Image Cache pane in the Preferences dialog box for Photoshop

2

Getting the Picture

Getting the Picture

*T*HE UNIVERSE OF PHOTOSHOP USERS IS BOTH wide and deep; people use Photoshop for everything from purely creative works to precise scientific imaging and processing. It naturally follows that there are many ways for an image to find its way into Photoshop. For years, many Photoshop images would start out as files from a scanner, but now many images arrive directly from a digital camera. Many fine artists and graphic designers start by "painting" on the proverbial blank canvas.

However, digital cameras have become so ubiquitous and scanners have become so cheap that it's easy to find yourself with hundreds of new digital photos each day. Opening each image at a time is not always practical, so the trick is to see how efficiently you can process massive numbers of images— preparing them for a Web site or a printer. We wrote most of this chapter to help you become as efficient as possible, using not only Photoshop but the cool (and super powerful) "Cracker Jack" toys you also received in the box along with Photoshop CS2: Adobe Bridge and Camera Raw.

Creating and Opening Files

New Document Secrets

? I've noticed that when I choose New from the File menu, the document size numbers sometimes change. Not only that, but sometimes the numbers mysteriously become exactly what I need. What's going on and how can I control this?

✓ The New dialog box has a few tricks up its sleeve. When you choose File > New, Photoshop automatically guesses the specifications for the document. By default, the New dialog box displays the specifications from the most recent document you created.

If there's an image on the Clipboard, the New dialog box uses the specifications of that image (**Figure 2.1**). Accordingly, the Preset popup menu is set to Clipboard in this case.

You can also copy document settings from any document currently open in Photoshop. Just choose the document's name from the Windows menu on the menu bar (it's not in the New dialog box). This is one of those times when you can use the menu bar even though a dialog box is open.

Making Your Own Document Presets

? In my job, we create graphics for a few standard sizes. Is there a way to make Photoshop templates so that I don't have to keep checking all of my document specs every time I create a new document?

✓ If you often use certain new document settings that aren't already in the Preset popup menu in the New dialog box, the next time you enter those settings, click the Save Preset button to name and save your own preset.

Opening Digital Camera Photos

? What's the best and fastest way to bring digital camera photos into Photoshop? Some people tell me that I should use the included cable, while others tell me I need to buy a separate reader even though I already have a cable.

✓ You typically get a cable free with the camera, so it's an obvious, easy way to get pictures from your cam-

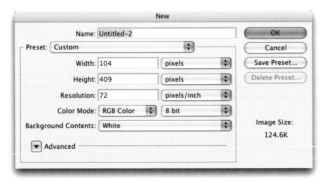

Figure 2.1: Set up new documents in the New dialog box. Here, Photoshop takes the default image specifications from the image on the clipboard.

era to Photoshop. However, it may not be the best way, for the following reasons:

- If you're shooting an event, you can't take any pictures while you're transferring photos.

- You spend precious battery energy for file transfer, leaving less energy for taking pictures, unless you plug an AC adapter into the camera during the transfer.

- Many cameras still transfer photos using USB 1.1 or the Full Speed version of USB 2.0, both of which are very slow. Hi-Speed USB 2.0 and FireWire are much faster.

- If a transmission glitch occurs, the glitch may ruin photos on your camera's memory card. It does happen.

What's the alternative? Instead of using a cable, use a card reader connected to your computer. Remove the card from your camera and insert it in the reader; you can then put another card into your camera and keep taking pictures during the transfer. A card reader is powered by your computer, so you don't drain your

TIP: Never edit digital camera photos directly off the camera or the card. This practice is unreliable and also very slow compared to a hard disk. First copy the images to a folder on your computer's hard disk, and then edit them. Professional photographers often make at least one backup copy of the untouched originals on CD or DVD before editing, in case something goes horribly wrong during editing or a batch process.

camera battery. FireWire and Hi-Speed USB 2.0 card readers are the fastest.

Also, consider using Adobe Bridge to preview, annotate, and open one or more images in Photoshop. If you are using raw camera files, in Adobe Bridge you can also choose File > Open in Camera Raw to make adjustments without having to open or tie up Photoshop.

Opening Images That Don't Want to Open

? Sometimes I double-click an image that's a file type Photoshop should be able to open, but instead the system tells me that it can't be opened, or a different program opens it. How can I fix this?

✓ Don't give up. A file can sometimes "forget" which application it belongs to as it's transferred over networks or across platforms. However, Photoshop can often look deeper into an image than the operating system can. Instead of double-clicking the image file, try opening it from Photoshop by choosing File > Open (or File > Open As in Windows) and selecting the file. You can also try dragging the file to the Photoshop program icon or to the Photoshop application window (Windows).

Also, check to see if the file has an extension at the end of the filename, such as .TIF or .JPG. Sometimes that's all the system needs to hook up the format with the default application that opens it. On the Mac OS, you can also select the file in the Finder and choose File > Get Info to set which application it belongs to. In Windows, open the Properties dialog box and click the Change button.

Become a Screen Shot Gunslinger

? In my job, I have to process a lot of screen shots. How can I streamline the process of cleaning them up?

✓ After you take your screen shots using your operating system shortcuts or a screen shot program, try these suggestions:

- If the screen shot is saved to the desktop (as on Mac OS X by default), drag it to Photoshop to open it. If you simply double-click the file, it will likely open in a program other than Photoshop.

- If the screen shot is on the clipboard (as in Windows, by default), choosing File > New in Photoshop enters the clipboard contents as the dimensions of the new document you're about to create. After the new document appears, all you need to do is paste.

- If you need to remove empty blank space around the screen shot (**Figure 2.2**), the easiest way is to choose Image > Trim. If the upper left pixel is the color of the area you want to remove, you can usually accept the default settings in the Trim dialog box and click OK.

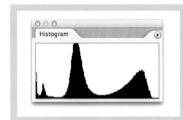 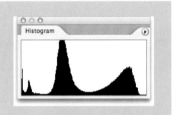

Figure 2.2: The Trim command can remove extra space (left) without cutting off a drop shadow (right).

Exploring Camera Raw

The Deeper Meaning of Camera Raw

? What is the point of Camera Raw? The files are bigger, they take longer to save, and are more complicated to process. My camera takes great pictures, and when I take them off the camera they're ready to roll. So why shouldn't I just use the JPEG format, which seems more convenient all around?

✓ Many people believe that the JPEG image that comes out of a camera is exactly what the camera saw. In fact, the raw sensor data needs a great deal of processing which digital cameras perform as you take the shot. A camera converts the raw data—which isn't even really RGB yet—into tones and colors, and applies other enhancements like sharpening. All of this processing affects the final JPEG image.

The problem with JPEG is the camera typically has a 12-bit sensor producing pure, uncompressed data, while JPEG is only an 8-bit format which is highly compressed to save space. This means the camera already throws out a lot of information before the image even reaches your camera's memory card. In addition, JPEG compression allows quality to degrade as you apply successive edits. However, if your camera can save its raw sensor data and if the camera's format is supported by Adobe Camera Raw, you can alter the judgments that would normally be applied by the camera, and you'll end up with higher-quality data.

If you want the most control in order to achieve the best quality, editing raw camera data is the best workflow in digital photography. If speed, convenience, and file size are more important to you, you may be happier shooting JPEG.

A useful analogy to editing raw camera data is developing your own film and prints in a darkroom. You can get exactly the quality you want because you have control over every step, but the process can be too daunting for casual users. Happily, learning Adobe Camera Raw is much faster and easier than learning how to use a darkroom!

When an Image Isn't in the Camera Raw Club

? I select images in Bridge and try to open them in Camera Raw, but instead they open directly into Photoshop. Also, the Open in Camera Raw command isn't available for these images. How can I edit these images in Camera Raw?

✅ The big question here is, are those images actually camera raw files? In Bridge, check the Document Kind field in the File Properties section of the Metadata tab. If it doesn't say Camera Raw, it won't open in Camera Raw.

Camera Raw only opens camera raw files. Image files in formats like TIFF, JPEG, and Photoshop must be opened in Photoshop itself. Only digital cameras can save camera raw files; you can't save or convert existing files to Camera Raw format. This is because a camera raw file is a record of a specific camera sensor.

If you're absolutely sure you're trying to open an actual camera raw file and this is the first time you've tried to do this, it's possible that your camera is not yet supported by Adobe Camera Raw. As of this writing, every camera's raw data is stored in a way that's unique to that camera, so every time a new camera comes out, Adobe must adapt Camera Raw and properly test the new camera before releasing an update to Camera Raw. Check the list of supported cameras at: *www.adobe.com/products/photoshop/cameraraw.html*

When you have a new camera that isn't yet supported by Camera Raw, you may need to convert the camera's raw files with the software provided by the camera manufacturer. Raw conversion software is typically included with cameras that can save raw data. You might not have as much control as you would in Camera Raw, but you'll be able to use your files.

Department of Redundancy Dept.?

? In Camera Raw, I see lots of functions that duplicate features in Photoshop itself, like Contrast and Sharpness. Do I apply these in Camera Raw, in Photoshop, or in both places?

☑ The general rule is, if you can do it in Camera Raw, do it there—you'll generally get a cleaner image with the controls in Camera Raw. For example, fixing white balance in Camera Raw preserves more image quality than converting a raw image at the wrong color balance and fixing it in Photoshop.

However, there are important exceptions. In some cases it may be better to apply sharpening and noise reduction in Photoshop rather than in Camera Raw.

In the Detail tab in the Camera Raw dialog box (**Figure 2.3**), the amount of Sharpness is best adjusted relative to the specifications of your final output. If you don't yet know the exact conditions of the output for the image, it may be better to apply sharpness later, after conversion. In addition, the Sharpness control in Camera Raw is rather basic; you can apply better sharpening techniques in Photoshop, including the wonderful Smart Sharpen feature (Filter > Sharpen > Smart Sharpen) in Photoshop CS2.

Similarly, the Reduce Noise feature in Photoshop CS2 provides different controls than the noise reduction features in Camera Raw (Luminance Smoothing and Color Noise Reduction in the same Detail tab). Depending on the noise reduction, you may want to use the Reduce Noise feature in Photoshop CS2 (Filter > Noise > Reduce Noise); in that case, set the Camera Raw noise reduction to zero.

In short, apply sharpening and noise reduction in either Camera Raw or Photoshop, but not in both. For all other Camera Raw options, it's better to apply them in Camera Raw, and it's OK to fine-tune the image in Photoshop if needed.

Cracking the Camera Raw Code

? I'm confused. Camera Raw is supposed to help me get the most quality out of my digital camera. But for years, the experts have been warning us away from the Brightness and Contrast sliders in Photoshop, because they can wreck a photographic image. And yet I see Brightness and Contrast sliders prominently placed in Camera Raw. Does that mean it's OK to touch Brightness and Contrast now? And one more thing: What's the difference between Exposure and Brightness?

☑ It's true, there is some confusing terminology in the Adjust tab of the Camera Raw dialog box. Some of the labels in Camera Raw actually don't mean the same thing they do in Photoshop. The trick is to ignore what the labels say, and study what they actually do. Here's a head start:

- Exposure sets the value of the lightest level you'll convert. To adjust Exposure, enable the Highlights checkbox at the top of the Camera Raw dialog box. This marks clipped highlights (lost details in bright areas) in red. Now drag the Exposure slider as far to the right

Figure 2.3: The Adobe Camera Raw dialog box with the Detail tab visible on the right side.

as you can without blowing out details in the highlights.

- Shadows sets the value of the darkest level you'll convert. Enable the Shadows checkbox at the top of the Camera Raw dialog box to mark clipped shadows (lost details in dark areas) in blue. Now drag the Shadows slider as far to the right as you can without blocking up shadow details.

- Brightness is nothing like the Brightness control in Photoshop, so you don't have to be afraid of it. Brightness actually sets the image's midtone for the conversion. Always get Exposure and Shadows right before adjusting Brightness.

- Contrast is not as destructive as the Contrast control in Photoshop, so it's really not scary either. In Photoshop, contrast pushes tones apart and lets them clip. In Camera Raw, Contrast applies an S-curve around the midtone you set using Brightness. While the S-curve doesn't clip tones, if you turn it up too high it can still push midtones

TIP: There is so much more that we could say about Camera Raw but couldn't fit in this book—that one Camera Raw dialog box is deeper than it looks. If you love (or want to learn to love) what Camera Raw does, you should read either *Real World Photoshop CS2* or *Real World Camera Raw with Adobe Photoshop* (both Peachpit Press), written by our esteemed colleague Bruce Fraser.

too far into the harder-to-reproduce highlights and shadows.

- Saturation, fortunately, does exactly what it says, and has the same implications as it does in Photoshop. Saturation simply controls the intensity of color.

There's one more control to mention here, and that's the Curve tab. If you're a Photoshop veteran, you might instinctively bypass the Adjust tab and run straight to the Curve tab. In Camera Raw, don't do that. The Curve tab applies after the Adjust tab, so to apply Curves to the best possible source data, first get the Adjust tab right, and then use Curve for fine-tuning.

Raw Files Cooked to Order

? Every time I convert camera raw files, they come out as 8-bit AdobeRGB files. I like to work in 16-bit ProPhoto RGB. Is there a way to change the conversion?

☑ At the bottom of the Camera Raw dialog box, enable the Show Workflow Options checkbox. In the rest of the dialog box you control how the image looks, and you use the workflow options to control the specifications of the converted file. Here are your options:

- The Space popup menu determines the color space. It defaults to Adobe RGB, but you can change it. This is where you can convert the raw data into a nice ProPhoto

RGB image for fine-art printing, or as 8-bit sRGB for the Web.

- The Depth popup menu determines the bit depth. If you want 16 bits per channel, set it here; there's no point in converting to 8 bits per channel and later changing to 16.

- Size is the dimensions of the image in pixels. Sizes with a minus or plus sign after the dimensions are downsampled or upsampled from the original, respectively. However, the more advanced resizing choices in the Image Size dialog box in Photoshop are superior to resizing in Camera Raw, so if you'd rather resize in Photoshop, leave the middle (original size) command selected in Camera Raw's Size popup menu and resize in Photoshop later.

- Resolution is the same as setting the resolution in the Image Size dialog box and is included here only for convenience. Changing resolution here doesn't add or remove any image data (changing Size will, though).

TIP: When you select a camera raw image in Adobe Bridge, you can choose to open it in Bridge (via File > Open in Camera Raw) or in Photoshop (via File > Open With > Adobe Photoshop CS2). The first methods opens Camera Raw inside Bridge without tying up Photoshop. The second method opens Camera Raw inside Photoshop without tying up Bridge.

Mixing Up a Big Batch

? **There are days when I'll bring home a couple hundred images and look at them in Bridge. I edit one and I like how it looks, but there are fifty more just like it that need the same correction. Can I transfer my corrections to other raw images?**

☑ Yes, you'll be able to convert so many at once that you'll feel like the leader of a trendy cult. There are several great ways to edit in bulk.

You can open a folder full of raw images in Bridge and select a range of images that are similar. From there, you can open all those images in Camera Raw (see tip on opposite page for details of how to open images in Camera Raw). Once Camera Raw opens, you see all the images in filmstrip mode (**Figure 2.4**). If you select more than one of those images, any edits you make apply to all the images selected in Camera Raw.

Alternately, you can play around with one image in Camera Raw and arrive at a good set of corrections that you'd like to apply to a bunch of other images. Fortunately, this is easy to do. If you're still in Camera Raw with a set of similar images selected, click the Synchronize button. You can then select which attributes to apply to the other selected images. Note that there are two selec-

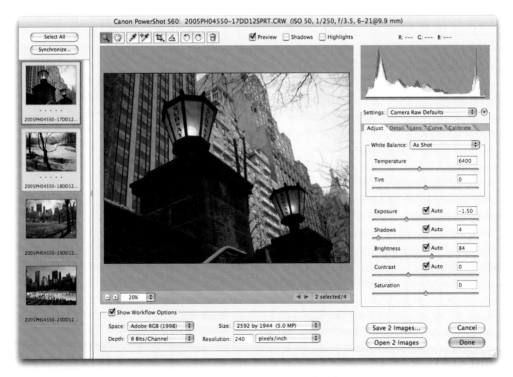

Figure 2.4: Along the left edge of the Camera Raw dialog box, you see multiple raw images opened from Adobe Bridge ("filmstrip mode"). The first two images are selected. The image at the top has a thicker border, so it's the image being viewed. Any changes to the viewed image apply to all selected images.

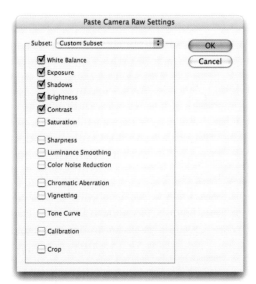

Figure 2.5: When you Synchronize or choose the Paste Camera Raw Settings command in Aoobe Bridge, you can specify which settings to transfer to other raw files.

tion levels in Camera Raw: The images highlighted with a lighter background, and the one image highlighted with a thicker border. When you synchronize, it's the image with the thicker border that becomes the source of the synchronization for other selected images.

Finally, if you aren't even in Camera Raw anymore, you can still apply one image's settings to others. In Adobe Bridge, select a properly corrected camera raw image and choose Edit >Apply Camera Raw Settings > Copy Camera Raw Settings. Next, select the other images you want to change, and choose Edit >Apply Camera Raw Settings > Paste Camera Raw Settings. You'll get the same dialog box you see when synchronizing in Camera Raw (**Figure 2.5**); just set it and click OK.

Door #1, #2, #3... or #4?

 Can you help me understand the difference between the Save, Open, Cancel, and Done buttons at the bottom of the Camera Raw dialog box?

That we can do. For the buttons in Photoshop CS2:

- Save creates a new DNG, JPEG, TIFF, or PSD document.

- Open converts and opens the converted image in Photoshop.

- Cancel exits Camera Raw—and this part is important—discards all edits you made in the current Camera Raw session. Don't click Cancel unless you really want to!

- Done saves the changes you made in the current Camera Raw session, closes the image, and returns you to Bridge or Photoshop without creating or opening anything.

When you press the Option/Alt key, two of the buttons change. The Save loses

TIP: Use caution when pressing the Esc key in Camera Raw. When the cursor is in a numerical field, Esc simple cancels what you changed there; Esc also cancels out of an active tool such as the Crop tool. However, if cursor focus is not on a tool or text field, pressing Esc closes Camera Raw without saving *any* changes you made to any of the images you've got open in it—game over, dude!

its ellipses, meaning it saves using the last-used settings, bypassing the dialog box of save options. Option/Alt also changes the Cancel button to Reset, which discards changes but keeps Camera Raw open so you can try again.

In Photoshop CS, there are two buttons: OK and Cancel. Pressing Option/Alt changes them to Update (same as Done in CS2) and Reset, respectively.

Jane, Stop This Crazy Thing!

? **In Camera Raw, I noticed that I can turn off the Auto checkboxes, and I like that better, but I'm getting tired of turning off those little boxes over and over again. Can I permanently turn off the Auto checkboxes?**

✓ The Auto values are Camera Raw's "best guess" for the correct settings, and you should use them as a starting point. The result may look different than what other raw converters may display. Some converters prioritize

> **TIP:** Camera raw files are read-only, so changes you make in Camera Raw are saved either in a central Camera Raw database or in an XMP metadata file stored alongside your camera raw files. In Camera Raw Preferences, you can control where the changes are stored. If you use XMP metadata files, use Adobe Bridge to move and rename the raw files; Bridge makes sure each XMP file is moved and renamed with its Camera Raw file.

contrast over tonal quality, while Adobe Camera Raw tries to preserve more tonal quality in the shadows and highlights so that you have more flexibility and potentially lose fewer tones when you edit.

You can turn off all Auto settings for an image by disabling Use Auto Adjustments. This command is in the menu you get when you click the round button to the right of the Settings popup menu (**Figure 2.6**). If you don't like the Auto settings and would like to have them off as the default, first turn them all off for the selected image, and then choose Save New Camera Raw Defaults from the same popup menu.

Alternately, you can press Command/Ctrl-U as a shortcut for the Use Auto

Figure 2.6: You can turn the automatic adjustments on or off from this menu in Adobe Camera Raw, and you can also use this menu to save your favorite Camera Raw settings as the default settings.

Adjustments command. This is a great way to quickly see what an image looks like with and without the Camera Raw auto adjustments.

Scanning

Scanning Essentials

? I love my digital camera, but I have a lot of print and film images that I need to convert to digital through scanning. Do you have any tips for wading through the endless number of controls in my scanning software?

☑ There are a few basic steps to getting a good scan. Like car dashboards, scanning controls may seem to vary across different scanning programs, but they usually work the same way. Whichever scanning software you use, the most important steps in relation to Photoshop are these:

1. Don't scan without first using the Preview button in the scanning software to help determine what scan settings to use.

2. Crop unneeded areas to scan faster and use less disk space. You can rotate and flip if you want, but you can do that in Photoshop too.

3. Set the resolution and dimensions based on your final output.

4. Set the black point and white point (**Figure 2.7**). The black point and white point define the darkest and lightest tones, respectively, that you'll scan from the original. Too narrow a range wipes out detail in

the shadows and highlights. Too wide a range will lack contrast. If you're a pro scanning at 16 bits per channel, it's possible to skip this step and fine-tune the black and white points later in Photoshop.

5. Adjust the color balance. If you aren't comfortable with the color balancing controls in the scanning software, you can skip this step and fix the color in Photoshop.

6. When everything looks good, you can finally click the Scan button in the scanning software.

Batch Scan Directly into Photoshop… Not!

? I like to scan photos right into Photoshop so I can edit them right away. This doesn't work well for batch scanning because the scanning plug-in ties up Photoshop, and all these windows of unsaved scans pile up (seems risky). Is there a better way?

☑ Scanning directly from within Photoshop is convenient for occasional scans. However, for maximum productivity see if your scanning software is capable of running as an independent program. If it can, you can work on completed scans in Photoshop while

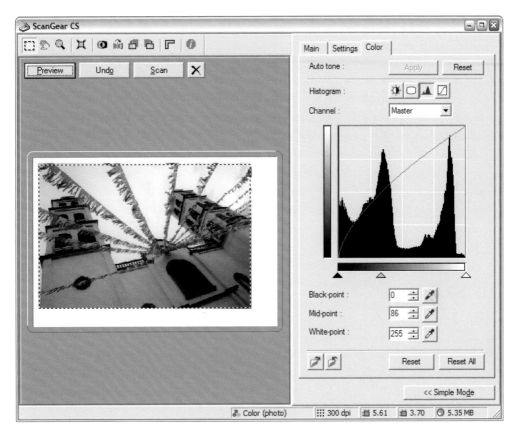

other scans are in progress in the scanning software. You can use the following technique to set up an efficient scanning and editing workflow with Photoshop.

1. Open Photoshop, Adobe Bridge, and your scanning software.

2. Set your scanning software to save completed scans to a folder.

3. In Adobe Bridge, locate and view the folder you set up in Step 2.

4. Use your scanning software to scan an image or two. You'll see your scans appear in Adobe Bridge as the scanning software saves them, so you can monitor the progress of the batch scanning operation.

5. In Adobe Bridge, select a scan and choose File > Open (or just press

Figure 2.7: Main scanning window of a typical scanning utility (Canon ScanGear shown as an example). Here, the color and tone controls are visible, along with the main toolbar that includes cropping and scaling tools.

TIP: Some scanning software lets you apply digital restoration and enhancements, like scratch and dust removal, grain enhancement, and color restoration for faded originals. If you're scanning an old or damaged original and your scanning software has those features, feel free to use them. The restoration features in today's scanners are often faster and more effective than performing the same tasks in Photoshop.

Return or Enter). The scan opens in Photoshop, and you can work on it as your scanner works on another image.

6. If you save your edited scans to another folder, you can open an additional window in Adobe Bridge (File > New) to monitor the folder containing edited scans. You can monitor progress of scanned and edited images simultaneously.

Turn a Negative into a Positive

? I've scanned lots of slides, but negatives really throw me for a loop. The color and contrast never look right after I invert them and try to color-correct them.

☑ Color negative film can be a challenge to scan. On negative film, the image is both inverted and has an orange-colored mask, so arriving at a final image requires some interpretation. Fortunately, there are a couple of quick ways to handle scans of color negatives.

If your scanning software provides a selection of presets for color negative film types, select your film type if available. If your scanning software doesn't have any color negative conversion options, try this manual and somewhat more involved Photoshop method.

1. Scan at 16 bits per channel, and apply no tone or color corrections in the scanning software. Don't even invert the image.

2. Open the color negative scan in Photoshop and choose Image >

Adjustments > Invert. Don't expect it to look good yet (**Figure 2.8**).

3. Open the scan in Photoshop, choose Layer > New Adjustment Layer > Levels, and click the Options button (**Figure 2.9**).

4. In the Auto Color Correction Options dialog box, click Find Dark & Light Colors and Snap Neutral Midtones. If the color balance is unrealistic, disable Snap Neutral Midtones and try different options in the Algorithms section.

5. If you want, adjust the Clip values for Shadows and Highlights (we tend to use smaller values than the defaults). When you're done, click the OK button.

6. If the image is still too dark or light, drag the Input midtone slider left

Figure 2.8: Original color negative (top), and after inverting (bottom).

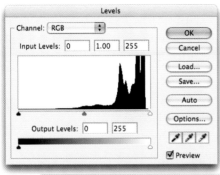

Figure 2.9: The Levels dialog box (top), the Auto Color Corrections Options dialog box (center) opened by the Options button, and the resulting image.

or right in the Levels dialog box. If you realize the black or white point needs adjustment, click Options and change the clip values instead of dragging the black point or white point sliders in the Levels dialog box—you'll get more balanced results.

7. When you're satisfied with the overall tonal range and color bal-

ance, click OK until both the Auto Color Correction Options dialog box and the Levels dialog box are closed. The image should now be at a stage (**Figure 2.10**) where you only need to fine-tune it.

Figure 2.10: The image after adjusting the Input midtone slider in Levels.

Scanning Line Art

? **What's the best way to scan line art for Photoshop? I set my scanner to the Line Art setting, but the results are sometimes uneven or blocked up.**

If you've ever tried to copy line art with a photocopier, you know that the machine itself can alter the image. This is sometimes the problem with using a scanner at its Line Art (or Black and White) setting. For more control, try a method that lets you tweak the line art easily in Photoshop:

1. Scan the original line art in gray-scale mode—8 bits per channel—at the optical resolution of your scanner (**Figure 2.11**).

2. Open the image in Photoshop.

3. Choose Filter > Sharpen > Unsharp Mask, setting Amount to 500 percent, Radius to 1, and Threshold

Figure 2.11: For best results, scan line art in grayscale mode (left) and then process it to create a Bitmap image (right).

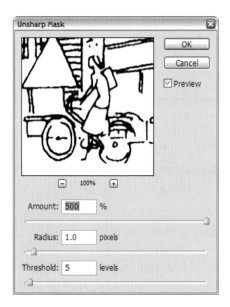

Figure 2.12: Applying Unsharp Mask tightens up the scanned grayscale edges.

to 5. You may need to increase the Radius or Amount at higher resolutions (**Figure 2.12**).

4. Choose Image > Adjustments > Threshold (or add a threshold adjustment layer) to adjust the level where gray pixels jump to

white or black (**Figure 2.13**). You're controlling the edge of the line art. Aim for a value that looks right, above the point where lines break up and below the point where spaces between lines block up.

5. Choose Image > Mode > Bitmap (**Figure 2.14**). Choose 50% Threshold from the Method popup menu, and click OK. This step freezes your edits into a final 1-bit line art file. If the document has layers, changing modes flattens the document.

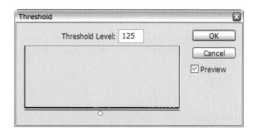

Figure 2.13: The Threshold Level controls which grayscale levels convert to line art.

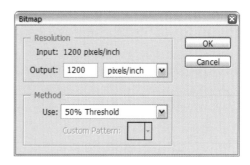

Figure 2.14: Converting the grayscale scan to a 1-bit bitmap.

Descreening a Scan

? A client asked me to include a photo from one of their old catalogs. When I scanned it, there was a terrible pattern across it. I asked if there were better copies of the photo, but there aren't. I have to use the one from the old catalog. How do I get rid of that pattern?

☑ Before printing an photograph on a typical printing press, an image must be converted to halftone dots. If you scan an image that's already been printed on a press, the halftone dots can appear as a distracting moiré pattern (**Figure 2.15**) due to the interference pattern between the halftone dots and the scanner's pixel grid.

The best way to remove the halftone dot pattern is to use a descreening feature on your scanner, if it has one. The most important setting in a descreening feature is lines per inch (lpi); entering a value that matches the actual lpi

of the print is most likely to produce a clean result. If your scanning software doesn't have a descreening option or you were given an image that was scanned by someone else, you can try these tips:

- If you have access to the printed original, scan it at an odd angle (try between 6 and 10 degrees) and set the scanner to a higher resolution than normally needed (try an additional five to ten percent more resolution). The purpose of this step is to avoid aligning the halftone screen with the scanner's pixel grid. After trying some of the techniques below, straighten the scan again.

- In Photoshop, experiment with the Median filter (Filter > Noise > Median) (**Figure 2.16**) or Gaussian Blur filter (Filter > Blur > Gaussian Blur) with different settings.

- For color scans, experiment with Filter > Noise > Reduce Noise, and

Figure 2.15: The rosette pattern visible in a halftone image, which can cause a moiré pattern when scanned.

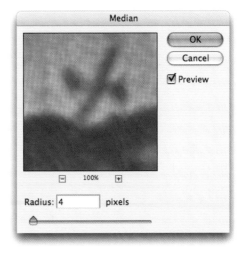

Figure 2.16: The Median filter can sometimes help smooth out distracting scanned halftone screens.

try increasing the Reduce Color Noise value without obliterating the details.

- If you scanned the image at a higher resolution and at an odd angle as we suggested in the first item on this list, your last step should be to downsample and straighten the image. Choose Image > Image Size, check the Resample Image box, and set the image to the desired dimensions and resolution. Then straighten the image; see the topic "Rotating an Image the Fast, Precise Way" in Chapter 3, *Image Editing Basics.*

There isn't one solution for all descreening problems, because screened images are printed to many different specifications, which can create varying patterns. You'll typically need to experiment with different combinations of the ideas above, until something works.

Mystery of the Awful Black-and-White Scans

I'm trying to scan black-and-white negatives for Photoshop, but they look awful no matter what I do! What's strange is that color negatives come out great.

Try turning off any dust or scratch-removal features in the scanning software. Dust and scratch removal is a useful feature in newer scanners, and it really does work… on most originals. Defect removal may not work on silver-based black-and-white film—compared to the flat dye layers in color film, the non-flat silver grains are perceived as dust by the defect-removal software. Dye-based (chromogenic) black-and-white films, such as Kodak BW400CN, work fine with scanner-based defect removal.

3

Image Editing Basics

Image Editing Basics

*T*HE IMAGE WINDOW OPENS BEFORE YOU FOR THE FIRST TIME, and you take a deep breath as you look it over and realize all the little things that need to be fixed before the image can be unleashed upon the public. What to do first? How to turn this into a masterpiece? Many images need only tone and color corrections plus a little sharpening before they're ready to go out the door. Other images need a few physical adjustments such as cropping and straightening, or may suffer from lens distortion that you'd like to remove. For these images, it's good to take care of physical corrections before you start adding layers and elements that depend on where things are in the image.

Before we get into the tone and color corrections in the following chapter, we want to spend a little time covering the ins and outs of image editing basics: resolution, transformations, and selecting areas and objects. Once you get a handle on these methods, it becomes much easier to apply tone and color corrections exactly where you want them.

All About Resolution

Don't Forget Your Resolutions

? If there's one thing that always trips me up, it's the concept of resolution. Is it just me, or does the word resolution have multiple meanings?

☑ In the strict sense, resolution is a measure of how fine the image dots are, by dividing the number of pixels by the physical size (as in "300 dots per inch"). But the exact meaning of that number does change depending on where and how an image is used, and where it is in the capture-to-output workflow. Knowing your resolutions is important when you're communicating with someone else. Here's how we've boiled it down (**Figure 3.1**):

- **Sampling resolution.** If you're using a scanner, this is the resolution at which a scanner samples the original. This number describes, in samples per inch (spi), how pre-

cisely an image was scanned. You control sampling resolution using your scanning software. For digital cameras, sampling resolution doesn't really apply: You could be taking a photo of a landscape 3 miles wide or a close-up of a 3-inch-wide flower, making "dots per inch" quite arbitrary.

- **File resolution.** When you save an image from Photoshop or other software, the software writes an image resolution into the file. File resolution doesn't mean much unless you print the image, because it doesn't refer to the number of pixels in the file. Some digital cameras write 72 ppi into a file just to put a number in that field.

- **Effective resolution.** This is the resolution of an image at its final output dimensions. For example, a 1600×1200-pixel digital camera photo scaled to 2.5 inches wide on a layout, creates an effective reso-

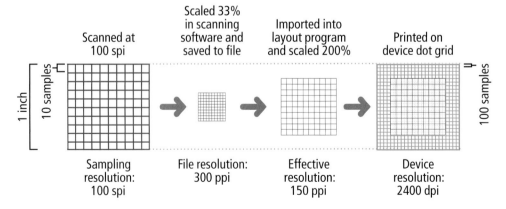

Figure 3.1: How the meaning of resolution changes as you move an image from capture to output.

lution of 1,600 pixels ÷ 2.5 inches or 640 ppi. If you scale up an image too far, its effective resolution drops below the value required for good quality.

- **Device resolution.** This number isn't part of the image at all, but is the resolution of the output device. For example, a monitor might be 96 dpi, and a platemaker might be 2,400 dpi. For print, an image doesn't need to match the device resolution. For example, you don't need to send a 5,760 ppi image to a 5,760 dpi inkjet! A 360 ppi image prints very well.

If you aren't printing an image, don't worry about dpi at all. Just pay attention to the image dimensions in pixels (e.g., 1600×1200 pixels). That's how image sizes are measured on monitors.

Finding Out the File Resolution of an Image

? I do a lot of print work, so I do need to be aware of the effective resolution of my images. Our publication requires images to have a resolution of 300dpi or higher. How do I use Photoshop to find out the resolution of an image?

You may not even need to use Photoshop! If you view an image in Adobe Bridge and display the Metadata panel (View > Metadata Panel), you'll see Resolution listed there. If you've already got the image open in Photoshop, you've got options (**Figure 3.2**):

- To display the file resolution in the document window status bar, click the black triangle next to the status bar and choose Document

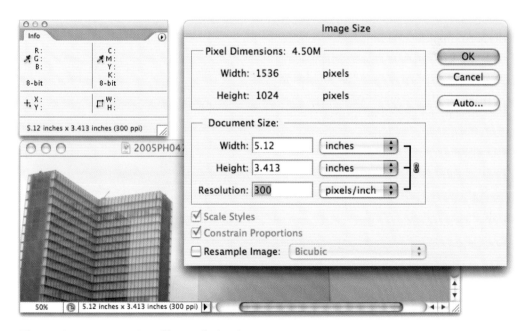

Figure 3.2: You can view file resolution in the Info palette (top left), document window status bar (bottom left), and in the Image Size dialog box (top right).

Dimensions. The status bar displays the file resolution after the dimensions, in parentheses.

- To display the file resolution in the Info palette, choose Palette Options from the Info palette menu and enable Document Dimensions.

- Choose Image > Image Size, and you'll find the Resolution option in the Document Size section. What happens when you change the Resolution value depends on if you enabled the Resample checkbox; see the topic "To Resample or Not to Resample" on the next page.

Kenneth, What's the Effective Resolution?

? I sent a digital photo to a magazine editor, but he told me that its resolution was too low. The magazine requires 300 ppi, and he said my image wasn't acceptable because it was 180 ppi. I was told that a 6-megapixel camera can produce quite good quality for an 8×10 image, and I didn't crop my image or change its resolution before I sent it to him. So why does he think the resolution is too low?

✅ The editor is making a classic, common mistake: evaluating file resolution when he needs to be looking at effective resolution instead. In other words, he didn't take the final output size into account when looking at your image.

Let's examine at a 6-megapixel image and look at its resolution properly. One

popular 6-megapixel digital SLR produces an image with dimensions of 2000×3008 pixels. The resolution means nothing until you state the size at which it will be printed, so let's state some sizes. Use the Image Size dialog box in Photoshop to do the math for you:

1. With the image open in Photoshop, choose Image > Image Size (**Figure 3.3**).

2. Make sure the Resample Image checkbox is disabled.

3. In the Document Size section, enter the width or height at which you want to output the image.

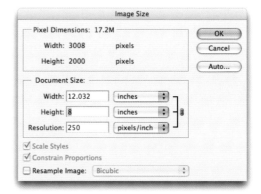

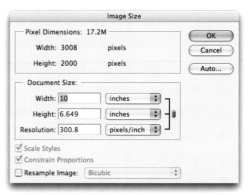

Figure 3.3: To determine the effective resolution of an image in the Image Size dialog box, disable the Resample Image checkbox and change Width and Height.

4. The Resolution value now tells you the resolution the image can inherently provide at that size.

The 2:3 frame proportions of the image don't match the 3:4 proportions of an 8×10-inch image, so we try entering 8 inches wide and Photoshop tells us it'll be 12 inches tall and 250 pixels per inch. A little low, but most magazines aren't 12 inches tall.

That still leaves one big question: Why does the editor see the image as 180 ppi? Digital cameras have no inherent resolution, but some would find it odd to have an empty Resolution field, so digital cameras tend to embed an arbitrary ppi value into their files. You could pull 3 different 6-megapixel cameras off the shelf, take a picture with each one, and compare the dpi values in the images. The image from one camera might claim 180 ppi, the second 300 ppi, and the third 350 ppi—even though all three actually produced the same number of pixels.

To Resample or Not to Resample...

When should I enable or disable the Resample Image checkbox in the Image Size dialog box?

That little Resample Image checkbox at the bottom of the Image Size dialog box (**Figure 3.3**) is a frequent source of confusion.

When Resample Image is on, pixels are added or subtracted during resizing (**Figure 3.4**). Resampling is usually a good idea when you make an image smaller, and occasionally a good idea when you enlarge an image. Resampling during reduction can remove unnecessary image data so that the file size doesn't take up too much disk space. Resampling during enlargement can help avoid jaggies in the image, but only to a point. Even with the best resampling methods, you

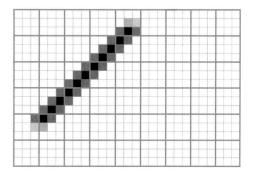

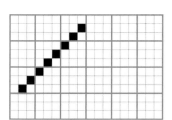

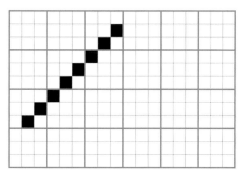

Figure 3.4: When the original image (top) is enlarged with resampling on (top right), Photoshop creates more pixels to keep the resolution constant. When enlarged with resampling off (bottom right), the number of pixels must stay constant, causing the resolution to drop—the pixels get bigger.

can enlarge an image only so far—typically less than 200 percent—before it no longer looks sharp. Resampling carefully can help keep an image within that happy medium between too little detail and an unnecessarily dense image file.

You can experiment with resampling if you have an image open in Photoshop. First choose Image > Image Size. When you enter new values for Width and Height under Pixel Dimensions and Resample Image is turned on, the file size changes but Document Size stays constant.

Going Bicubic

? **I have an image that I need to resample, but I don't know which of the five resampling choices to use. Should I simply leave it at the Bicubic default?**

☑ There isn't one best method for all situations, so Adobe provides five ways to resample (**Figure 3.5**):

- Nearest Neighbor duplicates a sample by simply copying a pixel next to it. This doesn't make photographic images look good, but is often better for some 1-bit-per-channel or indexed-color images.

- Bilinear duplicates a sample by averaging the pixels on either side of it. It's faster than the Bicubic options, but doesn't look as good.

- Bicubic looks at the samples on all four sides, averages them, and applies that value to the new sample point. Bicubic is slower than Bilinear or Nearest Neighbor, but yields the best quality with continuous tone images.

TIP: When talking about resolution, you may see references to samples per inch (spi), pixels per inch (ppi), and dots per inch (dpi). Strictly speaking, these terms help distinguish sampling and file resolution from effective and device resolution, to avoid the various kinds of resolution confusion we talk about in this section. In casual conversation, however, it's OK to use these units of measure interchangeably.

- Bicubic Smoother is a version of Bicubic that often works better when enlarging an image.

- Bicubic Sharper is a version of Bicubic that often works better when reducing an image.

The bottom line? When working with photos, use one of the Bicubic options. Because actual results depend on the image content, you might want to try each option when you're working with critical images.

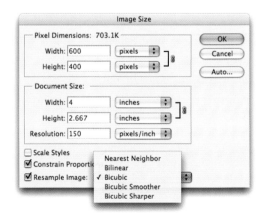

Figure 3.5: The resampling choices in the Image Size dialog box.

Image Size vs. Canvas Size

? What's the difference between Image Size and Canvas Size?

☑ The simplest explanation is that the Image Size command (Image > Image Size) affects the image, and Canvas Size (Image > Canvas Size) affects the document. If you enlarge the Canvas Size, you end up with more space around the image. If you reduce the Canvas Size, part of the image is chopped off.

A common use for Canvas Size is adding more area to a document while preserving the existing image size (**Figure 3.6**). A great example of this is when you're assembling several photos into one big document. You can start with one photo and enlarge the Canvas Size to make room for adding and arranging other photos.

Resizing a Batch of Variously Sized Images

? I've got a folder full of images that my boss wants me to put up on our web site. I've got two problems here. One, the images are print-sized, so I have to reduce them for the Web. Two, they're all different sizes, so the Image Size command won't work right in a batch action. What can I do?

☑ Use Fit Image (File > Automate > Fit Image) instead of the Image Size command. You can set a width and height within which each image is resized to fit. And it works great as part of a Photoshop action.

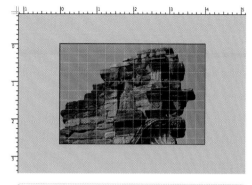

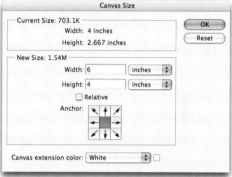

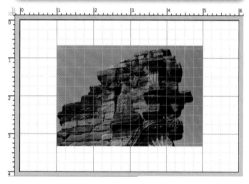

Figure 3.6: Original image (top), Canvas Size dialog box with new document dimensions entered (center), and the resized document (bottom).

TIP: In the Canvas Size dialog box, you can avoid doing math by enabling the Relative checkbox and entering just the difference between the old and new sizes. For example, to add 1 inch to the document height, just enable Relative and enter 1 inch. No need to work out the new height!

Cropping

Keeping What You Cropped

? Is there a way to restore an area I've cropped out of an image? Before you ask: Yeah, I already saved and closed the file.

☑ By default, the crop tool permanently deletes the cropped area, and you can't recover that area after saving. However, if you check out the Options bar for the Crop tool, you'll find two Cropping Area options: Delete, and Hide (you only see these after drawing the cropping rectangle). The Hide option is unavailable if you're cropping an image with a Background in the Layers palette, so the first step is to convert Background to a layer.

1. In the Layers palette, Option/Alt-double-click the Background layer to convert it to Layer 0.

2. Select the Crop tool, and drag a crop rectangle.

3. In the Options bar, click the Hide button (**Figure 3.7**).

4. Press Enter or Return.

Because you clicked the Hide option, there are two things you can now do that you couldn't before. First, you can reposition the cropped image using the Move tool (wow!). And second, at any time you can restore the cropped area by choosing Image > Reveal All.

You can also recover any part of the hidden area by dragging the Crop tool beyond the edge of the image.

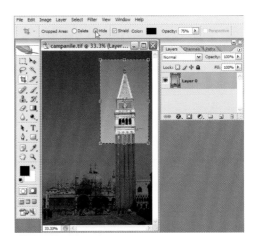

Figure 3.7: Clicking the Hide button on the Options bar for the Crop tool while a crop area is active. The Layers palette shows that the default Background was converted to a layer so that the Hide button would be available.

The area cropped out by the Hide option stays around even after you save and reopen the document, as long as you don't flatten the image. Because documents cropped with the Hide option look the same as documents cropped with the Delete option, you might want to add a note to the document using the Notes tool, to remind you that there is extra image area that needs to be preserved.

TIP: The Crop tool snaps to the edges of the document if the View > Snap To > Document Bounds command is enabled. If you want to temporarily prevent the Crop tool from snapping to the edges of a document, hold down the Ctrl key after you start dragging the Crop tool.

Removing Perspective With the Crop Tool

? Is it true that you can actually use the Crop tool to correct perspective distortion in an image?

☑ It sure is! There's a Crop tool option called Perspective, which is yet another crop tool option that's only visible when a crop area is active:

1. Using the Crop tool, drag a crop rectangle. Don't worry about precision at the point.

2. In the Options bar, check the Perspective option (**Figure 3.8**).

3. Drag corner handles to line up the edges of the crop area with perspective lines in the image.

4. Press Enter or Return to commit the crop area. The Crop tool uses your modified crop area to remove the perspective distortion.

Figure 3.8: Dragging crop area handles (bottom left) to match perspective lines in the image, made possible by the Perspective checkbox in the Options bar for the Crop tool (top) while a crop area is active. When you commit the crop, the Crop tool removes the perspective distortion (bottom right).

Living on the Edge

? The Crop tool is hard to control when it's right up against the edge of the window. I notice this most when I'm trying to move crop area handles in Perspective mode. If I drag a crop handle outside the window, I can't get it back. If I zoom out to see the area outside the image, I can no longer position the handle with precision. Is it possible to have more control over cropping near edges while I'm zoomed in close on the image?

✓ Yes. If you're viewing a document in the default window view (Standard Screen Mode), you may find it difficult to start or stop dragging precisely at the edge of an image . It's much easier if there's space around the image. Either zoom out or enlarge the window slightly to reveal the area outside the image, and you'll now be able to snap exactly to the image edge when you start or stop dragging (**Figure 3.9**). If you're viewing the document in Full Screen mode or Full Screen with Menu Bar mode, either choose View > Fit on Screen or zoom in and use the Hand tool to scroll past the edge; either method allows tools to snap to the edge.

Figure 3.9: In Standard Screen Mode (top), it's possible to drag a crop area handle past the window edge. To reach that handle after you release the mouse, you'd have to zoom out. If you work in one of the Full Screen modes (bottom), you can reach handles outside the crop area without having to zoom out.

Cropping with the Marquee Tool

? When I use the Crop tool Options bar to crop to a specific dimensions, it changes the resolution of the image. How can I crop to specific dimensions without altering the resolution of the image? I just want to clip some pixels off of the sides of the image.

✓ When you use the Crop tool and in the Options bar you specify a fixed size while leaving Resolution blank, the size of the crop area you drag determines the resolution of the resulting image. For example, if you set the Crop tool for 4 inches wide, any crop area you drag must be resized to fit into 4 inches. If one crop area you drag is twice as large as another, that's double the pixels to fit into four inches; therefore the resolution doubles.

Figure 3.10: The Options bar for the Marquee tool includes a Fixed Size option that you can use to crop an image without altering the file resolution.

To crop to specific dimensions without altering the resolution, you can use the Rectangular Marquee tool:

1. Select the Rectangular Marquee tool.

2. On the Options bar, choose Fixed Size from the Style popup menu, and enter the size you want, such as "4 in" or "200 px" (**Figure 3.10**).

3. Drag the Rectangular Marquee tool to position the selection marquee. You can only reposition the marquee; you won't be able to resize it because you used the Options bar to lock the dimensions.

4. Choose Image > Crop.

5. Choose Select > Deselect.

Why not just fill in the Resolution field in the Options bar for the Crop tool? If you do this, the Crop tool resamples the image, so if you're trying to avoid resampling, don't fill in the Resolution field.

Cropping in Camera Raw

? I see that Camera Raw also has a Crop tool. When should I use that one?

✓ We think you should crop in Adobe Camera Raw whenever possible. If you crop in Camera Raw, you'll reduce the amount of data that's passed to Photoshop in the first place. Also, the Crop tool in Adobe Camera Raw is nondestructive, so if you screw up a crop, just go back to Camera Raw, edit the crop, and re-convert the raw image to Photoshop. Nondestructive cropping in Camera Raw is much easier than using the Hide feature in the Options bar for the Crop tool.

One big advantage to cropping in Camera Raw is that Camera Raw remembers the crop. If you ever need to convert the raw image again, your previous crop is already there. If you crop a converted raw in Photoshop and you need to convert the raw file again, you have to somehow re-create the same crop.

Camera Raw records your crop area along with your other raw adjustments, saving it all to the Camera Raw database or in the image's XMP file, depending on how you've set your preferences. That's how it remembers the crop.

TIP: You can use the Crop tool to extend the canvas size, by dragging a crop rectangle that's larger than the canvas area. The catch is that you have to drag the crop tool to the document edge and let go; only after the crop area exists are you able to drag the crop area past the edge of the image. The new area uses the background color by default. If you want to added area to have a particular color, set the background color before you add to the canvas area.

Changing the Frame Aspect Ratio

? I need to get an image into an aspect ratio of 16:9 for an HDTV project. What's the fastest way to do that?

✓ If you know the pixel dimensions of the new aspect ratio, such as 1280×720 pixels, simply choose the Crop tool and enter the new dimensions in the Crop tool's Options bar before you start dragging the crop rectangle.

However, the Crop tool doesn't provide a way to enter an aspect ratio, such as 16:9, without also changing the dimensions of the image. If you want to crop to a specific aspect ratio (outside of Camera Raw), you can use the Marquee tool.

1. Select the Rectangular Marquee tool.

2. On the Options bar, choose Fixed Aspect Ratio from the Style popup menu, and enter the aspect ratio you want. For example, to set a 16:9 aspect ratio, enter 16 into the Width box and 9 into the Height box.

3. Drag the Marquee tool to position the selection rectangle (**Figure 3.11**). If you want to reposition or resize the selection rectangle after you release the mouse, choose Select > Transform Selection and Shift-drag a corner handle to resize it proportionally (and then press Enter).

4. Choose Image > Crop.

Frame and pixel aspect ratios

Aspect ratio exists at both the frame and pixel level. Frame aspect ratio relates to the entire frame, while pixel aspect ratio relates only to the pixels themselves. For example, computers use square pixels, while televisions use rectangular pixels that are taller than they are wide. If you draw a square on a rectangular-pixel system like a television graphics workstation, then move that file to a square-pixel system like a Mac OS or Windows computer, the square will look unnaturally thin because the square computer pixels aren't the same proportions as the rectangular TV pixels.

The pixel aspect ratio of a DV (digital video) pixel is .9:1, which means its width is .9 times its height. Photoshop lets you choose a pixel aspect ratio when you create a new document. Photoshop also uses the Pixel Aspect Ratio submenu on the Image menu to indicate the pixel aspect ratio of an existing document. On both places, the aspect ratio's scaling factor is at the end of each menu item. The only video formats that use square pixels are certain digital high-definition standards, because they have more in common with computer formats than traditional video formats.

The important thing is to not confuse the aspect ratios of the image and its pixels—don't change pixel aspect ratio if you intended to change the image aspect ratio.

Feather: 0 px   ☐ Anti-alias   Style: Fixed Aspect Ratio ▾   Width: 16 ⇄ Height: 9

⊟ aspect ratio.psd @ 50% (RGB/8*)

50% ⊙ sRGB IEC61966-2.1 (8bpc) ▶

Changing the Pixel Aspect Ratio

If you import an image from a video capture (such as a frame from iMovie) and the contents appear distorted in Photoshop, you may need to assign a different pixel aspect ratio to the image. Simply choose the pixel aspect ratio of the source video from the Image > Pixel Aspect Ratio submenu.

Assigning a pixel aspect ratio doesn't alter the image data at all. It only corrects the display to account for the pixel aspect ratio under which the image was created. If you want to see what the image looks like without the pixel aspect ratio correction and without losing the assigned pixel aspect ratio, you can turn the command View > Pixel Aspect Ratio Correction on and off. You can assign a pixel aspect ratio to a new document, too.

Figure 3.11: To crop an image to a new aspect ratio without altering its resolution, use the Marquee tool in Fixed Aspect Ratio mode.

In the New dialog box (File > New), click the triangle next to Advanced and enter a Pixel Aspect Ratio.

> **TIP:** When all you want to do is remove extra blank space around a graphic, choose Image > Trim as a fast alternative to manual cropping. The Trim command works when the area you're removing is all one color or tone; it won't work if there are stray pixels or a texture. We mentioned the Trim command before for screen shots, but we mention it here again because it's good for cropping more than screen shots.

Selection Strategies

Lasso Like a Cowboy

? Are there secrets to using the Lasso tool? I never get a perfect selection and I hate having to start over because of stray bumps and missed areas.

☑ No one makes a perfect selection with the Lasso tool the first time. First, make an initial selection that's close enough for you to fine-tune. You can then make additional passes to refine the selection until it's just right. As is so often the case, the secret lies within modifier keys you can press to change the behavior of the lasso tool as you draw:

- To add to an existing selection, start with the mouse button up and then Shift-drag the Lasso tool through the existing selection (**Figure 3.12**).

- To subtract from an existing selection, start with the mouse button up and then Option/Alt drag through the existing selection.

- When you Option-Shift-drag/Alt-Shift-drag a selection tool through an existing selection, what's left is the intersection between the two selections.

You can use these techniques with any tool that creates a marquee (that "marching ants" effect), such as the Magic Wand, Magnetic Lasso, or Elliptical Marquee tools. As you memorize the modifier keys, you can get into a rhythm where you "sculpt" rough initial selections into precise selections over multiple passes.

TIP: To draw a perfectly straight segment while you're dragging the Lasso tool, hold down Option/Alt, keep holding down Option/Alt as you release the mouse button, then click. As long as you keep holding down Option/Alt, clicking creates straight segments and dragging creates freeform segments. When you release the Option/Alt key, the lasso tool returns to its usual mode.

Figure 3.12: To add to an existing selection, Shift-drag the Lasso tool.

Selecting with the Magnetic Lasso

? Can you give me an example of when I might want to use the Magnetic Lasso tool? It doesn't seem to work too well when I drag it.

☑ The Magnetic Lasso tool can be a godsend when an edge is so complicated that dragging the Lasso tool along it would be extremely tedious. As you move the Magnetic Lasso tool (**Figure 3.13**), it looks for contours in the form of contrasty edges, and it creates a selection along the contour it finds.

You don't need to constantly press the mouse button as you use the Magnetic Lasso tool. After you first click the tool to set the starting point of the selection, you can let go of the mouse button and simply move the pointer along the contour you want the magnetic lasso to follow, and the magnetic lasso can usually follow it. If it goes off course, you can then back up and drag, or back up and click to put down a control point.

Figure 3.13: The Magnetic Lasso tool automatically follows an edge formed by obvious contrast between colors or tones.

Selecting by Color or Tone

? **What's the easiest way to select all the parts of an image that are the same color?**

☑ If you just want to select a few regions of the same color, the simplest way is probably to click the region with the Magic Wand tool.

If you want to select all areas of a color and the color appears in many separated

Polygon Lasso and Magnetic Lasso Tips

The Polygon Lasso and Magnetic Lasso seem different on the surface because each tool selects areas in very different ways. But because they both operate in a segment-to-segment manner, they share certain shortcuts.

The Polygon Lasso marks changes in direction with corners, and the Magnetic Lasso tool marks changes in direction with control points to mark changes in direction. If you don't like the location where either tool changes direction, press Delete/Backspace to remove the last corner or point (and

the preceding corners/points if you press Delete/Backspace again).

To immediately complete the selection by having the Polygon Lasso or Magnetic Lasso tool automatically close the selection, press Return/ Enter. The farther apart the ends of the existing selection, the more guesswork Photoshop will have to do to close it up.

If you give up and want to start over with either tool, press Esc, but make sure your really want to: the entire existing selection goes away!

areas throughout the image, the Color Range tool is probably a more efficient way. The Color Range command lets you click the color you want, and provides a Tolerance value so you can interactively include or exclude a range of variations in your target color. Unlike the Magic Wand tool, the Color Range command always selects all instances of your target color. Even though the feature is called Color Range, you can also use it to select a particular tone in a black-and-white image. To use the Color Range command:

1. Choose Select > Color Range.

2. In the Color Range dialog box (**Figure 3.14**), set the color or tone to select by choosing it from the Select popup menu, or clicking the color in the image window.

3. If you want to select more or fewer pixels based on their similarity to the color you clicked, drag the Fuzziness slider.

4. To add or subtract colors from the selection, use the eyedroppers with the plus or minus sign, respectively, to click colors in the image.

5. Click OK.

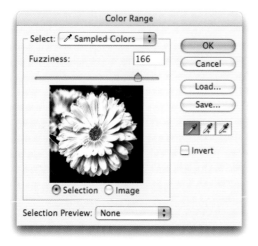

Selecting by Threshold

? **It looks to me like the Threshold feature would work much like the Color Range command. Right?**

✓ Not exactly. Color Range can select a range starting from any color or tone in the image, and provides ways to customize the selection. Threshold only lets you select a range of tones starting from black or white. Also, you can't go straight from the Threshold dialog box to a selection; after you isolate the area you need to click it with the Magic Wand tool.

However, when you quickly want to select a range based on the very lightest or darkest tones in the image, Threshold is a fast way to get it done (**Figure 3.15**). Follow these steps:

1. Choose Layer > New Adjustment Layer > Threshold and click OK.

2. Drag the slider until you see the edge you want to define, and click OK.

3. Select the Magic Wand tool, and click either the white or black area.

4. In the Layers palette, click the eye icon for the Threshold adjustment layer to hide it, and select the layer where you want to apply the selection. The selection marquee now applies to the selected layer. (If you don't need the Threshold layer any further, you can delete it.)

Figure 3.14: The Color Range dialog box after clicking the flower color to mark it for selection. The white areas will be selected.

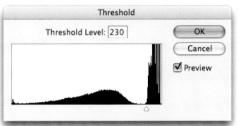

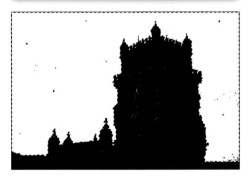

Figure 3.15: The overcast sky in the original photo (top) is nearly all white, making it a good candidate for isolation with the Threshold dialog box (center). Once the desired range is isolated, you can select it by clicking with the Magic Wand tool (bottom).

TIP: Some selection tools can result in sloppy selections that have many little bumps in them. To smooth these out, choose Select > Modify > Smooth. Enter a value large enough to remove unwanted bumps but small enough to preserve important details along the selection.

Selecting from a Channel

? I've heard of people making selections through channels. What does that mean, how do I know when this is a good idea, and then how do I do it?

☑ An object with a dominant color has more color contrast in some color channels than in others. For example, if you have an RGB image of a landscape with a blue sky and you use the Channels palette in Photoshop to look at each channel individually, the sky stands out very clearly in the blue channel. This is similar to how Color Range works: If you want to select an area already isolated in one color channel, you can save a lot of time and effort by using that channel as a starting point for selection.

Keep in mind that image channels look different when you convert the image to different color modes. If the RGB channels of an image don't reveal any selection shortcuts, try duplicating the image and converting it to CMYK or LAB before checking the channels. If you're isolating an area defined by light and dark, you may find a selection shortcut in the K channel of a CMYK version of an image, or in the L channel of a LAB version of an image. To make a selection from a channel:

1. In the Channels palette, click each of the different channels to see which one isolates your subject the best (**Figure 3.16**).

2. In the Channels palette, Command/Ctrl-click the channel you picked in step 1. The channel is now a selection.

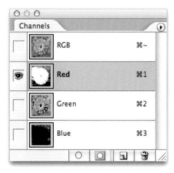

Figure 3.16: In this RGB image (far left), the flower's outline stands out clearly in the red channel (second from left). It's easy to make a clean selection from the red channel, though not from the green or blue channels (last two top images). At left is the Channels palette with the Red channel selected.

3. If the subject or its edges need a little more isolation (it almost certainly will), you can use any other selection tools or Quick Mask mode to refine the selection into exactly the form you want. We discuss how and why to use Quick Mask mode in "Edit a Selection as a Quick Mask," later on in the chapter.

4. To save what you've done as a new channel (so you can recall it again later), click on the Save Selection as Channel button in the Channels palette.

TIP: To add the contents of a channel to an existing selection, Command-Shift-click/Ctrl-Shift-click a channel in the Channels palette. To subtract channel contents from an existing selection, Option-Shift-click/Alt-Shift-click a channel.

Remove a Difficult Background

? I'm trying to get rid of a background in an image, and all of the suggested methods so far are too tedious. Is there anything left in the Photoshop bag of tricks?

✓ You're nowhere near out of options! When you try to select along a very complex edge like hair, where contrast isn't consistent, selecting the edge you want may still be a challenge even with an intelligent selection tool like the Magnetic Lasso tool. The Extract feature is a way of indicating an edge through painting instead of drawing. Like other methods, it's not a cure-all, but when you need it, you need it. To use Extract:

1. In the Layers palette, drag the layer you're working with to the New Layer button to duplicate it, then click the eye icon for the original layer to hide it. This step backs up

the original layer data in case you want to try again.

2. Choose Filter > Extract.

3. Select the Edge Highlighter tool, and drag it to paint an outline along the edge you want to define (**Figure 3.17**). When dragging the brush, keep it over the edge you want to define. It's better to keep the brush center on the subject's side of the edge.

4. When you're done painting the outline, select the Fill tool and click inside the area you want to keep.

5. Click Preview to check the separation of foreground from background.

6. If needed, use the Cleanup tool to make unwanted areas transparent, or use the Edge Touchup tool to define the edge of the subject more cleanly.

7. When you're done, click OK.

TIP: You can view each channel of an image without having to open the Channels palette; just use keyboard shortcuts. Press the Command/Ctrl key with number keys 1 through 3. For example, press Command/Ctrl-1 to display the red channel of an RGB image or the L channel of a LAB image. For CMYK images, Command/Ctrl 1 through 4 display each of the CMYK channels. In any color mode, Command/Ctrl-~ (tilde) displays all channels. And you can add the Option/Alt key to load the channel as a selection!

One of the interesting things about the Extract feature is that it actually performs "edge-spill decontamination." That is, it gets rid of those ugly halos around the selection by removing the background color from the remaining edge pixels. Cool!

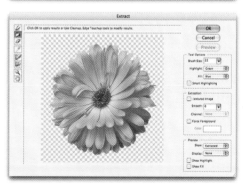

Figure 3.17: Working in the Extract dialog box: After dragging the Edge Highlighter tool (top), after clicking with the Fill tool (center), and after clicking the Preview button (bottom).

Edit a Selection as a Quick Mask

? I was editing a selection once and the image turned red. I think it's because I pressed a key. When I restarted Photoshop, everything was back to normal. What was that all about?

✓ You accidentally put Photoshop into Quick Mask mode. This is not a bad thing. Quick Mask mode simply displays your selection as a channel instead of as a selection marquee (**Figure 3.18**). Anywhere you paint in the Quick Mask becomes a selection when you exit Quick Mask mode. Use Quick Mask mode whenever you think it would be easier to define a selection through painting black and white rather than by using a selection tool.

Now back to the main question: How did you accidentally get into Quick Mask mode? Normally, you'd enter or exit Quick Mask mode using the Standard Mode and Quick Mask Mode icons in the toolbox. You probably pressed the keyboard shortcut for Quick Mask mode, which is Q. If your selection goes Quick Mask red all of a sudden, all you need to do is press Q again (or click the Standard Mode icon in the toolbox). Or, you can edit your selection in Quick Mask mode before returning to Standard mode.

Sculpting Selections with Masks and Channels

Even when you're armed with all of the best shortcuts for editing a selection marquee, it can sometimes be a royal pain to surround just the right pixels with selection tools. Clicking in the wrong place can drop the entire selection, and the shimmering "marching ants" effect can be awfully distracting when you're trying to do precision work.

There is another way. In addition to being able to convert a channel into a selection, you can also store selections as masks or extra channels, where white areas are inside the selection, and black is outside the selection, and gray areas are partially selected through the use of transparency.

What's valuable about working with selections in channels and masks is that you can "sculpt" selections using any painting tools to the precision you want. You can extend a selection area by painting with white, and reduce the selection area by painting with black. You can use a bigger brush to paint a selection into a larger area, or a very tiny brush to edit a selection edge very precisely.

Another advantage of editing selections as bitmaps is that it can be much easier on your wrist than attempting to exercise tight, precise control of your mouse or stylus while dragging one of the Lasso tools. With masks and channels, you can paint in a portion of a selection, relax your hand and sit back to check your work, then go back in and paint in or erase another area of the selection.

Figure 3.18: When the Quick Mask button is active (left), a selection (center) appears as red pixels (right) so that you can use painting tools to edit the selection.

You can use selection tools to help you paint or erase in Quick Mask mode, but don't let that confuse you. The only areas that convert back into a selection when you leave Quick Mask mode are the areas that are colored when you're in Quick Mask mode.

If you don't like the red color, you can change it by double-clicking either the Standard Mode or Quick Mask Mode icon in the toolbox.

TIP: If you accidentally deselect a selection, choose Edit > Undo right away and you'll restore the selection. Selection actions are added to the History palette, so you can undo selections or step backward or forward through them in the History palette. You can also try choosing Select > Reselect if you don't want to undo intermediate steps.

Convert between Mask, Selections, and Channels

? I just painted a great Quick Mask, but I'd like to keep it around. But as soon as I deselect the resulting selection, I lose the Quick Mask. How can I save a Quick Mask with the document?

✓ You can save the Quick Mask selection as an extra "alpha" channel. In the Channels palette, click the Save Selection as Channel button (**Figure 3.19**)—or Option/Alt-click the button if you want to name the channel right away. A new channel based on the selection appears in the Channels palette. (Note that while you work in Quick Mask mode, a temporary Quick Mask channel appears in the Channels palette.)

Once you save a selection as a channel, you can convert the channel back to a selection by Command/Ctrl-clicking the channel name in the Channels palette.

When you select your new channel in the Channels palette, you see the contents of the channel. You can edit a channel much like you would a Quick Mask—with painting tools. If you want to see the channel and the main image at the same time, enable the eye icons for both the channel and the main image in the left column of the Channels palette.

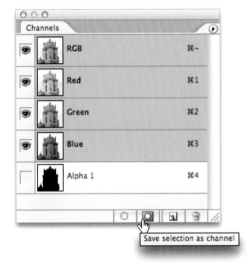

Figure 3.19: Click the Save Selection as Channel button to convert the current selection to a new channel.

TIP: When you want to copy the pixels inside a selection, but the contents of the selection exist on different layers, you don't have to flatten the document to copy the selection the way you want to. Simply make your selection and choose Edit > Copy Merged, and Photoshop merges all visible layer contents to the clipboard.

Convert between Selections and Layer Masks

? Making a selection into a channel is a nice trick, but what I do most often with selections is try to separate a subject from its background. Can I go straight from a selection to background removal?

✓ Yes, by converting a selection to a layer mask. It's quite common to create a selection and then turn that into a layer mask. If you can create a selection that defines the outline of a subject, you'll be able to separate it from its background rather quickly.

1. Create a selection (**Figure 3.20**).

2. You must be working with a layer that isn't the Background in the Layers palette. If the subject you want to mask is part of the Background, first Option/Alt-double-click the Background to convert it to a layer.

3. Make sure the subject's layer is selected in the Layers palette and click the Add Layer Mask button in the Layers palette.

4. A new layer mask appears (**Figure 3.21**). If needed, use any painting or editing tools to refine the layer mask by painting with black or white.

As with channels, you can convert the layer mask to a selection at any time: Just Command/Ctrl-click the layer mask icon in the Layers palette. If these shortcuts don't work, make sure the document is in Standard mode, not Quick Mask mode.

Figure 3.20: The Layers palette (left) contains two layers: the foreground objects with the sky selected (center) on the top, and a more dramatic sky on a lower layer (right).

Figure 3.21: Clicking the Add Layer Mask button with the sky selection active adds a layer mask (left) to the current layer. Because the sky is selected, the new mask keeps the sky visible and hides the rest (center). This is the opposite of what we want, so with the layer mask selected in the Layers palette, we choose Image > Adjustments > Invert. That inverts the mask and gives us what we want: a mask that makes the old sky transparent and reveals the new sky.

Comparing Channels to Layer Masks

? But… if channels and masks are both ways to store and use selections as pixels, what exactly is the difference between a channel and a layer mask?

✔️ Extra channels (those other than the image's own color channels, such as RGB) don't directly affect the final look of the document (unless you export one along with an image, as an alpha channel). Compared to a channel, a layer mask does affect the final look of a document by applying transparency to a layer.

You'd typically create a new channel to store selections or transparency away in a file for later use, and you'd typically create a new mask to create transparent areas on a specific layer right now.

Scaling, Rotating, or Distorting a Selection Marquee

? I created a selection that was just right, except that I needed to rotate and scale the entire selection. When I tried using the Free Transform command, it rotated and scaled the selected pixels, not the selection. How can I transform the selection but not the pixels?

☑ As you discovered, the transformation commands on the Edit menu affect only pixels, not selection marquees. Instead, choose Select > Transform Selection (**Figure 3.22**). With Transform Selection, the transformation bounding box works the way it does for the Edit > Free Transform command but only affects the selection marquee, not the image. When you're done, commit the transformation by pressing Enter or Return.

Spreading Out or Pulling In Selections

? I want to make a selection slightly larger, but because it isn't a uniform shape, the selection becomes distorted if I try to enlarge it using Transform Selection. What now?

☑ Sounds like you'll find the answer in the Expand/Contract commands. They don't scale selections—they offset them inward or outward. To spread out or pull in a selection, choose Select > Modify > Expand or Contract (**Figure 3.23**). However, for really fine control over spreading or choking a selection edge, switch to Quick Mask mode, run a small Gaussian Blur filter on the mask (perhaps 1 pixel), then open the Levels command (Image > Adjustments > Levels). Drag the gray midpoint slider to expand or contract the selection in the channel, then click OK and leave Quick Mask mode.

Figure 3.22: Using the Transform Selection command to rotate and scale an elliptical marquee to match the perspective of the clock face.

  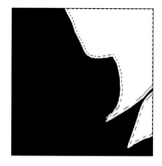

Figure 3.23: Original selection (top left) and Expand Selection dialog box (left). Selection after entering 5 in Expand Selection dialog box (top center) and after entering -5 (top right).

Using a Selection as a Line Instead of an Area

? How can I paint along a selection edge with a line, instead of filling it?

✓ You can choose between two options in this case. To paint the selection marquee with a simple stroke, choose Edit > Stroke, enter a width and other options, and click OK.

Alternately, you can be more creative with that border, such as painting it with an interesting fill, by choosing Select > Modify > Border. After you enter a Width and click OK, the selection encloses the border of the original selection, instead of enclosing an area. Now fill it with something interesting, or run a filter.

> **TIP:** Choose Select > Inverse (press Command/Ctrl-Shift-I) to select what's outside the selection instead of what's inside it. The Inverse command is useful whenever the selection is the opposite of what you want, or when you think it's easier to select everything other than the subject.

Blurring the Edge of a Selection

? What's the best way to soften the edge of a selection?

✓ When a selection is active, simply choose Select > Feather and enter the width of the edge blur you want (**Figure 3.24**). Keep in mind that there won't be any visible change to the selection marquee after you feather the selection—you'll only see the effect of feathering after you apply a change to the selection in some way, such as filling it.

For more control over the softening the edges of a selection, try these steps:

1. Make a selection.
2. In the Channels palette, click the Save Selection As Channel button

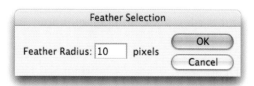

Figure 3.24: Choose Select > Feather to soften the edge of a selection.

to make a new channel from the selection.

3. Apply a blur filter to the channel (**Figure 3.25**). If you want, you can use other blur filters and tools to get exactly the blur you want.

4. In the Channels palette, Command/Ctrl-click the channel to convert it back to a selection. Because blurring the channel created grayscale values, the selection is feathered.

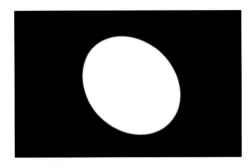

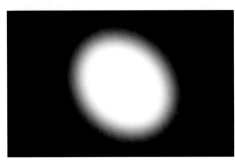

Figure 3.25: A channel resulting from a selection (top), and after applying the Gaussian Blur filter (bottom). When the channel is converted back to a selection, the selection border will be feathered by the blur created in the channel.

Transferring a Selection to Another Document

? I made a selection in one document, and I realized that I have a use for that same selection in another document. How can I quickly transfer a selection from one document to another?

✓ Piece of cake! Photoshop makes it possible to move selections between documents in two ways: as a "marching ants" selection or as a saved channels. To move the selection itself, make sure both documents are visible and drag the selection from one window to the next using any of the selection tools. If you want to center the selection, hold down the Shift key while dragging. (If the two images have the same pixel dimensions, the Shift key will make the selection appear in the same position as in the original file.)

Alternately, you could save the selection in the Channels palette and then drag the channel tile across to the other document or use the Duplicate Channel feature in the Channels palette flyout menu to copy it into the other file.

TIP: When converting between a mask (or channel) and a selection, Photoshop has to draw the selection line somewhere. For a mask that contains only black and white, the border is easy to figure out. For grayscale masks, the selection border is drawn at the 50-percent value of the grayscale image that forms the mask. If a selection edge isn't falling exactly where you expected, you can fine-tune the resulting selection by first using Levels or Curves to adjust the contrast in the mask. And if you're painting in a mask, a harder-edged brush makes it easier to tell where the selection border will fall.

Selecting with Pen Tool Paths

? I was looking at the Paths palette and I found a button that can convert a path to a selection. When is this useful?

✓ Many people who are fluent with the Pen tool find it easier to set up selections by drawing a path and then converting the path to a selection. Paths can be much easier to edit for subjects that involve precise lines and curves. Instead of having to drag the mouse so carefully, as you must do with the marquee and Lasso tools, with the Pen tool you can adjust paths precisely by dragging handles, points, and segments as needed.

Another advantage of paths is that you can draw multiple paths, store them in the Paths palette, and convert them to selections at any time. Here's how:

1. Select the Pen tool and click the Paths icon in the Options bar.

2. Use the Pen tool to draw the outline you want (**Figure 3.26**).

3. Paths are temporary unless you save them. To save the path with the document, double-click the temporary Work Path in the Paths palette to name it as a new entry.

4. To save more paths, click in the empty area of the Paths palette and draw and save another path.

5. In the Paths palette, Command/Ctrl-click the Work Path to create a selection from the path. (Or press Command-Return/Ctrl-Enter.)

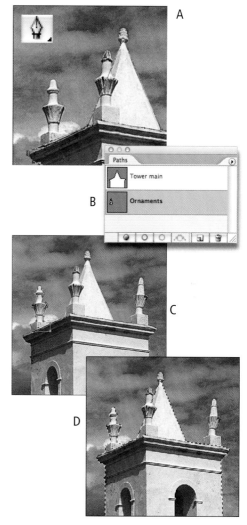

Figure 3.26: A path around the top of the tower drawn using the Pen tool (A). The path saved in the Paths palette (B). This is repeated with a path drawn around a tower ornament (C). After Command/Ctrl-clicking the first path, Command/Ctrl-Shift-clicking the next path adds it to the selection (D).

6. To build a selection out of multiple paths, Command/Ctrl-click a path in the Paths palette, and then Command/Ctrl-Shift-click the other paths.

Using Selections to Save Multiple Crops

? **Is there a way to save multiple crop areas within a single document? We've worked out preferred crop areas for various media like 4:3 aspect ratio TVs and widescreen TVs, and we'd like to save these crop areas in the master image.**

☑ Once you crop an image with the Crop tool and save the document, you can't retrieve the deleted area unless it still exists in a history state, or you applied the crop in Adobe Camera Raw, or you turned on the "Hide" feature in the Options bar with the Crop tool (see "Keeping What You Cropped," earlier in this chapter). However, you can sort of store multiple crop areas by saving selections in the Channels palette.

1. Use the Rectangular Marquee tool to draw a selection rectangle around the crop area you want to save.

2. In the Channels palette, click the Save Selection as Channel button, as we described earlier in this chapter.

3. Repeat steps 1 and 2 for other crop areas you want to save.

4. When you want to use a saved crop area, Command/Ctrl-click it in the Channels palette, and then choose Image > Crop. You might want to do this to a duplicate of the original image.

Amazing Transformations

Rotating a Layer vs. the Entire Document

? **How can I rotate an entire document? The commands on the Edit > Transform submenu rotate only one layer at a time.**

☑ Photoshop has two sets of rotation commands. One rotates layers and objects, and the other rotates everything (**Figure 3.27**). When you want to rotate just one layer or object (like a path), select a layer in the Layers palette, then choose a command from the Edit > Transform submenu.

When you want to rotate absolutely everything in a Photoshop document, including the document dimensions, choose a command from the Image > Rotate Canvas submenu.

Rotating an Image the Fast, Precise Way

? **I've used the Arbitrary rotation option, but it takes a lot of trial and error. How can I tell how much an image needs to be straightened?**

 When you want to straighten an image but you don't know the

exact angle you need, the Measure tool can help you (**Figure 3.28**):

1. Select the Measure tool. It normally hides in the toolbox under the Eyedropper tool; if the Measure tool is hidden, hold down the mouse on the Eyedropper tool to reveal it.

2. Drag the Measure tool along a line in the image that should be perfectly horizontal or vertical.

3. Choose Image > Rotate Canvas > Arbitrary. The angle from the Measure tool is entered automatically, so just click OK and the image should straighten perfectly.

  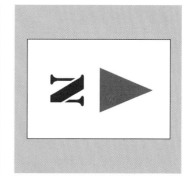

Figure 3.27: The original (left) has two layers: One with the triangle, and the other with the letter N. In the center image, only the triangle layer is rotated, using Edit > Transform > Rotate 90° CW. In the right image, the entire document is rotated, using Image > Rotate Canvas 90°CW.

Figure 3.28: Dragging the Measure tool along a line in the image that should be vertical (top with detail view); Rotate Canvas dialog box with the Measure tool angle entered automatically (center); canvas straightened by the angle entered in the Rotate Canvas dialog box (right).

Rotating in Camera Raw or Bridge

? I see the same rotation features in Photoshop, Camera Raw, and Bridge. When is it better to rotate in Bridge or Camera Raw rather than Photoshop?

☑ Adobe Bridge is great for applying 90-degree rotations to a bunch of images at once. You'd usually do this when you import scans or digital camera photos that don't automatically rotate. Camera Raw is the best place to straighten many crooked digital camera photos at once. Use Photoshop for any remaining rotational needs that aren't met by Bridge or Camera Raw.

To apply 90-degree rotations in Bridge, select an image and click one of the Rotate icons at the top of a Bridge window (**Figure 3.29**). Note that you can select multiple images and rotate them all at once much faster than you can in Photoshop.

Camera Raw also sports these same Rotate icons. However, Camera Raw also lets you rotate at any angle with its Crop tool. If you drag a crop rectangle in Camera Raw and position the pointer outside the crop rectangle, you can drag to rotate the crop rectangle (**Figure 3.30**). The rotation takes effect when you open the raw image in Photoshop; rotation and cropping are applied during the conversion.

In both Camera Raw and Bridge, the rotation information is saved with the object's metadata, which means you always retain the complete original image in case you want to edit the rotation later.

Figure 3.29: In any Bridge window, you can rotate one or more selected images 90 degrees at a time using the two rotate icons in the middle of the toolbar.

Figure 3.30: Dragging from just outside the top right corner of a Crop Tool rectangle to rotate an image in Camera Raw.

Instant, Direct Straightening

? I see a Straighten tool in Camera Raw. How does this compare to the Photoshop Measure tool method you covered earlier?

☑ Both Adobe Camera Raw and the Lens Correction filter include a Straighten tool that directly corrects crooked images. If you thought the Measure tool trick was cool (see "Rotating an Image the Fast, Precise Way," earlier in this section), the Straighten tool does the same thing in fewer steps:

1. Open a raw image in Camera Raw, or if you already have an image open in Photoshop, choose Filter > Distort > Lens Correction.

2. Select the Straighten tool from the Camera Raw or Lens Correction toolbox.

3. Drag the Straighten tool along a line in the image that should be perfectly horizontal or vertical (**Figure 3.31**). In Camera Raw, the crop rectangle rotates, but the image itself remains unrotated during conversion from raw format. In Lens Correction, the image immediately rotates according to the angle formed by the line.

4. Click OK when you're done making all corrections in Camera Raw or Lens Correction. The rotation is applied to the image.

Transforming with Total Freedom

? **Is there a way to transform with a bounding box or by typing numbers, as you can in Illustrator or InDesign?**

In a word: Yes. The Free Transform command does it all. When you choose Edit > Free Transform, a bounding box appears around the current layer. You can, of course, use the bounding box to transform the layer. What most folks don't notice, however, is that when the Free Transform bounding box is active, numeric entry options appear in the Options bar, too! So you can move, rotate, or scale the layer by entering precise values and then pressing Return or Enter.

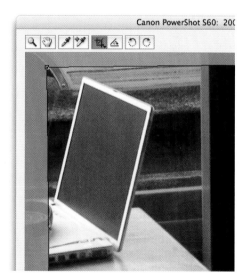

Figure 3.31: After dragging the Straighten tool in the Camera Raw dialog box (left), the crop rectangle rotates to match, so that the image will be straightened when converted from raw format.

But for those who want to work visually rather than numerically, here's a quick guide to the Free Transform bounding box:

- To rotate, position the cursor outside the bounding box until you see the double-arrow rotation icon, and drag (**Figure 3.32**).

- To scale, drag any handle.

- To skew, Command/Ctrl-drag a handle.

- When using the bounding box, add the Shift key to transform proportionally, or add Option/Alt to transform from the center.

Correcting Lens Distortion

? Is there anything I can do about the barrel distortion that's produced by my camera lens, particularly in wide angle shots?

✓ Photoshop CS2 includes the new Lens Correction filter, which is great for removing various types of visual distortion which are usually most obvious in images shot using wide-angle lenses. Start by choosing Filter > Distort > Lens Correction (**Figure 3.33**).

It's a good idea to straighten the image first. Select the Straighten tool and drag it along a line in the image that should be perfectly horizontal or vertical, and Photoshop rotates the image accordingly. If the result is just a little bit off, click in the Angle value and press the up and down arrow keys. That's usually an easier and more precise way to adjust the value, rather than dragging the Angle control.

Then, to correct the barrel distortion, increase or decrease the Remove Distortion amount. Check your progress by keeping your eye on the grid.

To correct perspective distortion, increase or decrease the Vertical Perspective or Horizontal Perspective values. It's usually easier to see what you're doing here after you've straightened the image and removed barrel distortion.

As you make corrections, Photoshop automatically sizes the image. If you think too much of the edges are cut off, reduce the Scale value at the bottom of the dialog box. Click OK when you're done.

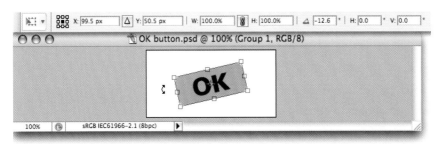

Figure 3.32: Rotating with the Free Transform bounding box (notice the Options bar).

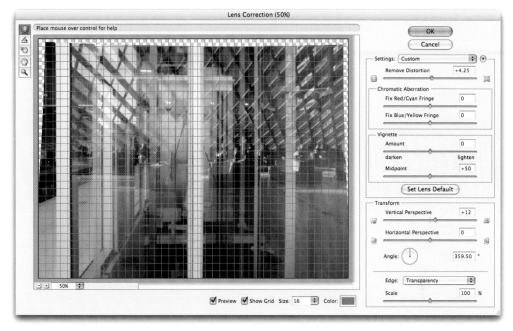

Figure 3.33: Formerly distorted vertical bars are straightened after adjusting the Remove Distortion, Vertical Perspective, and Angle options in the Lens Correction dialog box.

Duplicate Anything

Duplicate an Entire Document

? I sometimes want to make a quick copy of a document so I can try out an idea. Is there an easier way than closing the document and duplicating it on the desktop?

☑ No need to run off to the desktop; you can duplicate a document from within Photoshop. Choose Image > Duplicate, name the duplicate, select Duplicate Merged Layers Only if you want the duplicate to be a flattened version of the current document, and click

OK. The duplicate document appears as a new window.

Or even faster: Add the Option/Alt key when you choose Image > Duplicate and you'll get a copy without the annoying dialog box!

A document you create with the Duplicate command doesn't exist as a file until you save it, even though you see a named title bar at the top of the duplicate document.

Duplicate documents can be useful for creating variations on a document, or for quickly experimenting with techniques on a flattened or downsampled version of a document.

Duplicate Layers

? What's the best way to duplicate a layer? And can a layer be copied to another document?

✓ There are lots of ways to duplicate a layer, depending on what you're trying to accomplish.

To duplicate the current layer using the Layer menu, choose Layer > Duplicate Layer. In the Duplicate Layer dialog box, you have the option to create the duplicate in another open document or in a new document. This is a great way to "send" a layer to another document. The Duplicate Layer command also appears on the Layers palette menu.

Another, faster way to copy a layer is to select the Move tool and Option/ Alt-drag anywhere in the image. This is a good option if you don't want the duplicate to be in the exact same position as the original layer.

Or, to duplicate the current layer using the Layers palette, drag a layer to the New Layer icon.

A type object exists on its own layer, so you can use any of these methods to duplicate a type object too.

Duplicate a Path or Shape

? How can I duplicate a path or shape without duplicating the entire layer? I just want to make a copy of the vector object on the same layer.

✓ It's a simple matter of changing the tool you're using to select. To copy a path or shape without making

a new layer, Option/Alt-drag the path or shape using the Path Selection tool (the black arrow tool), not the Move tool (**Figure 3.34**).

Figure 3.34: Duplicating the original path (top) by Option/Alt-dragging the path with the Path Selection tool (bottom).

Create a Step-and-Repeat Layout

? I don't have a layout program and I sometimes need to create step-and-repeat layouts, like a page full of business cards. It's easy enough to copy layers, but when the original needs to be updated, I have to set up the copies all over again. Is there an easier way?

✓ Thanks to the new Smart Objects feature in Photoshop CS2, it's now practical to create step-and-repeat jobs right in your favorite image-editing program. You can create a single graphic, make a Smart Object out of it, and duplicate the Smart Object as needed. If you edit the contents of the Smart Object, all of the Smart Object duplicates update automatically. Here's how it works:

1. In the Layers palette, select the layers you want to repeat, and choose Layer > Smart Objects > Group Into New Smart Object (**Figure 3.35**).

2. Make sure the image canvas is large enough to contain all the duplicates you're going to make (see "Image Size vs. Canvas Size, earlier in this chapter). Or, probably better, just create a new document large

enough, and drag your new smart object layer into it.

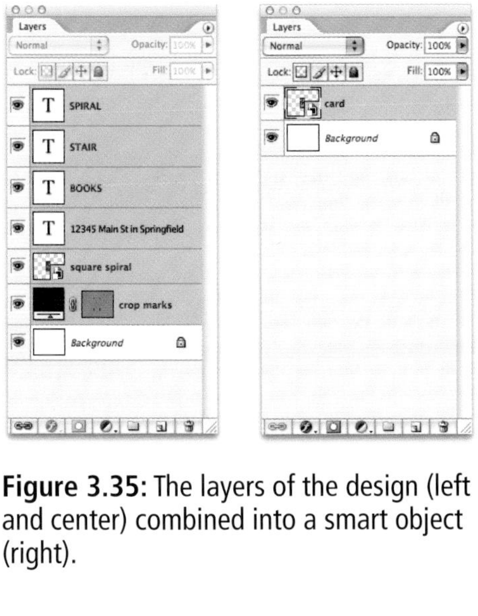

3. Using the Move tool, position the Smart Object in the top left corner of the document.

4. Using the Move tool, Option-Shift-drag/Alt-Shift-drag the Smart Object to make and position a duplicate next to the original. Repeat until you've created an entire row of duplicates (**Figure 3.36**).

Figure 3.36: The smart object Option/Alt-dragged across four times to create a complete row.

Figure 3.35: The layers of the design (left and center) combined into a smart object (right).

5. If you didn't space the layers evenly while drawing, you can do it now. Select all of the layers making up the row and choose Layer > Distribute > Horizontal Centers.

6. In the Layers palette, select the layers you created. Choose Layer > Group Layers The layers are now grouped in a folder in the Layers palette.

7. You can now Option-Shift-drag/Alt-Shift-drag a copy of the group downward from the original, repeating until you have the number of rows you want.

8. To update all of the smart objects at once, double-click any of them in the Layers palette, or choose Layer > Smart Objects > Edit Contents (**Figure 3.37**).

9. The contents of the smart object open in a temporary window. Edit it as needed then save it and close the window.

When you close that editing window, Photoshop updates all of the smart object copies in the document!

> **TIP:** When you edit a smart object, there's behind-the-back document magic going on. When you choose Edit Contents and see the smart object opening in another window, it's opening as a temporary file stored in a hidden folder on your disk. When you close the edited smart object, the temporary file closes and is embedded back into the main Photoshop document.

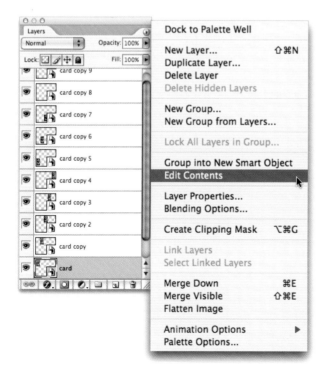

Figure 3.37: The Edit Contents command on the Layers palette menu (left) opens a smart object for editing. Here, the background image in the smart object was flipped (above). Saving this smart object updates all instances of that smart object in the document.

Correcting Images

Corrections Images

*T*HIS IS THE PART WHERE YOU GET TO PLAY DOCTOR. The image is your patient, of course, and the first thing you do is look over the image and take a few notes on areas that need improvement. Shadows that aren't black enough, an overall purple cast, some dust specks picked up during the scan or a pimple that showed up on the raw camera file, and so on. Once you've got an inventory of ailments to address, you can plan your procedures and the order in which you'll perform them.

Once you complete your diagnosis, you can place your patient on the operating table, surround it with all kinds of monitoring equipment (such as the Info palette and the Histogram), and whip out your precision tools—like the Smart Sharpen filter and the Healing Brush tool. (We're sure there are medical doctors out there who wish they had one of those!)

When you've got the right Breakthrough tips and tricks, you can cure whatever ails your images. Because there are already 1,000-page Photoshop books out there that show you the long way around (David has even written some of them), we've concentrated on the quickest, easiest techniques. Image correction shouldn't be brain surgery!

Evaluating an Image

Who's on First?

? When I have a new image in front of me, what should I do first—do some retouching or fix the tone and color?

☑ Typically, it's best to correct tone and color first. It can be easier to spot abnormalities like dust spots if the image generally looks normal. Unlike scans, digital camera images won't have surface defects, so those images can always go straight to color correction.

The important thing is to complete both basic color correction and remove unwanted blemishes (such as pimples and telephone wires) before you start making copies for different media, or moving on to deeper edits. If you ever need to go back to your master image, you don't want to have to re-create changes you made later in the process. For example, let's say you crop and resize an image and then remove unwanted telephone wires. Later you realize you need another version of the master image with a different crop. The telephone wires weren't removed in the master, so you'll have to remove them again.

Give the image a quick check again after you apply sharpening. Sometimes sharpening brings out blemishes or film scratches that were not visible before.

> **TIP:** You can see all of the view shortcuts in the Photoshop Help file. They're in the topic "Keys for Viewing Images."

Checking an Image for Surface Defects

? When I correct my scanned images, I fix any scratches and dust I can find, but later I often notice areas I missed. What's the best way to inspect an image without missing anything?

☑ Photoshop power users have a systematic way of carrying out search-and-destroy missions in search of image defects. When the image contains many more pixels than the screen, a popular method is to use keyboard shortcuts to scroll to check the image sector by sector. Here's how to do it:

1. Click one of the Full Screen mode icons on the toolbar (or press F), and press Tab to hide all the palettes.

2. Press Command-Option-zero/Ctrl-Alt-zero to jump to Actual Size.

3. Press the Home key to scroll to the upper left corner of the document. Inspect this portion of the image for defects, and fix them if needed.

4. Press Command/Ctrl-Page Down to scroll the document one screenful to the right. Inspect this area and fix defects as needed, then scroll another screenful to the right (**Figure 4.1**).

5. When you reach the right edge of the document, press Page Down to go down one screenful. Inspect and fix as needed.

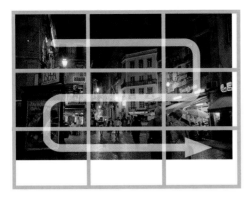

Figure 4.1: A screen-scrolling pattern for inspecting an image; each square is the area a monitor might see when viewing a large image at Actual Pixels magnification.

6. On this row, press Command/Ctrl-Page Up to scroll the document one screenful to the left, inspecting and fixing until you reach the left end of the row. Keep moving back and forth, row by row, until you reach the end of the image.

Some defects are easier to see when zoomed in, so you may prefer to perform your inspection at 200% even though covering the image may take longer.

Scrolling with a Laptop Keyboard

? Now wait a minute. I have a laptop, and the keyboard doesn't seem to have Home, End, Page Up, and Page Down keys. Am I out of luck?

✓ Because laptop keyboards are smaller than desktop keyboards, they often don't have dedicated Home, End, Page Up and Page Down keys. If you use such a laptop, find out if those keys are accessible through function key combinations. For example, on an

Apple PowerBook, Home is printed on the same key as the left arrow, and the left arrow is the default function. To use the Home function of that key, press Fn-Left Arrow.

Persistent Spots on Digital Camera Images

? There's a tiny black spot in the same location on a whole bunch of frames I just downloaded from my digital SLR. It looks like I'll have to hit every frame with the healing brush. Is there a problem with my camera?

✓ It's possible for dust to affect a digital camera image if it gets into the camera and lands on the image sensor. Dust can enter a digital SLR when you change the lens. If you see the same spot on your photos over and over, your sensor may be dusty. You may be able to locate some dust on the sensor by shooting a bright light source at a small aperture like f/22. While cleaning kits and techniques exist, the sensor is extremely delicate, and you risk causing irreversible damage to the sensor if you make a wrong move. It may be best to have the sensor cleaned by an authorized service center.

Reading a Histogram

? Everyone tells me to check the histogram when I'm evaluating image quality, but to me, it's just a graph. What am I looking for when I view a histogram?

✓ For a typical image, a good histogram shows a full, solid range of tones from black to white. When you evaluate a histogram, you're keeping an eye out for two things: gaps and clipping (**Figure 4.2**):

- A gap at the left side means no pixels in the image are black. If you want black pixels, adjust the black point in the Levels or Curves dialog box, or the Shadows slider in Camera Raw.

- A gap at the right side means nothing in the image is white.

- Gaps in the middle mean there are tones where no information exists. Small gaps are rarely a problem, but if there is a regular pattern of gaps, you might see posterization or stair-stepping in the image's gradations.

- If the histogram falls off abruptly at the left or right edge, too many levels may be clipped—you may have lost shadow or highlight detail. Look into this further in the topic "Checking for Clipping."

Keep in mind that there's no ideal histogram; it all depends on the image. If you take a picture of a cloudy sky, there won't be any black in the image, therefore it would be normal to see most of the image's tones at the right side of the graph.

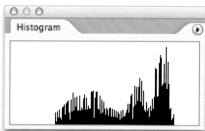

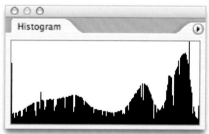

Figure 4.2: An image lacking contrast (top) and its histogram (second from top) revealing a lack of any tones in the shadows and highlights; next, an image with proper contrast (third from top) with its histogram (bottom).

TIP: For some other ways to view the Histogram palette, try the alternate views in the Histogram palette menu. For example, All Channels View lets you see a histogram for each color channel individually.

Checking for Clipping

? How can I tell if the shadows or highlights of an image are clipped?

✓ These tips can help you locate clipping in Photoshop.

- In the Levels dialog box, press Option/Alt while dragging the black or white Input sliders to see which pixels get clipped at a given level (**Figure 4.3**).

- If you see many levels bunched up against the left or right side of the Histogram palette, check for clipping. Levels at the ends of the histogram don't necessarily indicate that anything important is clipped, because the clipped levels may be absolute black shadows or white specular highlights.

- Adding a Threshold adjustment layer can show which pixels exist at a given level, so that you can note the shadow and highlight levels at which meaningful details are clipped. You can then use those values in the Levels dialog box.

- In Camera Raw, enable the Shadow and Highlight checkboxes at the top of the Camera Raw dialog box to display blue pixels if shadows are clipped, or red pixels if highlights are clipped.

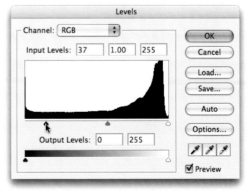

Figure 4.3: Original image (top left), image when Option/Alt-dragging the black Input Level slider in the Levels dialog box to reveal clipping at level 0 (top center), and increased clipping revealed (top right) when Option/Alt-dragging the black slider to level 37 (right).

Using the Info Palette

? What's the Info palette good for? How can I use its readouts?

✓ The Info palette is like a trusted advisor who constantly whispers valuable guidance into your ear about the current tool, selection, or document. Photoshop CS2 adds even more display options to the Info palette. Maximize the usefulness of the Info palette (**Figure 4.4**) with these tips:

- To customize the information displayed in the Info palette, choose Palette Options from the Info palette menu.

- The Info palette displays the same list of items as the status bar. This may sound minor, but if the status bar is hidden—such as when you work in full screen mode—it can be a significant advantage to display your favorite status bar items in the Info palette instead.

- In the Info Palette Options dialog box, turning on Show Tool Hints displays useful text that typically

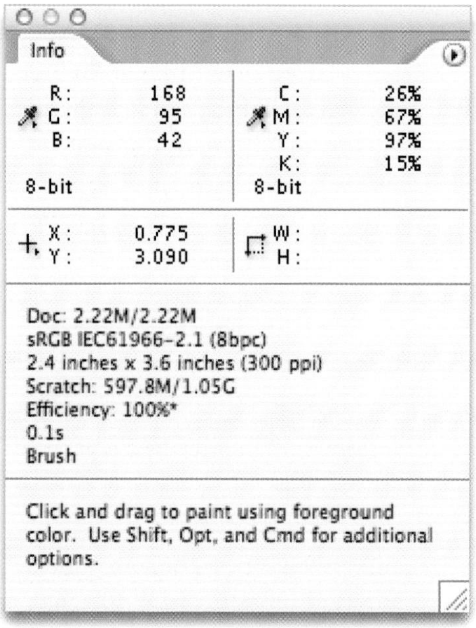

Figure 4.4: Info palette fully decked out with many readout options turned on, including status bar items in the middle section and tool hints at the bottom.

describes not only what the current tool does, but also extra functions when you also press a modifier key such as Shift. We think it's a great middle ground between the too-brief tool tips and having to navigate the help file.

Making Global Corrections

Removing Defects with Filters

? What are the most useful filters for removing defects like dust and scratches?

✓ First of all, if you're scanning and your scanner has defect-removal features, use them first. Photoshop provides techniques for "painting in" corrections where you want them, preserving the quality of the rest of the image (we cover those in the section "Making Local Corrections," later in this chapter). However, if an image has small defects throughout the whole image, you may want to use a Photoshop filter for defect removal. The best ones are on the Filter > Noise submenu (**Figure 4.5**):

- Despeckle applies a quick blur and can be useful for some types of noise. However, it isn't adjustable.

- Dust & Scratches is a step up from Despeckle, because it provides controls. Dust & Scratches looks for defects based on their size (controlled by the Radius option) and the amount of difference between their tone and color and the surroundings (controlled by Radius). Start with low values and increase them, but back off when the image starts to lose actual detail.

- Median isn't adjustable because it simply assigns a pixel the median value of the pixels of similar brightness surrounding it. As you might remember from math class, the median is not the average value; it's halfway between the minimum and maximum. This method tends to locate and then de-emphasize pixels that are significantly brighter or darker than their surroundings, which is how defects often appear.

- Reduce Noise is the newest and most sophisticated filter in this group. We cover it in the topic "Don't Bring the Noise." Like the filter name says, Reduce Noise is optimized for locating and reducing digital camera noise, so if you want to remove film grain from print or film scans, you may want to try a plug-in such as Grain Surgery by Visual Infinity (*www. visinf.com*). Reduce Noise isn't designed for removing dust and scratches, either.

Most defect removal filters share an important limitation: It's hard for software to tell the difference between details and defects. Just when you think you've applied a filter at sufficient strength to wipe out dust or noise, you notice that you're losing important details like stone textures or blades of grass.

Figure 4.5: The Filter > Noise submenu contains filters that can be useful for minimizing noise and surface defects.

Correct Quickly with Auto Color

? What's the fastest way to color-correct an image?

☑ The Auto Color command in Photoshop can be a quick and convenient way to correct images that should have a fairly typical color balance—particularly if you quickly become lost when making manual Levels and Curves adjustments. But avoid choosing the Auto Color command from the Image menu's Adjustments sub-menu. Instead, you can control this feature more precisely through the Levels dialog box (**Figure 4.6**). Thanks to Bruce Fraser for showing us this cool technique.

1. Create a new Levels adjustment layer.

2. Click the Options button in the Levels dialog box.

3. In the Auto Color Correction Options dialog box, select the Find Dark & Light Colors and Snap Neutral Midtones options. If the image doesn't look right, try other Algorithm options. Turning off Snap Neutral Midtones may improve the image if there aren't any neutral gray tones in the image.

4. Fine-tune the Clipping values. Default clipping values should be set to between 0 and 0.5% as a starting point. Then you can move up from there in small increments by pressing the up arrow and down arrow keys on the keyboard. Back off when the image starts to lose

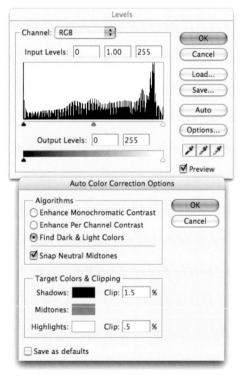

Figure 4.6: Original image (top), fixed version (second from top), and the Auto Color Correction Options that neutralized the color cast. You can monitor the Levels histogram as you adjust the options.

highlight or shadow detail. As an alternative, you can click the Shadow and Highlight boxes to set their target values with eyedroppers. If the adjustments you've made so far have not corrected the color balance, click the Midtones swatch and adjust the values; equal values in all three RGB channels neutralize a typical image.

5. Click OK. Photoshop might ask you if you want to save the current settings as the defaults. You can do so if you're going to work on more images that will need similar corrections. It's a good idea to save defaults that have Find Dark & Light colors selected and Snap Neutral Midtones turned on, because you're going to want those options to be on for most images.

Using Auto Color may not take care of every color problem, but if neutral shadows, midtones, and highlights existed in the original subject of the image, Auto Color can quickly give you a huge head start compared to using other methods. And because you applied this using an adjustment layer, you can always remove it or tweak it without degrading the image further.

Calibrating and Profiling Your Monitor

If you want to do the best job of correcting your images, make sure your monitor is, at the very least, profiled—and calibrated if possible. When your monitor is calibrated and profiled, the images you produce are more likely to print reliably and appear consistent when you send them to other people or publish them on the Web. Calibrating and profiling make it possible for today's color management systems to do their job.

There's more than one way to calibrate and profile your monitor. You can use the calibration software you already have; this is the least expensive—and least accurate—method. On Mac OS X, you can use the Apple Display Calibrator Assistant; open the Displays system preference, click the Color tab, and click the Calibrate button. On Windows, use the Adobe Gamma utility that comes with Photoshop. Both work similarly; just follow the instructions.

A better way is to use a hardware calibrator, such as the GretagMacbeth Eye-One. Instead of relying on your eyes, a hardware calibrator uses a precise instrument to measure the color response of the monitor and build an accurate profile. Photoshop can use the profile to compensate for how the monitor shows color.

Whether you're calibrating and profiling an LCD or CRT monitor, calibration and profiling work best if the monitor has warmed up to its optimum operating temperature. That can take about half an hour, to be on the safe side. Working in a darkened room also helps.

The Curves Dialog Box in Five Minutes or Less

The Curves dialog box is intimidating at first, but mastering Curves is the key to many advanced techniques. To help you get there, we put together this cheat sheet to help you figure out which way is up in the Curves dialog box.

At the bottom of the Curves dialog box is a gradient that tells you which side is white and which side is black. You can switch the orientation of black and white by clicking the gradient. All of the tips below show the RGB curve where white is on the right by default.

The default curve is a 45-degree line because which indicates that no changes have been made (all of the output values equal all of the input values). When you steepen a segment of the curve above a 45-degree angle, you add contrast. Combine that knowledge with the figures on this page, and you'll know which way to drag points in the Curves dialog box.

It's useful to know that the Levels and Curves dialog boxes do the same thing; the main difference is that Curves gives you more control points to work with so that you can make more subtle changes. The Curves dialog box doesn't offer the histogram that's included in the Levels dialog box, but that's easy to address: simply leave the Histogram palette open and in view as you work in the Curves dialog box.

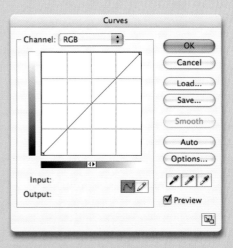

The default Curves dialog box for an RGB image. The 45-degree angle of the curve shows that no changes have been made. You can adjust the curve for each of the RGB color channels by selecting a channel from the Channel popup menu at the top of the dialog box. A grayscale image has only one channel, while a CMYK image has four.

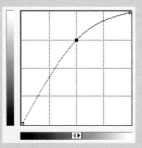

To brighten a tone in an image, click a point (usually a midpoint) and drag it up. Drag the point down if you want to darken that tone.

You can add a point for any exact tone in an image: While the Curves dialog box is open, Command/Ctrl-click the image to add a point on the curve precisely at that tone. Then drag the point around.

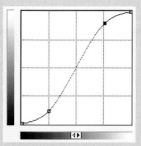

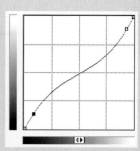

Where the curve rises more than 45 degrees, contrast goes up. This is a classic S-curve that increases contrast in midtones, but that means the highlights and shadows lose some contrast.

This curve is the opposite of the one on the left. It decreases contrast in the midtones, and increases it in the shadows and highlights.

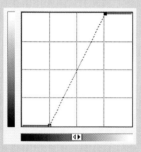

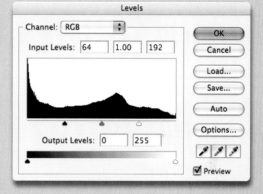

The curve above does the same thing as the positions of the Levels sliders on the right. The settings clip the shadows and highlights significantly.

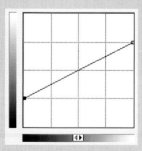

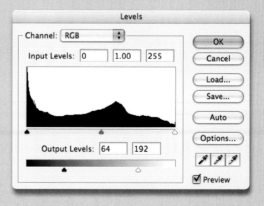

The curve above limits the final shadow and highlight values, just like the Levels sliders on the right.

Enhance Shadow and Highlight Details

? **What can I do when most of the important tones in an image are in the very light and very dark areas? Any move I make in Levels or Curves either blows out the highlights, plugs up the shadows, or flattens the midtones.**

☑ Some images have detail across such a large dynamic range that it's time-consuming or difficult to make both the shadows and the highlights look good using Levels and Curves. The Shadow/Highlight command uses advanced blending techniques that can't be duplicated using Levels or Curves alone, and Shadow/Highlight can often get you where you want in one step:

1. Choose Image > Adjustments > Shadow/Highlight (**Figure 4.7**).

2. If there's detail in the shadows that you want to lighten, increase the Shadow value. While the dialog box defaults to 50, for many images we recommend starting at a low value like 5. Many digital cameras and scanners are noisy in the shadows, and pushing shadows too far can emphasize existing noise.

3. If there's detail in the highlights that you want to darken, increase the Highlights value.

4. If the changes to the shadows and highlights are good, but midtones are now flat, enable the Show More Options checkbox and increase the Midtone Contrast value.

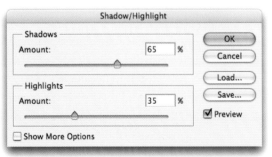

Figure 4.7: Original image (top left), improved version (top right), and the Shadow/Highlight settings that improved this particular image (left). Increasing the Shadows value opens up the shadows, and increasing the Highlights value restores detail to the sky.

Punch Up an Image with Blending Modes

? I'm a little confused about blending modes. There's a long list of them and they're everywhere—in palettes, dialog boxes, and the Options bar—yet I still don't know why most of them exist. Got an answer for that?

☑ Blending modes can be hard to understand because their effect depends on the layers you apply them to. If you try them out, it's obvious that they can radically alter the appearance of an image in "cool" ways, but they can appear to be unpredictable and their practical uses aren't apparent at first.

It can help to understand how a blending mode works. To use a blending mode, you need at least two layers. You apply the blending mode to any layer other than the bottom layer. The blend-

ing mode compares a pixel on the upper layer to a pixel on the lower (base) layer, and applies some math to the color or tone values of both pixels. Sometimes the math is as easy as adding, subtracting, multiplying, or dividing. For RGB images, pixels get lighter when the pixel values increase, and get darker when the pixel values decrease, and that's how the blending mode affects the appearance of the image. Color changes result when the math changes the values in each color channel.

We can tell that you're already recoiling from this page because we used the word "math." Relax... it's possible to understand blending modes without touching any numbers at all. Use the sidebar "Blending Modes: Justify Your Existence," on the next page, to help figure out if a blending mode can help solve a problem for you.

Change Blending Modes with Shortcuts

? Is there a way to change blending modes using the keyboard?

☑ If you're not sure which blending mode to use, you can quickly cycle through every one of them using keyboard shortcuts. Press Shift-+ (plus sign) to apply the next blending mode in the blending mode popup menu, or Shift-− (minus sign) to apply the previous blending mode. Every blending mode also has its own direct shortcut—such as Option/Alt-Shift-S for Screen or Option/Alt-Shift-M for Multiply. To learn them all, open Photoshop Help and search for "blending mode keys."

Blending Modes: Justify Your Existence

The differences between blend modes in Photoshop often come down to variations in color intensity and contrast. The modes are divided into groups, marked by dividing lines in the blend mode popup menu you see throughout the program.

Normal and Dissolve

Normal mode simply displays applied colors, unchanged, over the base layer. Layers behind the applied colors show through transparent pixels on that layer. Dissolve expresses transparency using a random dither pattern.

Modes that Lighten

Lighten, Screen, Color Dodge, and Linear Dodge lighten image areas. No part of the base image becomes darker, and black is the neutral color for these modes—black areas don't change the underlying color. When experimenting, start with Lighten and Screen. Lighten compares the applied and base pixels and keeps the lighter pixel. Screen produces a more intense version of Lighten because it multiplies the inverse of the two pixels' color values. Color Dodge colorizes lighter base pixels with the applied color; darker base pixels don't change as much. If Color Dodge is too extreme, try Linear Dodge, which is a lower-contrast version of Color Dodge.

The upper (applied) and lower (base) layers used in the examples. Watch what happens to white, black, 50% gray, color, and the semi-transparent circle in the lower right corner of the top layer.

Modes that Darken

Darken, Multiply, Color Burn, and Linear Burn modes darken image areas. This mode group has the opposite effect of the modes that lighten. For example, Color Dodge colorizes lighter base pixels with the applied color, while Color Burn colorizes darker base pixels. The neutral color for these modes is white, not black.

| Normal | Lighten | Screen | Color Dodge | Linear Dodge | Difference |

| Dissolve | Darken | Multiply | Color Burn | Linear Burn | Exclusion |

Difference Modes

Difference and Exclusion modes amplify differences between applied and base color values. The bigger the difference, the more intense the color. Exclusion is a lower-contrast version. You get a neutral result (black) if the applied and base pixels are identical.

Light Source Modes

Overlay, Soft Light, Hard Light, Vivid Light, Linear Light, and Pin Light modes alter color based on whether the applied or base pixels are lighter or darker than 50 percent gray—the neutral color for these modes. The main differences among these modes have to do with the amount of contrast they produce. Overlay and Soft Light are frequently used because they're the least extreme modes in this group.

Color Component Modes

Hue, Saturation, Color, and Luminosity transfer specific color components of the applied pixel to the base pixel. Hue replaces the base color's hue with the applied color's hue, but preserves the base color's lightness and saturation. Saturation replaces the base color's saturation without affecting its hue and lightness. Color replaces the base color's hue and saturation without affecting lightness. Luminosity replaces the base color's lightness without affecting hue and saturation.

Painting Modes

You only see the Behind and Clear modes in the blending modes popup menu when you use painting tools.

The Behind mode creates the illusion of painting the applied color behind the base color, by painting only the transparent pixels on a layer. Clear let you "paint transparency." Any pixels it touches become clear, revealing any layers behind. For these modes to work, Lock Transparency must be turned off in the Layers palette. The Replace mode is used only by the Healing Brush tool, to help preserve details like texture and grain.

In the Behind and Clear examples below, we painted the top layer with the Brush tool and a yellow color.

Overlay   Soft Light   Hard Light   Hue   Saturation   Behind

Vivid Light   Linear Light   Pin Light   Hard Mix   Color   Luminosity   Clear

Making Local Corrections

Heal, Spot, Heal!

? **I usually do touch up with the clone stamp tool, but Photoshop keeps adding more touch-up tools. When's the best time to use the Clone Stamp tool versus the other, newer healing tools?**

☑ The pattern we've observed is that each new touch-up tool the Photoshop team adds has a bit more smarts than the older tools.

The Clone Stamp tool is the oldest and most literal of the touch-up tools. You Option/Alt-click to set a source point on the image and then click or drag to paint a copy of the source point. This direct cloning makes no attempt to adjust the clone to the new area, so you have to set your source point carefully.

For isolated defects like a dust speck, click or drag the Spot Healing Brush. For example, if you click the Spot Healing Brush on a dust speck, it tries to fill the spot you clicked with whatever surrounds it (**Figure 4.8**). If the surrounding area is uniform like a sky, this works great. If not, the results may not match properly.

When the Spot Healing Brush doesn't do the job, move on to the Healing Brush tool. Like the Clone Stamp tool, you Option/Alt-click to define the source point and then click or drag to paint over the defect. Unlike the Clone Stamp tool, the Healing Brush tool attempts to blend the source and the destination. The Spot Healing Brush and Healing Brush tools are often best for removing skin blemishes.

The Patch Tool is like the Healing Brush except it works with selected areas instead of brush strokes. You draw a selection with the Patch tool and drag

Figure 4.8: Original image (top left), blue spot removed by clicking with Spot Healing Brush tool (highlighted top right), and crack repaired with Clone Stamp tool (highlighted bottom right).

the selection to another area. The Patch Tool can work in one of two directions. If Destination is selected in the Options bar for the Patch tool, the selection you drag patches the location you drag it to. If Source is selected in the Options bar, the selection you drag picks up the area you drag to and uses it to patch the original selection location.

> **TIP:** If you have a scroll wheel mouse, you can use the scroll wheel to move up and down in a document. Want to go left and right? Press Command/Ctrl as you turn the scroll wheel. If your scroll wheel zooms instead, press Option/Alt to scroll. Scrolling vs. zooming is controlled by the Zoom with Scroll Wheel preference in the General Preferences dialog box; pressing Option/Alt temporarily switches to the other behavior.

Using Selections to Control Filters

? I sometimes try to control where a filter is applied by selecting an area first, but it doesn't always match up with the surroundings very well. How can I make a filtered area blend into its surroundings more seamlessly?

✓ Selections are certainly a quick, easy way to limit a filter, although not quite as reversible as using a layer mask. These tips can help you get exactly the selection you need:

- After you make your selection, choose Select > Feather to blur the

selection edge. This helps to avoid an obvious visual break where the filtered area meets the original (non-selected) area.

- If the result of a filter significantly changes the overall texture of the selection, the filtered selection will no longer match its surroundings. If this happens, right after applying the filter choose Edit > Fade with its Preview option on and see if you can reduce the opacity to a point where defect removal is balanced with maintaining a match with the surroundings. Don't forget to try the modes in the Fade dialog box; start with the Luminosity mode.

- If you're not handy with the lasso tool, you can make selections by painting over defects in Quick Mask mode. See "Edit a Selection as a Quick Mask" in Chapter 3, *Image Editing Basics*.

Dodge and Burn with Overlay Mode

? I've played with the Dodge and Burn tools, but they seem hard to control. Is there a better way to lighten and darken specific areas of an image?

✓ The Dodge and Burn tools in Photoshop are like the proverbial crazy aunt—they're there, but we prefer not to talk about them. Why? Because they're hard to control, difficult or impossible to reverse later, and they make it a little too easy to overwork an image.

Instead, you can apply reversible and precisely adjustable dodging and burning with a new layer filled with 50-percent gray, then painting with white or black to dodge and burn, respectively. This technique is made possible by the Overlay blending mode (**Figure 4.9**).

1. Option/Alt-click the Create a New Layer button in the Layers palette.

2. In the New Layer dialog box, choose Overlay from the Mode popup menu, and also turn on the Fill with Overlay–neutral color (50% gray) checkbox. This automatically fills the layer with the layer color that doesn't alter the image in this mode.

3. Enter a layer name (such as "Dodging and Burning") and click OK.

4. Now, in the Tool palette, select the Brush tool.

5. Click the Default Foreground and Background Colors icon, or just press the D key which does the same thing.

6. Paint on your new Overlay layer. To dodge an area, paint it with white. To burn an area, paint it with black. To restore the original image levels to an area, paint it with 50-percent gray.

If the effect is too strong or hard-edged, use the Options bar to reduce brush opacity, and use the Brushes palette to adjust the brush Hardness and Shape. Press X to switch between the foreground and background colors.

The Magic of Layer Masks

? What are layer masks good for? They seem somewhat complex to use, so I'm not sure if I want to learn about them.

☑ Layer masks have two great advantages. First, they make it easy to apply changes to very specific areas of a layer. Second, they make it easy

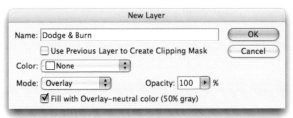

Figure 4.9: Original image (top left); setting up the new layer (left); painting over the walkway with black and painting over the mossy rock with white on the Dodge & Burn layer (top right).

to reverse any changes you later don't like. You can restore all of the layer's original appearance, even if you're unable to do so in the History palette. The disadvantage of layer masks is that they consume quite a bit of disk space and memory, because the document has to carry around that extra layer and layer mask. Here's one way to use layer masks (**Figure 4.10**):

1. Apply the correction on a separate layer. Use an adjustment layer if possible. If not (for example, you're applying a filter), duplicate the original layer and apply the change to the duplicate.

2. With the new, edited layer selected, Option/Alt-click the Add Layer Mask button in the Layers palette. This adds a layer mask filled with black; the filtered layer will seem to go away but don't be alarmed about that. The black layer mask has simply made the entire duplicate layer transparent.

3. Select the Brush Tool and set the foreground color to white.

4. Zoom into an area where you want the change to be visible.

5. With the layer mask active in the Layers palette, paint the area where you want the change to be visible. Painting white on the layer mask makes that portion of the layer opaque, revealing the edited pixels on the duplicate layer.

6. To reverse corrections at any time, set the foreground to black.

Figure 4.10: Camera raw file converted to show shadow detail (top left), and a second conversion added to the same file, showing highlight detail (center) placed on a lower layer. We added a layer mask to the upper layer (left), then applied a simple gradient and other touch-up brushwork in the layer mask to merge the best of both images.

Merge Edits by Changing History

? I'm not really into planning ahead with layers and masks—it doesn't fit my creative style. Is there a less structured way to apply filters interactively, maybe with a brush?

✓ A popular and very interactive technique involves time travel: painting between two history states in the History palette. You apply the filter, back up one history state (undo), and then use the History Brush and the History palette to paint back the filtered version in only the areas you want to fix. Here's how (**Figure 4.11**):

1. Apply an edit (like a filter or tonal change) at the maximum strength you want in the image.

2. In the History palette, click on the state one step back (the one just before applying the filter).

3. Click in the column to the left of the history state for the edit you applied. This sets the source state of the History Brush tool.

4. In the document window, paint with the History Brush to apply the corrections only in the areas where they're needed.

When painting in corrections with the History brush or a layer mask, use brush options for finer control. For example, reduce the Opacity in the Options bar to allow more gradual application of the brush. If you use a pressure-sensitive stylus, you may also be able to control brushstroke opacity and width through stylus pressure, depending on the settings in the Brushes palette.

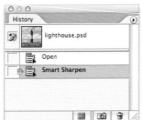

Figure 4.11: Original (left). Smart Sharpen was applied using settings perfect for the lighthouse (center) but otherwise too strong. By moving back a History step and setting the History Brush source to the Smart Sharpen state (right), the sharpened version could be painted on just the lighthouse using the History Brush.

Maintaining Image Quality

Keep Your Adjustments Neutral

? Sometimes when I apply a filter or sharpen, I notice color fringing or color shifts. How can I avoid these?

✓ Image processing can sometimes introduce color artifacts or distortion, which you might not want if you're trying to keep an image looking realistic. To avoid causing color problems, try these tips:

- Always start from a color-balanced image. If you manipulate an image before you've color-balanced it, image manipulations can exaggerate any unresolved imbalances in the image and make them harder to correct.

- Use the Fade command. If an effect creates unwanted color artifacts, choose Edit > Fade immediately after applying the effect, then choose Luminosity from the Mode popup menu. Luminosity applies

the effect by changing only the brightness of pixels, not their colors. Because the colors are left alone, they don't go out of control. If you don't want to completely apply the results of the effect, lower the Fade percentage.

- Convert to LAB color mode and edit in the L channel only. The LAB color mode separates lightness from color. If you apply an effect or other change to just the L (lightness) channel, the change won't affect the red-green (A) and blue-yellow (B) channels, leaving the image colors alone. when you're done, you'll probably need to convert the image back to RGB or CMYK for your final output. This is a pain, so we'd rather just use the Luminosity fade mode.

Don't Bring the Noise

? I've used a third-party plug-in to reduce digital camera noise. I see that Photoshop CS2 has a Reduce Noise filter. Is this a reasonable alternative to third-party noise filters?

✓ The new Reduce Noise command (Filter > Noise > Reduce Noise) in Photoshop CS2 is designed to help minimize noise in digital camera images. Reduce Noise tries to identify typical noise patterns so that it can isolate and remove them. Film grain is different than digital noise, so if it's grain you want to remove, you'll probably get better results

---

TIP: People often ask for "filter layers" in Photoshop—layers that apply but which can be made visible or hidden at will. While Photoshop doesn't yet offer this, you can simulate it by duplicating a layer and applying a filter to it. Or hold down the Option/Alt key while selecting Layer > Merge Visible to create a new layer that merges all the visible layers in your document.

using a plug-in such as Grain Surgery (*visinf.com*). Here are some tips that can help you get the most out of the Reduce Noise filter (**Figure 4.12**).

- Make basic tone and color corrections before you apply Reduce Noise.

- When you turn up the settings, aim to reduce noise as much as possible without obscuring actual details in the image. Use the Preview checkbox to watch how the filter affects the image as a whole.

- As you increase the Reduce Color Noise value, watch out for color shifts in highlights—especially a decrease in saturation. Lower the value if you start to see color shifts.

- If you have trouble working out the right settings, click the Advanced radio button and click the Per Channel tab to see if the noise is particularly pronounced in one channel or another (the blue chan-

TIP: Having a little trouble working out the right settings in the Reduce Noise filter? For some images, we find it's faster to simply run the Despeckle filter (Image > Noise > Despeckle) a few times on each of the color channels individually, until the noise goes away.

nel is usually the worst). After you take care of a particularly noisy channel, the remaining noise may be easier for you to fix.

- Applying noise reduction may soften the image a little, but you can try gently applying Smart Sharpen after Reduce Noise. Compare the History Palette states before applying Reduce Noise and after applying Smart Sharpen to make sure your Smart Sharpen settings aren't too strong. If you apply sharpening too strongly after noise reduction, you may end up re-creating the noise.

Figure 4.12: The Reduce Noise filter can minimize both noise in image brightness and noise in color channels. It's especially useful for photos taken with digital cameras at high ISO settings.

Productivity Perks

Preserve Options with Adjustment Layers

? **Some of the commands on the Image > Adjustments submenu are repeated on the Layer > New Adjustment Layer submenu. Which should I use?**

☑ The commands on the Image > Adjustments submenu are ordinary commands. Once you apply them, they permanently alter the image. The commands on the Layer > New Adjustment Layer submenu are only adjustment *layers*—they keep corrections on a separate layer so that you can edit, turn off, or remove them at any time without altering the original image (**Figure 4.13**). The changes you make with an adjustment layer aren't actually applied until printing or exporting, or when you flatten the image's layers.

Adjustment layers have another advantage: unlimited undo. While Photoshop has multiple undo, it's limited by the number of history states you've allowed in the History palette, and you can't recover undo steps after you've closed a document. But with an adjustment layer, you can change the adjustment at any time, even weeks later. You can even keep multiple versions of adjustments in the same file and turn them on or off as needed; for example, in one image you could store different tone and color correction adjustment layers for the various printers and papers you use.

If you have a choice between applying an adjustment as a regular command or as an adjustment layer, it's typically best to apply the change as an adjustment layer.

Figure 4.13: An image with an adjustment layer that applies sepia-tone colorization (top, left), and the original version restored simply by turning off the adjustment layer (left, and top right).

Why Isn't the Future Here Yet?

? If adjustment layers are so great, and the Shadow/Highlight command is so useful, why isn't Shadow/Highlight an adjustment layer?

☑ The Shadow/Highlight command is so effective and useful that Adobe gets this question a lot. The reason Shadow/Highlight isn't an adjustment layer is that it would cause long delays in screen updates. An adjustment layer compares a pixel on the adjustment layer to the same pixel on the layer(s) behind it. However, Shadow/Highlight compares a layer's pixel to the pixels around it—it's really more like a filter in this way. The amount of calculation involved if Shadow/Highlight were an adjustment layer would slow down screen redraw, even with just a small number of layers.

Until computers become a lot faster, if you want a little more flexibility with Shadow/Highlight you can apply the command to a duplicate layer.

Moving Corrections to Other Images

? I perfected corrections to an image. Yay! But now I want to apply those same corrections to a bunch of other images without starting from scratch. How can I do that?

☑ If you apply corrections using adjustment layers, you can save time by correcting one image and then transferring the corrections to any number of other images.

1. Open an image that's representative of the set you want to correct.

2. Create a new adjustment layer for the correction you want to apply. You can use the Create New Fill or Adjustment Layer button in the Layers palette, or choose an adjustment from the Layer > New Adjustment Layer submenu.

3. Make the adjustment and click OK.

4. Open another image, and choose Window > Arrange > Tile Horizontally or Tile Vertically.

5. Drag the adjustment layer from the Layers palette in the first document and drop it on the second (**Figure 4.14**).

TIP: Use caution when dragging an adjustment layer between documents that have different color modes or document profiles—the adjustment may not have the same effect. Also, layer masks you transfer fit only other documents that have the exact same dimensions.

Using a Batch Action to Copy Corrections

? What if I want to apply the same adjustment layer to a large numbers of images automatically? I sure don't want to process 100 images by hand!

☑ You can't automate dragging adjustment layers to other documents, but there is another way. When you're happy with the settings in an adjustment dialog box (such as Curves),

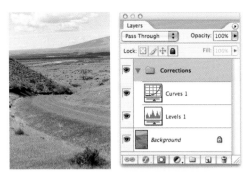

Figure 4.14: An image corrected with Levels and Curves adjustment layers (top). The next frame in the shoot needs similar corrections (center). Just drag the group of adjustment layers from the Layers palette to the second image (bottom), bringing it to a good starting point.

click the Save button in the adjustment dialog box, and save the corrections to a file on disk. Then record an action that adds a new adjustment layer of the same type and loads the file you just saved. You can now use the File > Automate > Batch command to run that action on as many images as you want.

TIP: If you're working on Camera Raw images, transferring settings among images is even easier. In Adobe Bridge, you can copy and paste settings from one Raw image to any number of others by using the commands Edit > Apply Camera Raw Settings > Copy Camera Raw Settings or Paste Camera Raw Settings. In Camera Raw itself, you can use the Synchronize button if you opened multiple images.

Storing Favorite Adjustment Layers

? I'd like to save some adjustment layers as files for future use, but I can't seem to find a way to delete everything but the adjustment layer. What am I missing?

You're not really missing anything. You can't store an adjustment layer alone in its own file—Photoshop wants a background or at least one layer in the document. However, you can create a Photoshop document with a small image size and store as many adjustment layers in it as you want. However, if you want to store adjustment layers with masks, you'll need to store them in a Photoshop document with a big enough image size to accommodate the size of the largest mask.

Note that the Save button in an adjustment layer dialog box only saves the settings inside the dialog box. The Save button can't save layer options such as opacity, blending mode, or masks.

Make Do with Low-Resolution Images

? I always get clients who send me web images that they want in their print jobs. When I ask for a higher-resolution version, they either tell me that the one on the web site looks sharp enough to them, or they don't know where the higher-resolution versions are. Is it possible to make web images look good in print?

☑ When you are forced to prepare low-resolution images for high-resolution output, use the following tips to try to rescue them. Not all of the tips work in all cases, and these tips will never make a low-resolution image look as good as an image at the proper resolution, size, and color depth. But if these tips keep your project going, they can be well worth the effort.

- If you were given a GIF, convert it from Indexed Color to RGB (Image > Mode > RGB Color). Once a GIF image is in 8-bit RGB mode, you can easily resample and apply all kinds of filters and effects that aren't available in Indexed Color mode. Many of the following tips won't work unless the image uses at least 8 bits per channel.

- Apply noise reduction (Filter > Noise > Reduce Noise). If the image contains dithering, Reduce Noise may help smooth it out. For low-resolution images, start with Strength set to 10 and Preserve Details and Sharpen Details both set to 0. For JPEG images, try selecting the Remove JPEG

Artifact box. You can also try the Despeckle or Median filters.

- Resample to print resolution. Choose Image > Image Size, select the Resample Image box, and enter the final dimensions you want.

- Apply Smart Sharpen (Filter > Sharpen > Smart Sharpen). Start with an Amount of 100% and a Radius of 1 pixel, and find a combination that makes the image crisper without bringing back the original pixelation.

- If photorealism isn't required, try resampling to print resolution and then applying a creative filter to it, such as Filter > Distort > Diffuse Glow, or Filter > Noise > Add Noise. Applying a filter at the new, higher resolution can help hide the evidence of resizing.

- Instead of printing the image as a normal halftone, consider printing it using a diffusion dither or stochastic screening (also called FM screening). Stochastic screening usually requires much less resolution than a normal halftone. To print with this method, you'll likely need a special utility (such as Isis Imaging's Icefields), or a special setting on the imagesetter's RIP.

Preserving a Document's History

? Is there any way to save history states with a document?

☑ One of the few shortcomings in the very powerful History palette is that you lose all of your history states when you close the document. In earlier versions of Photoshop, there was nothing you could do about that. In Photoshop CS, Adobe added a preference for keeping a history log you can review at any time. You can study how an image got to its current state, particularly with features that involve numerical settings. It's a great way to look up what values you entered into a filter you applied, for example.

You'll find the History Log preferences in the General panel of the Preferences dialog box (**Figure 4.15**). You can save the history log to the document's metadata, to a separate text file, or both. If you store the history log in metadata, you can read it in the Edit History panel in Adobe Bridge when the document is selected. You can also inspect the same history log by choosing File > File Info and clicking History. Although it doesn't say so anywhere, you can click in the History panel where the log is, press Command/Ctrl-A, switch to a text editor, and paste the log there for printing or easier reading.

Unfortunately, the history log doesn't actually save the history states with the document; you still can't go backwards after closing it. The history log also can't record mouse movements such as brush strokes. But we still find it useful.

Using the Measure Tool

? What's the Measure tool good for? Is it just a ruler on the screen?

The Measure tool doesn't get a lot of air time, because it doesn't do anything flashy. However, like many Photoshop tools, the Measure tool does have some hidden talents, which we point out in these tips:

- The Measure tool doesn't work alone. You use the Measure tool together with the Info palette. After you drag the Measure tool, the Info palette reports the measuring line's position, distance, and angle for your convenience.

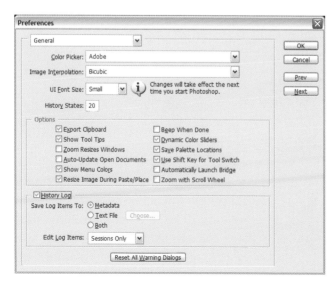

Figure 4.15: Options at the bottom of the General pane in the Preferences dialog box let you record the History Log to the document's metadata, a text file, or both.

- After you drag the Measure tool, the resulting measuring line remains in place. Choosing another tool makes the measuring line disappears, but choosing the Measure tool again displays the measuring line again.

- The Measure tool provides a cool way to quickly straighten an image. Drag the Measure tool along an edge in the image that should be perfectly horizontal or vertical, then immediately choose Image > Rotate Canvas > Arbitrary. Photoshop automatically fills in

the Angle field from the measuring line you drew. All you have to do is click OK, and your document is perfectly straightened.

- You can create a second measurement segment by Option/Alt-dragging from either end of an existing measurement line. This is useful as a protractor—you can easily measure angles this way (**Figure 4.16**). When you have two measurement lines, their distances are listed as D1 and D2 in the Options bar and in the Info palette.

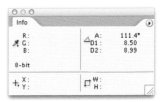

Figure 4.16: The Measure tool drawn to match an angle in the image (left), and the measured angle appearing in the Info palette (right).

Sharpening

Basic Sharpening with Unsharp Mask

? Everyone says to use Unsharp Mask to sharpen, but I don't quite understand what the sliders do. Can you enlighten me?

Sharpening is a tricky subject, even for those of us who have been doing it for years. Unsharp masking works by enhancing your perception of edges. Unsharp masking emphasizes the contrast along that edge where two tones meet. The name comes from traditional prepress, where a slightly blurred (unsharp) negative copy of an image created the necessary emphasis along image edges.

The Unsharp Mark dialog box has just three options: Amount, Radius, and Threshold. Here's our quick cheat sheet for unsharp masking (**Figure 4.17**):

1. Begin by adjusting the Radius. For a good starting point, divide the image's output resolution by 200. Back off if ugly halos appear.

2. Increase the Amount value, but back off when sharpening starts to look unnatural.

3. Set Threshold high enough so that you're only sharpening details. If you see that noise or grain is being sharpened, you're probably set Threshold too low. When sharpening faces, try starting at 4 to 8 levels to avoid sharpening skin blemishes.

When you're done, use these tips to check your work:

- View your results in Actual Pixels magnification (View > Actual Pixels). Zooming in or out won't show sharpening accurately.

- To change the preview, click on the image outside the dialog box.

- Monitors don't always show sharpness accurately for print, so test your sharpening settings on a press proof if available.

- You may need (and you can get away with) somewhat stronger sharpening settings if the image will be viewed at a distance, such as on a poster or billboard.

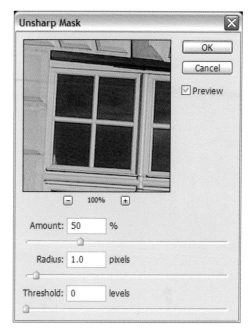

Figure 4.17: The Unsharp Mask dialog box.

Better Sharpening with Smart Sharpen

? Tell me about the new Smart Sharpen command. How is it different than Unsharp Mask? Do I use it with Unsharp Mask, or instead of it?

✓ The Smart Sharpen command, new to Photoshop CS2, could be considered a more intelligent version of Unsharp Mask. If you want, you can use Smart Sharpen to apply different amounts of sharpening to highlights and shadows, and you can even remove special types of blur. Here are a few pointers (**Figure 4.18**):

- Set Amount and Radius using the same guidelines as in the "Basic Sharpening with Unsharp Mask" topic.

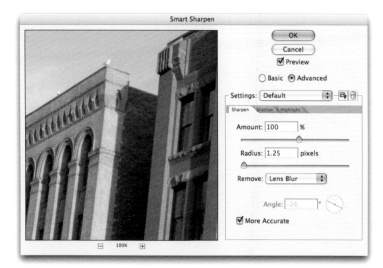

Figure 4.18: The Smart Sharpen dialog box, including the tabs made available by clicking the Advanced button.

- In the Remove popup menu, you've got three choices. Gaussian Blur is basically the same as Unsharp Mask. Lens Blur is a new, smarter version of Unsharp Mask. It tries to preserve detail and suppress halos, so you might be able to get away with higher sharpening values than with Gaussian Blur or the Unsharp Mask command. You can use Motion Blur and Angle to try to remove blur caused by camera or subject movement.

- For best results, turn on the More Accurate option. More Accurate improves the sharpening by repeating it in stages. However, More Accurate makes the sharpening process take much longer.

- Click Advanced to independently control the amount of sharpening in very light and very dark areas.

Smart Sharpen has an Advanced mode that activates Shadow and Highlight tabs. Here's how those work:

- Increase the Fade Amount to preserve more of the original, non-sharpened image.

- Increase the Tonal Width to extend the range of sharpening toward the midtones.

- Adjust the Radius value in the same way you would for the Sharpen tab or Unsharp Mask command; it's available in the Shadow and Highlight tabs so that you can assign a different Radius value for sharpening those tonal ranges.

Suppress Digital Noise when Sharpening

? **I need to sharpen a digital camera image, but the noise is sharpened, too! How can I keep the noise from being sharpened along with the details?**

You've got a couple of options. You can use the Advanced mode in Smart Sharpen to help keep shadow areas smooth. In Smart Sharpen, click

The Stages of Sharpening

Hardcore sharpening geeks tell us that the different stages of image production require different kinds of sharpening. You don't want to apply too much sharpening before you're done editing the image. And different types of output require different levels of sharpening. The conventional wisdom is that sharpening strategies should be based on the following stages:

Capture Sharpening

Because of the way digital sensors work, an unretouched digital capture is slightly softer than the original. This is true whether the image is captured by a digital camera or a scanner. Right after scanning or downloading a digital camera image, apply just a touch of sharpening to reduce the softening effect of digitizing an image.

Camera raw files may need more sharpening than JPEG files from the same camera. JPEG files are typically sharpened by a camera as part of its post-shot processing. By definition, raw files leave the processing to you, so the amount of sharpening they undergo depends largely on the sharpening settings in the raw converter you use, such as Adobe Camera Raw.

Creative Sharpening

One part of an image may need a little more sharpening than the rest of an image, or an area may simply need to look its best because it's an important region of interest in an image. You can use various methods to apply more or less sharpening to image areas, such as using layer masks or painting from history states. See the section "Making Local Corrections."

Sharpening for Output

Even if you don't apply any other kind of sharpening, you'll probably sharpen your images for output, because the final result counts—you want the image to be sharp when it's published on your web site or in your print project. There is no magic set of sharpening settings, because sharpening has to be customized to the many different kinds of output requirements and resolutions. However, the sharpening guidelines we give you in the "Basic Sharpening with Unsharp Mask" topic are useful starting points.

For the Web, sharpening is more straightforward, because you're previewing sharpening settings on the output device. If it looks right, it is.

the Shadow tab and increase the Fade amount until the noise level goes down. Sharpness in dark areas is usually not critical.

You can also try applying the Reduce Noise filter before applying Smart Sharpen, so that there's less noise there to be sharpened in the first place!

Actions and Batches

I'd Like to See the Menu, Please

? There are some commands I can't record as an action—they don't even register when I record them. An example are the zoom commands. Is there a way to include those menu commands in an action?

☑ There is a way. You can add any menu command to an action by choosing Insert Menu Item from the Actions palette menu (**Figure 4.19**).

The Insert Menu Item command is also useful when you want to play back a command that opens a dialog box, and you want the dialog box to open without being influenced by whatever settings were in effect when the action was recorded.

Run Actions on a Batch of Images

? I'm having fun putting actions together; I can see how they'd save time. But in the Actions palette, I'm not seeing where I can run an action on multiple images. Where is that?

☑ To process multiple images with an action, you need to use the Batch command. And for some odd reason, the Batch command is nowhere near the Actions palette. But we know where it is:

1. Choose File > Automate > Batch. Or, from Adobe Bridge, choose Tools > Photoshop > Batch (**Figure 4.20**).

2. In the Play section popup menus, choose the Set containing the action you want, then choose the Action itself.

3. From the Source popup menu, choose the location of the images you want to process. Note that a source can be the images currently selected in the active Adobe Bridge window, if you choose Bridge.

4. Choose a Destination and set options. It's best to choose Folder; see the topic "Protect Originals From a Few Bad Actions."

5. Click OK.

Figure 4.19: Using the Insert Menu Item command, you can add any menu command to an action… even the commands that aren't recordable.

Figure 4.20: In the Batch dialog box, you can apply any action to all files in a specific folder, the currently open files, files you import, or files selected in Adobe Bridge.

Cropping a Batch of Images

? **I've got a bunch of images and I need to clip one inch off of the bottom of each one. Can I avoid carpal tunnel syndrome by having Photoshop do them all?**

☑ Try the following procedure. It'll work great if you can crop from the center, a corner, or an edge.

TIP: To resize many images to the same size, include the File > Automate > Fit Image command in a Photoshop action. You'll find the details in the topic "Resizing a Batch of Variously Sized Images" in Chapter 3, *Image Editing Basics*.

1. In the Actions palette, click the Create New Action button, name it, and click Record. The action begins recording.

2. Choose Image > Canvas Size.

3. Enable the Relative checkbox.

4. Enter how much you want to crop the Width or Height. In the example you asked about, you'd enter 0 for Width and -1 inches for Height (**Figure 4.21**).

5. In the proxy, click the edge or corner where you want to anchor the crop. If you want to crop off the bottom, click one of the squares in the top row of the proxy.

6. Click OK and then click Proceed.

7. In the Actions palette, click the Stop Recording button.

8. In Adobe Bridge, select all of the files you want to crop, and choose Tools > Photoshop > Batch. Select the Set and Action at the top of the Batch dialog box, specify Bridge as the source, specify options, and click OK.

TIP: If you used the Actions palette in previous versions of Photoshop to assign shortcuts to menu commands or to override the built-in menu command shortcuts, you can now use the Keyboard Shortcuts command in Photoshop CS2 to do so. The great thing about using the Keyboard Shortcuts command instead of the Actions palette is that you're no longer be limited to the function keys for shortcuts.

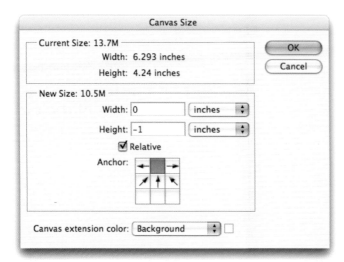

Figure 4.21: The Canvas Size dialog box set up to remove the bottom inch from the current image, by anchoring at the top edge and reducing the height.

Protect Originals From a Few Bad Actions

? **I guess I should have spent a little more time testing an action before running it, because it processed a whole folder of images the wrong way, and the changes can't be undone. Help!**

✓ Actions blindly do what you tell them to do, and when the results aren't quite what you anticipated, you can end up with a folder full of ruined images. For example, an action that works great on your test image might do something unexpected on an image of a different size or color mode. Here are a few tips that can help ensure that if one of your actions does go haywire, it won't be your originals that are irreversibly mangled.

- Run actions on duplicates of the originals in a separate folder from the originals, or back up the originals before you start.

- Always check all of the resulting images after running an action for the first time.

- In the Destination popup menu in the Batch dialog box, don't choose the Save and Close option. Instead, choose Folder and specify a folder that isn't the original folder so that the processed documents don't replace or get mixed up with the originals.

- If the action creates a copy of the original, such as the way Save for Web exports in a different format, it may be acceptable to open original files if you add a step at the end

TIP: If you use the Batch command all the time, you might get tired of digging through submenus to get there. To make the Batch command more accessible, you can use the Edit > Keyboard Shortcuts command to assign a keyboard shortcut to the Batch command.

You can also put the Batch command on the Actions palette—just use the Insert Menu Item on the Actions palette menu.

that closes each document without saving changes.

- Consider setting up an Input and Output pair of folders that you use solely for actions. Put copies of your originals in the Input folder, and point the action or the Batch dialog box to the Output folder for the processed images. After you approve the processed images, move them to their final destination.

Avoiding Batch Processing Errors

? What can I do to prevent batch-processing errors? I get them far more often than I want to. I guess I don't want to get them at all!

✓ Batch processing can go astray in an astounding number of ways. The cause can be something as easy to overlook as a missing color profile that generates an alert dialog box. Here are a

Getting Some Good Keyboard Action

You might already know the basics of Photoshop shortcuts: Menu command shortcuts are visible on the menus, and tool shortcuts are visible on Tool palette tooltips. But Photoshop goes further than many programs in how and where you can add or edit shortcuts. If you're a big fan of keyboard shortcuts, these tips can help you get the most out of Photoshop's shortcut features.

- Photoshop makes heavy use of modifier keys (Command, Shift, and Option on the Mac, and Ctrl, Shift and Alt on Windows) to alter the behavior of tools. In the past, you had to look up modifier key functions in online help. In Photoshop CS2, you can see the selected tool's modifier key hints in the Info palette. To enable this, choose Palette Options from the Info

palette menu and enable the Show Tool Hints checkbox.

- Any Action can have a function key shortcut, so if you perform an action frequently, assign a function key shortcut to it. In the Actions palette, double-click to the right of the action name to open the Action Options dialog box, and choose a function key from the Function Key popup menu. You can add the Shift or Command/Ctrl key to the function key.

- If you want to add or edit keyboard shortcuts, Photoshop CS2 give you near-total control over them. Choose Edit > Keyboard Shortcuts and make the changes you want. See "Your Keyboard, Your Way" in Chapter 1, *Photoshop Essentials*.

few tips you can follow to prevent common errors and even speed up actions processing.

- Read and verify the whole Batch dialog box and verify the selected action, source, and destination before clicking OK. The defaults may not be what you want.

- When recording actions, don't touch anything that you don't want to change. Options that aren't changed during recording respect each individual image's values for those options when you run the action, and changing a value will affect every image in the action.

- Add steps that standardize and streamline the documents before the steps that make up the main part of the action. For example, Conrad's action for generating Web images flattens documents, converts them to sRGB, and resizes them before opening Save for Web. Before he added these steps, high-resolution documents or documents with many layers took much longer to process, had the wrong colors on the Web, or errors would stop the process.

TIP: If you want to leave notes for other people who may need to edit a Photoshop document when you're not around, such as a client, use the Notes tool in Photoshop. These notes are persistent: If you save the document in Photoshop PDF format and open it in Adobe Reader or Acrobat, you'll see the notes you entered, and the notes won't affect the output.

- If something does go wrong, use the error-reporting feature at the bottom of the Batch dialog box to help debug actions. Also, you can monitor action testing more closely by choosing Playback Options from the Actions palette menu and selecting Step by Step or Pause to slow down the action for observation.

- If you're trying to record an Open step for Adobe Camera Raw, enable the Override Action Open Commands checkbox in the Batch dialog box. Otherwise, the action will always open the same image you used to build the action.

Working with Layers

Working with Layers

THE ROMANS HAD A CONCEPT THAT WE STILL USE TODAY: "Divide and Conquer." According to this principle, a major challenge can be solved by breaking it down into smaller, more easily manageable components. That's the general idea behind using layers in Photoshop. By breaking up an image into components, you can control your edits more precisely, protect different parts of the image from editing, and generally make it easier to change your mind later.

In this chapter we'll offer a number of solutions for getting the most out of Photoshop's Layers palette. Adobe beefed up the functionality of the Layers palette significantly in CS2. Some of the changes are subtle, but if you use a lot of layers, you'll be a happy camper with these new features.

Managing Layers

Choice Selections

? When I work with many layers, it's hard to select exactly the layer I want. In a complex document, I might see 20 layer names in the Layers palette, and I may not know which name refers to each layer—especially if someone else created the document.

☑ Once in a while, it's good to say to the Layers palette, "You think you're so special? Well guess what, I don't need you." When you select the Move tool, the Options bar at the top of the screen displays additional selection options: Auto Select Layer and Auto Select Groups (**Figure 5.1**). If you enable Auto Select Layer, you can select a layer just by clicking on any pixel belonging to that layer with the Move tool. Auto Select Groups is similar, but selects an entire group containing the layer you clicked.

It can be tough to use Auto Select Layer and Auto Select Groups when layers are close together, have soft edges, or are semi-transparent. When layer edges are hard to see, you may not know where to click! So instead of simply clicking on layers, we recommend Ctrl-clicking/right-clicking them with the Move tool. A context menu appears with the names of all layers containing a painted pixel that's right under the location you clicked. This method is more precise than using Auto Select Layers, because you can specifically choose which layer you want to select.

> **TIP:** If you work with layers that have a smaller area than the document, make sure the View > Extras command is on, and choose View > Show > Layer Edges. Seeing layer edges can help you identify which layer is selected.

The Search for the Missing Link

? What have they done? Before Photoshop CS2, I linked layers all the time. In Photoshop CS2, the linking column is completely gone!

☑ It's not a bug, it's a new feature! Actually, we're not joking about that. Links are less important now that you can select multiple layers. Linking is still supported, however. To link layers in Photoshop CS2, select the layers you want to link and then click the Link button at the bottom of the Layers palette (**Figure 5.2**). Note that the link icons aren't visible unless you select at least one of the linked layers.

Figure 5.1: Layer selection options are available at the left side of the Options bar when the Move tool is selected.

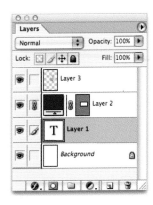
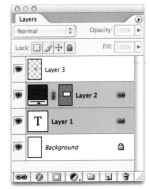

Figure 5.2: In Photoshop CS (left), layers could be linked using the second column in the Layers palette. In Photoshop CS2 (right), you link layers by selecting them and clicking the link button at the bottom of the Layers palette.

Why the change? Back in Photoshop CS and earlier, linking layers was the only way to apply a transformation to multiple layers, such as moving or rotation. In Photoshop CS2, Adobe added the ability to select multiple layers in the Layers palette (with the Shift and Command/Ctrl keys), making it less necessary to link layers. The new selection ability is more intuitive because it's consistent with the how selected objects behave in many other applications.

As in other applications, selection is meant to be quite temporary. Groups and links in Photoshop are now intended to provide a way to associate multiple layers persistently, and independently of selection. Links work better than groups when layers are so far apart in the layer stack that they can't be grouped. In favor of layer groups, you can have more than one group per document, while you can only have one set of linked layers per document. We talk about groups later in this chapter.

TIP: If you open a Photoshop document created in Photoshop CS or earlier and it has linked layers, don't worry—they'll still be linked in Photoshop CS2.

Total Pixel Lockdown

? I painted a layer that's just perfect, so it's frustrating when I accidentally paint on it. Is there a way to prevent painting on a layer while still keeping it visible?

✅ Click the Lock Image Pixels button in the Layers palette. You'll find it along the Lock row of icons in the Layers palette, the second icon from the left (**Figure 5.3**). Lock Image Pixels prevents any kind of painting or processing of pixels on a layer. You'll still be able to transform the layer. Filters and adjustments don't work on a layer with locked pixels, but adjustment layers work because they don't permanently change the layer pixels. The other buttons on that row are useful too:

- Lock Transparent Pixels lets you change the colors of already-

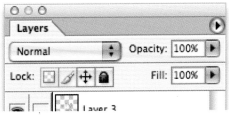

Figure 5.3: The Lock buttons in the Layers palette can prevent accidental edits.

painted pixels with the brush tool, while preventing paint from covering existing transparent pixels.

- Lock Position prevents all transformations to the layer, such as moving and rotating.

- Lock All does what it says. It's the same as selecting all of the other lock buttons.

Keeping Options Open

? My Photoshop ideas often go off in two or more directions, so I sometimes duplicate layers, give the duplicates different settings, and save them with the document. It's a chore to turn multiple layers on and off to view my alternatives. Is there an easier way?

✓ Luckily, there are two ways to maintain alternatives in the file. If you want to turn a few adjacent layers on and off at the same time, group them by selecting the layers and choosing Layer > Group Layers (Command/Ctrl-G). You can then show or hide the entire group by clicking the eye icon for the group, which uses a folder icon (**Figure 5.4**). (In Adobe Photoshop CS, layer groups are called layer sets).

If you want to control combinations of layers that aren't adjacent, or remember multiple states of the same layers, you can create layer comps in the Layer Comps palette. Layer comps are like history states you can save with the document. A layer comp remembers not only whether layers are visible or not, but can also remember its position and layer style. For each alternative version, click the Create New Layer Comp button in the Layer Comps palette. To view a different layer comp, select it in the Layer Comps palette.

In general, layer groups are intended to help you organize layers and control their structure, while layer comps are intended for storing versions of the same layers. For example, you can add a layer mask to a layer group to mask all of the layers inside the group. On the other hand, if you simply want to see different arrangements of the same five layers, you'd save each arrangement as a layer comp.

TIP: To temporarily disable a layer link, Shift-click the link icon of a linked layer. Shift-click the same link icon to enable the link again later. The link icon of a disabled link displays an X through it, you don't have to remember which layer you unlinked. That's why this is better than simply unlinking that layer.

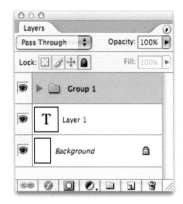

Figure 5.4: When you group layers, they're collected under a folder icon in the Layers palette that you can expand by clicking the triangle next to the folder icon.

Conserving History with Layer Comps

? Hey! I noticed that each time I apply a layer comp, the changes made to layers register as a new history state in the document. All I was doing was comparing two layer comps by switching between them, and I used up all my history states. How can I prevent this?

☑ Instead, click each layer comp you want to see once, and then use the History palette to alternate between the history states created by applying each layer comp (**Figure 5.5**). When you settle on a layer comp, that's a good time to finally apply the layer comp in the Layer Comps palette and then continue working.

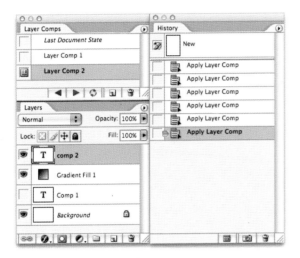

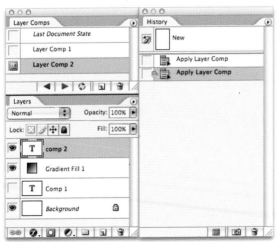

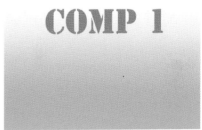

Figure 5.5: Each time you switch back and forth between layer comps (above), you use up History states (top left). To preserve the available History states, try each comp just once and use the History palette to switch between them (bottom left).

Aligning Layers

Smarter than Your Average Guide

? When I drag layers, I see horizontal and vertical lines appear and disappear. Is this some kind of bug?

✓ Photoshop CS2 includes a new Smart Guides feature that automatically helps you align layers. It's on by default. As you drag a layer close to the edge of another layer, a temporary magenta-colored Smart Guide appears when the two layers are aligned. As long as the Smart Guide is visible, you can drag the layer along it to keep the two layers aligned. You can control the Smart Guides color in the Guides, Grid & Slices panel of the Preferences dialog box.

Together We Can Rule the Document

? I was given some page specifications that I'm trying to set up in a Photoshop document. It's tedious to drag ruler guides to precise numerical locations. Is there a more exact way of adding guides than dragging them out of the rulers?

✓ Yes, this is. Choose View > New Guide, enter the orientation and exact position for the new guide, and click OK.

We Are All Lined Up

? I want to align some layers to each other, but the Align submenu under the Layer menu is dimmed. How do I make those commands available?

✓ Photoshop needs to know which layers you want to align, so select them first. In CS2, you can Shift-select or Command/Ctrl-select the layers you want to align in the Layers palette, and the alignment commands will be available. As a shortcut, you can click one of the alignment buttons in the Options bar (**Figure 5.6**). Those buttons have the same functions as the commands on the Layer > Align submenu, but they're a lot easier to get to.

In Photoshop CS, you have to link the layers together to make this work. But in CS2, simply linking layers no longer allows them to align. You need to select layers instead.

> **TIP:** Layers align to the outer dimensions of the layer contents. For example, a star-shaped layer aligns by the dimensions of the smallest rectangle that can enclose the entire star. If layers don't align the way you expect them to, check for stray pixels or partially transparent pixels that may extend the dimensions of a layer.

Figure 5.6: Layer alignment options are available at the right side of the Options bar when the Move tool is selected.

Layer Masks

Making Sense of Masks

? **Photoshop seems to have a million kinds of masks. How do I know which one to use at any time?**

☑ Photoshop offers so many ways to mask that you may not be sure which kind of masking to use. Each kind of masking has its own advantages and disadvantages, so use this tip to pick the best method for the task at hand.

- Use a Quick Mask as an alternative to drawing a selection with the lasso tool, so you can paint a selection instead of drawing one. See the topic "Edit a Selection as a Quick Mask."

- Use a layer mask when you want a mask that can have partial transparency. A layer mask is like a selection you can edit with brushes and filters. See the next solution for more on this.

- Use a vector mask when you want to draw a mask with the Pen tool or a shape tool. A vector mask is based on paths, so it always has hard edges and you can't paint on or apply a filter to it. See the topic

TIP: If snap to grids and guides aren't working, check two things. Make sure the View > Snap command is turned on, and make sure the types of objects you want to snap to (such as the grid) are turned on in the View > Snap To submenu.

"Create Transparency with a Vector Mask," on the next page.

- Use a clipping mask to mask a layer with another layer. A common example is when you want to add adjustment layers that affect just one layer. See "When a Layer is a Mask," later in this section.

TIP: If you don't use adjustment layer masks very often, you can prevent the default adjustment layer mask from appearing. Choose Palette Options from the Layers palette menu, and disable the Use Default Masks on Adjustments checkbox.

Create Transparency with a Layer Mask

? **I know how to use layer opacity to make an entire layer semitransparent. But what I want to do is make part of a layer transparent. How can I do that?**

☑ Add a layer mask. In a layer mask, white areas are 100-percent opaque, black areas are 100-percent transparent, and gray areas are partially transparent, with lighter areas being more opaque.

1. In the Layers palette, select a layer. You can add a layer mask to any layer except the default Background layer.

2. Click the Add Layer Mask button in the Layers palette.

3. Use any method to darken areas of the layer mask. The areas of the mask become darker, the more those areas of the layer become transparent (**Figure 5.7**).

You can also make layer areas transparent by using the Eraser or Background Eraser tool, if you're sure you'll never need to restore the areas deleted by those tools. However, the advantage of using a layer mask instead of erasing is that you can always restore areas you made transparent, by painting white in the layer mask.

Create Transparency with a Vector Mask

 I want to draw a curvy mask, but it's not easy to draw a smooth curve with the lasso tool. Is there a better tool?

☑ You can use a vector mask to hide parts of a layer using paths you draw with the Pen tool or the shape tools. Vector masks are great if you need a mask made up of straight lines and sharp edges, or smooth curves, which can be more difficult to draw in a bitmap-based layer mask.

1. In the Layers palette, select a layer. You can add a vector mask to any layer except the default Background layer.

2. Choose Layer > Vector Mask > Reveal All. Alternately, you can Command/Ctrl-click on the Add Layer Mask button in the Layers palette.

3. Use the Pen tool or a Shape tool to create a path on the vector mask.

Any area inside the path remains visible, and any area outside the path is hidden. (If you choose Layer > Vector Mask > Hide All in step 2, areas inside the path are hidden and areas outside the path are visible.)

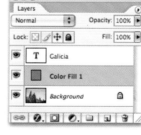

Figure 5.7: The goal is to show the photo on the bottom layer through the layer Color Fill 1 (left). First, add a layer mask to Color Fill 1. Then paint black on the mask to create a transparent area that allows underlying layers to be visible.

When a Layer is a Mask

? I want to apply an adjustment layer to an image layer, so I positioned it just above the image layer in the Layers palette. However, the adjustment layer affects everything below it. How can I make that adjustment layer affect only one layer?

☑ A clipping mask (not to be confused with a clipping path, which is quite different) lets you use any layer as a mask for any other layer—sort of like grouping two layers together—and it's very useful for situations like yours. To mask the layer with another one, first make sure that in the Layers palette, the layer you want to act as a mask (in this case the image you want to affect) is directly below the layer you want to mask (in this case, the adjustment layer). Position the cursor over the dividing line between the layers and Option/Alt-click. You can also select the layer above and choose Layer > Create Clipping Mask (or press Command-Option-G/Ctrl-Alt-G).

The masked layer becomes indented and marked with a bent arrow (**Figure 5.8**).

If you're familiar with layer masks, you should know that you can add a layer mask to a clipping mask for even more control over the effect.

Masking Adjustment Layers

? I applied an adjustment layer to an image, but I don't want the adjustment layer to affect the entire area of the document. How can I control the area affected by the adjustment layer?

☑ Each adjustment layer comes with a layer mask by default. That means you can apply an adjustment layer and then draw on its layer mask to limit the effect of that adjustment layer to specific areas.

1. In the Layers palette, click the Create New Fill and Adjustment

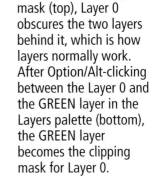

Figure 5.8: Before creating the clipping mask (top), Layer 0 obscures the two layers behind it, which is how layers normally work. After Option/Alt-clicking between the Layer 0 and the GREEN layer in the Layers palette (bottom), the GREEN layer becomes the clipping mask for Layer 0.

Layer button and select the type of adjustment layer you want to add.

2. Make the changes and click OK.

3. To reduce the effect of the adjustment layer, lower its opacity in the Layers palette. David likes to make adjustments a bit on the strong side so that it's easier to see the result, then he lowers the opacity to fine-tune the adjustment to the proper level.

4. To suppress adjustments in local areas, paint gray or black into the layer mask. White lets the adjustment layer apply at full strength, and darker tones reduce the strength of the adjustment.

- If you're painting in a mask with the Brush tool, adjust the brush's Hardness value to feather the edges of your brush strokes. To find the Hardness value, open the Brushes palette with the Brush Tool selected and click Brush Tip Shape.

- If you've already been painting in a layer mask with hard-edged tools and features and you realize you need to soften the edges, don't worry. Simply run a blur filter (such as Gaussian Blur) on the entire layer mask.

- If you just need to blur a few edges in a layer mask, use the Blur tool.

Softening Mask Edges

? I created a mask, but I don't like its hard edge. How can I soften the edge of a mask?

✓ When using masks to blend layers seamlessly, it's usually better for your layer mask to have a subtle feathered edge rather than a hard, obvious edge. However, hard mask edges often result from using selection tools or converting paths to selections. Here are some tips for softening hard mask edges.

- If you're defining a mask edge with a feature that has a Feather option, you can use it. For example, if you define an edge by making a selection, choose Select > Feather to specify how much the resulting selection edge should be softened when you fill the selection.

One Mask to Rule Them All

? How can I apply one mask that affects multiple layers?

✓ A layer group is the solution. In the Layers palette, Shift-click the first and last layers you want to mask and choose Layer > Group Layers. Then, with the layer group (folder icon) selected in the layer list, click the Add Layer Mask button at the bottom of the Layers palette, which is the same as choosing Layer > Layer Mask > Reveal All. In the Layers palette, you'll see that the mask is attached to the layer group icon instead of a layer (**Figure 5.9**). You can then paint in and filter the mask as you would with any other layer mask, and that one mask affects all layers in the layer group.

Figure 5.9: Before creating the group mask (top), any mask added to an upper layer would only mask its layer. After adding a mask to Group 1 (bottom), all layers in the group are masked by the single mask applied to the group.

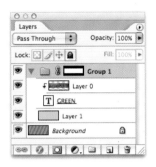

Combining Images

Remix Your Images

? **Layers look like a natural way to make digital collages and montages. How should I get started combining images?**

☑ You're right, layers do make it easy to create composite images. Adjustment layers and layer masks make it easy to change your mind without having to start over from the beginning. Use these layer tips to assemble composite documents.

- Put each image on its own layer so that you can reposition images at any time.

- To blend images, add a layer mask to each non-background image.

Paint black in the layer mask to make areas of a layer transparent. The advantage of a mask over simply erasing parts of the layer is that if you change your mind, you can paint white in a layer mask to restore deleted areas.

- To even out colors and exposure, add one or more adjustment layers to each image layer so that you can easily move back and forth among images, tweaking each image individually. To create an adjustment layer that only affects one layer, make sure the adjustment layer is selected and directly above its image layer in the Layers palette, and then choose Layer > Create Clipping Mask.

Stitching Small Images Into One Big Image

? I like to take several photos of very wide scenes. How can I quickly assemble all of these photos into one big panorama?

✓ If you shot a series of overlapping images specifically to create a larger image, such as a panorama, try the Photomerge feature (File > Automate > Photomerge). In the Photomerge dialog box, you can arrange photos into a larger composition, overlapping their edges (**Figure 5.10**). Photomerge can take it the rest of the way, merging edges and producing a seamless composite.

Photomerge works better if your exposure was consistent and the images aren't too distorted by shooting with a wide-angle lens. And Photomerge doesn't just create horizontal panoramas—you can combine images along any edge that matches.

Identify Identical Layers

? I have two images that look about the same, but I think one of them contains edits. They look nearly identical to the naked eye. Is there any way Photoshop can tell me if there are any differences between them?

✓ The aptly named Difference blending mode provides an easy way to find out, as long as the two images can be precisely aligned. First, Shift-drag one image to another, so that the dragged image becomes a new layer centered in the destination document. Make sure they're aligned down to the pixel. Then select the top layer and choose the Difference blending mode from the Layers palette.

When you apply the Difference blending mode to an image, any pixels identical to lower layers appear black. Any areas that aren't identical appear in

Figure 5.10: Photomerge can take several images with overlapping edges and combine them into a single seamless image, even if the original images aren't exactly the same size or angle.

color, and areas that are completely different appear white. If the entire document appears black, you'll know the two images are exactly the same. Any differences will be obvious, because they won't be black (**Figure 5.11**).

Subtle color differences don't show up well in Difference mode (they're very-near black), so you might also want to add a temporary Levels adjustment layer. In the Levels adjustment layer dialog box, move the gray midpoint slider far to the left to exaggerate brightness, which can help reveal subtle differences.

Figure 5.11: The differences between the two image versions (left and center) are not easy to spot just by looking. By setting up the images as aligned layers and applying the Difference mode to the top layer (right), the differences are revealed by any area that isn't black. Retouching is visible near the bottom left corner of the image, and a duplicated screw is visible near the top right corner.

Merging and Flattening Layers

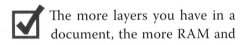

? What's the difference between merging and flattening layers? When would I want to do either?

☑ The more layers you have in a document, the more RAM and disk space the document requires. You can save RAM and disk space by merging layers, if you're sure that you won't need to change those layers any further.

When you flatten a document, you merge all the layers and remove any transparency. Merging layers retains any transparency (the checkerboard you can see). Flattening or merging a layered document is useful when you're sending the image to someone else and you don't want them to be able to arrange or adjust its component parts, or when you want to minimize the number of variables that can affect a job. These days, more applications can import layered Photoshop documents (particularly Adobe's other graphics and video applications), so you may not even need to flatten the document unless directed.

> **TIP:** If you shot separate panorama frames using the panorama mode of a digital camera, the camera may mark the frames in a way that allows the software that came with the camera to assemble the panorama automatically. If this is true, it may be faster for you to assemble the panorama in the digital camera's software than in Photoshop.

> **TIP:** Difference mode is useful for manually aligning overlapping image edges. You can use Difference mode to see how image edges line up.

Working with Type

Working with Type

WHEN YOU HEAR THE PHRASE "POWERHOUSE OF TYPOGRAPHY," photo and painting programs aren't usually the first to come to mind. But several years ago—after Adobe developed advanced typographical features for its other products (like Adobe InDesign and Adobe Illustrator)—a light went on over someone's head and they said, "Hey, why don't we throw some of this great code into Photoshop?" The result? Photoshop can now hold its own against other professional graphics programs, offering a wide variety of professional, precise, and versatile type features.

Photoshop has full-featured Character and Paragraph palettes, hanging punctuation, kerning, and other advanced spacing options. Want something a little flashier? Jazz things up with layer effects or type warping. People may still gloss over Photoshop type features on their way to the program's overwhelming graphics capabilities, but if you take a closer look and get to know how type works in Photoshop, you could just gain that extra little edge that makes your Photoshop work stand out a little more, or gain the flexibility that makes graphics production go a little more smoothly for you.

Creating and Editing Type

It's Not Just Bits

? **Photoshop is an image editor. Is there a reason I should set type in Photoshop, since it's all going to be jaggy bitmaps anyway?**

✓ Actually, type in Photoshop isn't always just a bitmap. In fact, when you use one of the Type tools to add text to a Photoshop document, it's maintained as a separate layer of vector type until you manually rasterize it or save in a format that doesn't support vectors. Type layers share many characteristics of vec-

tor shape layers (layer clipping paths). For example, you can apply layer effects to type layers, and the effects stay up to date as you edit the type.

Because each text object is its own layer, you can work with a text object in exactly the same way you would use any other layer (**Figure 6.1**). You can transform, mask, group, link, or rasterize a layer, and you can add adjustment layers to type.

Create Area or Point Type

? **Why is it that sometimes I get a single line of type that won't wrap at the edge of the image?**

✓ What you're seeing is point type, one of the two kinds of type objects you can create (**Figure 6.2**). With point type, the text doesn't wrap unless you type a new line character (Shift-Return/Shift-Enter) or type Return/Enter. (See "Make Your Exit," later in this section for more details.) With area type, text appears inside a bounding rectangle, and the text rewraps when you resize the bounding rectangle—just like adjusting the size of a text frame in InDesign or QuarkXPress.

You create point type by clicking the document when the Type tool is active, and you create area type by dragging the Type tool. If you aren't aware of this difference, you may not realize that dragging is different than clicking.

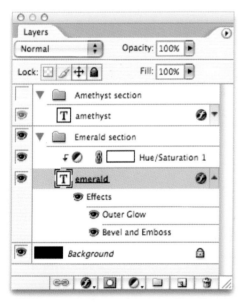

Figure 6.1: When you've got type, you've actually got a vector layer, along with all the benefits that entails.

Getting a Handle on the Handles

? The handles on a type layer sometimes don't do what I want. If I drag one, it sometimes scales both the type box and the type, and other times it only scales the box. Is there a pattern to this?

✓ When you click a Type tool in a text layer that contains area type (see previous solution for how this is different than point type), control handles appear around the type layer. They look like the same handles that you see on other layers or when the Free Transform feature is enabled, but they have a slightly different function. You can tell that the handles work differently because the layer bounding box has a dashed line instead of a solid line.

In an area text layer, dragging a control handle resizes the area in which text will flow, but doesn't stretch the contents. If the text contains multiple lines, dragging a handle can rewrap the text. To resize the contents, Command/Ctrl-drag the handle. (Holding down the Command/Ctrl key is like temporarily turning on Free Transform.) Watch the cursor carefully when you position it over a text layer handle: When you see a double-headed arrow, dragging the handle rewraps the text; when you see a arrowhead, dragging the handle stretches the text.

Import Text from Other Programs

? How can I import text into Photoshop? I tried pasting, but all I got was an ugly bitmap.

✓ Copying and pasting text is the only way to get text into Photoshop other than typing it in. That part might be obvious, but what isn't obvious is that you don't want to simply paste the text into the Photoshop document. By default, text pastes as a new bitmap layer using the Times font in a particularly ugly way, and because it pastes as a bitmap, you can't edit the text or change its attributes. If you want to be able to edit the pasted text, use this procedure instead:

1. Copy the text from the application.

2. Switch to Photoshop

3. Drag the Type tool to create a new text layer. Leave the blinking text cursor active.

4. Choose Copy > Paste.

When you paste text when the blinking text cursor is active, the pasted text takes on the type attributes of the type layer, as if you typed it in yourself. You can then edit the type or its formatting however you want.

Area type   **Point type**

Figure 6.2: Dragging the Type tool creates area type (left), and clicking the Type tool creates point type (right).

Moving Text Between Documents

? When I copy and paste text from one Photoshop document to another, I lose attributes of the text, such as effects I applied. I'm guessing there's a better way to do this?

✓ You guessed right. There's another way, and it's an easier way, too. You don't have to go through Copy and Paste steps when transferring text between Photoshop documents. Just drag the whole layer from one document window to another. You can drag the type layer from the Layers palette, or you can drag using the Move tool from one document to the other. Even better, hold down the Shift key when you drag the layer: If the two documents are the same pixel dimensions, the type layer will end up in the same place in the new document; if they have different dimensions, the layer will end up centered.

Quickly Select Ranges of Text

? Do I have to drag over the text I want to select? That's really annoying if I want a whole paragraph or something.

✓ All the Adobe Creative Suite application let you double-click to select a word, triple-click for a line, or click four times for a paragraph. But if you want to select all the text on a type layer, it's much easier just to double-click on the layer thumbnail in the left column in the Layers palette.

Change Type Defaults

? When I create a new type object, everything's wrong: The alignment, the font, the size, and so on. I have to format everything. How do I control the default settings for the Type tool?

✓ To change the default type settings, first make sure nothing is selected in the document window and that there isn't a blinking text cursor anywhere in the document. Once you've ensured that nothing is selected, change the type settings. That sets the defaults for all new type objects.

However, if you use two or more type formatting styles a lot, you should set up tool presets for each. Set the type formatting while no text is selected, then save a new Type tool preset (in the Tool Presets menu in the Options bar or in the Tool Presets palette; see "Give Tools a Memory" in Chapter 1, *Photoshop Essentials*). Now, when you need that formatting for some new text, just choose the tool preset from the popup menu or palette and you're good to go.

Make Your Exit

? Is there a way to commit text changes using the keyboard? In dialog boxes, I press the Return key to do that, but when I'm entering text, the Return key creates a new paragraph. I guess that makes sense, but I'd still like to commit text changes without reaching for the mouse every time.

✓ You've almost got it. To avoid the ambiguity of the Return/Enter key, add the Command/Ctrl key. In other words, press Command-Return/Ctrl-Enter to exit a type object while committing changes. To exit without saving your changes, press Esc instead. By the way, the Enter key on the numeric keypad also works by itself, because technically the Enter key and the Return key are not the same. On laptops, the keypad Enter key may be in a different location; on Apple PowerBooks the Enter key is along the bottom row next to the arrow keys.

Get Set with Type

Previewing and Selecting Fonts

? **I used to be able to see fonts in their actual typeface in the font menu, but for some reason it isn't doing it anymore. Do you know what happened?**

✓ Font previewing (**Figure 6.3**) is controlled by a preference, and that preference may have gotten turned off by accident. (Or perhaps a co-worker?) Choose Photoshop > Preferences > Type (Mac OS) or Edit > Preferences > Type (Windows), and enable the Font Preview Size checkbox. While you're working with fonts, here are some tips to make font selection even easier:

- If the font menu preview size is too large or too small for your monitor resolution, choose a size from the Font Preview Size popup menu, which is next to the Font Preview Size checkbox.

- If you click on the font menu to open it, you don't need to scroll manually; just start typing the font name and the menu scrolls right to that font.

- You don't have to open the Character palette every time you want to change type settings. Some type settings are available from the Options bar when the Type tool is active.

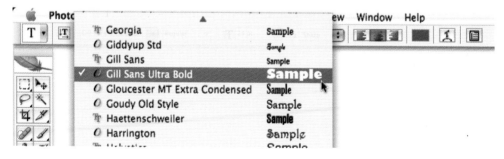

Figure 6.3: Photoshop can display fonts in their actual typefaces.

Format Type En Masse

? **Does Photoshop have text styles or another way to apply the same formatting to lots of text at once?**

✔ Photoshop doesn't have text styles of the kind you'd find in a word processor or layout program, but you can at least apply the same formatting to an entire type layer. Instead of selecting all the text with the Type tool, you can simply select a type layer in the Layers palette. Now any type settings you change are applied to all the text on that layer. When you're editing text with the Type tool, the Options bar displays type formatting options because the Type tool is selected. But when you select a layer in the Layers palette, you may be using a tool other than the Type tool and the Options bar won't include type options. Simply switch to the Type tool to see the formatting controls in the Options bar.

Stroking Type Outlines

? **How can I stroke the outline of a type character like I can in other graphics applications? I don't see any stroke commands in the type controls, and the Edit > Stroke command isn't available for text.**

✔ Yeah, well we never said Photoshop was perfect. It's true that applying a color to text applies only to the text's fill. But there's always a workaround: If you want to control the color and width of character outlines, apply a Stroke effect to a type layer (**Figure 6.4**):

1. Select a type layer.

2. In the Layers palette, click the Add a Layer Style button and choose Stroke from the popup menu.

3. In the Layer Style dialog box, the Stroke option is selected along the left side. Change the stroke options as needed, and click OK.

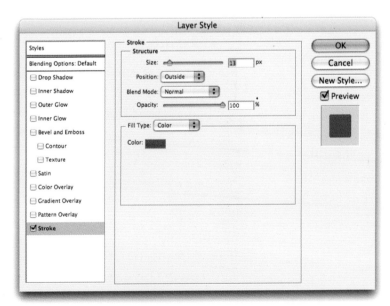

Figure 6.4: Use the Stroke effect to control the outline of type characters.

Note that in the Stroke effect panel, even though it says "Fill Type," it refers to "filling" the stroke—not the fill of the characters. The effect always applies to all the text on a layer, so you can't stroke just one or two characters.

Smoothing Type for Screen Display

? I'm setting type that's going to be exported as a bitmap for Web display, but I'm not happy with the way Photoshop renders the characters. What are my options?

☑ By default, Photoshop always anti-aliases text—simulating higher resolution by using shades and tones along edges. However, there's more than one way to anti-alias type, so Photoshop gives you a choice of several popular methods. To change the anti-aliasing, select a type layer and then choose an anti-aliasing option from one of the following:

- The Layer > Type submenu
- The anti-aliasing popup menu in the Options bar (available when the Type tool is selected) or in the Character palette (**Figure 6.5**)
- The context menu accessible by Ctrl-clicking/right-clicking the type

TIP: To change the color of all text at once, select the text layer in the Layers palette, pick a foreground color, and then press Option/Alt-Delete.

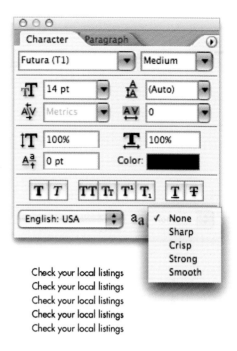

Figure 6.5: The anti-aliasing popup menu in the Character palette, and examples of each of these anti-alias settings.

Setting Type for Web Pages

? I'm trying to design a web page, but the type spacing looks uneven no matter what anti-alias setting I choose.

☑ Try choosing System Layout from the Character palette menu (**Figure 6.6**). The default display mode for type is Fractional Widths, which is more appropriate for high-resolution printed typography. System Layout uses the default type layout method used by your operating system, which is more appropriate for low-resolution screen display. However, this also turns off anti-aliasing.

Figure 6.6: The System Layout option sets type spacing more appropriately for screen display.

Convert Type to a Selection

? I want to paint with the brush tool inside text shapes. How can I use text outlines as a selection?

☑ There's more than one way to create a selection from type outlines:

- Command/Ctrl-click a text layer thumbnail (not the layer name) to create a selection from the character shapes. Then, to use the selection, choose the layer you want to affect. (Not the type layer because you can't paint or adjust a type layer.)

- Enter text using the Horizontal Type Mask or Vertical Type Mask tools. Clicking or dragging these tools puts the document window into Quick Mask mode. As soon as you commit the changes, the document returns to standard mode and the type becomes a selection.

- Press Q to jump into the Quick Mask mode, then use the regular Type tool. When you press Command-Return/Ctrl-Enter, you can manipulate the text (move it, scale it, and so on). Then press Q to leave Quick Mask mode.

You should also consider using type as a clipping mask, so that you can always go back and edit or change the text later. Using this method, you would paint on the layer above the type layer, then Option/Alt-click between the two layers. For more on setting up a clipping mask layer, see "When a Layer is a Mask" in Chapter 5, *Working with Layers*.

Type Along a Path

? How can I make type follow a path? It seems like it should be easy, but I'm baffled.

☑ You're right that it is quite easy, but only after you've done it once or seen how it's done. Just follow these steps:

1. Select a path or shape tool. For example, if you want to set type along a circle, use the Ellipse tool.

2. In the Options bar, click the Paths button (the second button from the left).

3. Create the path. It appears as the Work Path in the Paths palette in case you want to edit the path you created.

4. Now select the Type tool, position it over the path where you want to start the text, and click to insert a

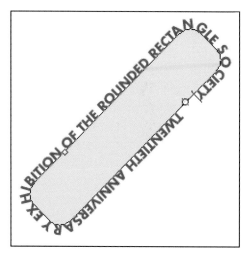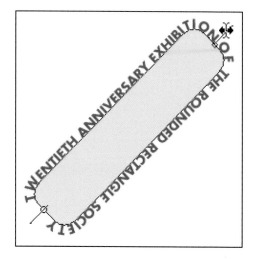

Figure 6.7: Type entered along a path (left) and being dragged along the path (right).

blinking text cursor. Type the text, and when you're done, press Ctrl-Enter (**Figure 6.7**).

If you later want to move the text to a different location along the path, switch to the Path Selection tool (the black arrow tool) and drag the text.

TIP: Don't like how punctuation like quotation marks push their way into a line of text in a paragraph? Open the Paragraph palette (Window > Paragraph), and choose Roman Hanging Punctuation from the Paragraph palette menu. No, "Roman" doesn't mean that it only works in Italian; it refers to the fact that this doesn't apply to punctuation in non-roman languages such as Japanese.

Warp a Type Layer

? I'm making a label for a soft drink can, and I need to simulate how the type will look when it's wrapped around a can. I have a photo of the can. How can I warp the type around the can?

To be honest, we like the 3D tools in Adobe Illustrator more for this kind of thing. However, the Warp Text feature in Photoshop can do the trick in some cases. Try these steps:

1. In the Layers palette, select the type layer you want to distort.

2. Select the Type tool and then choose Layer > Type > Warp Text.

3. Choose a warp (**Figure 6.8**). For a cylinder like the can example, start with the Arch warp.

4. Set options and click OK.

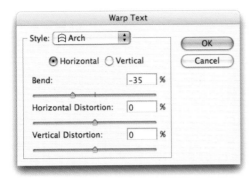

Figure 6.8: The Warp Text dialog box (top), and before and after applying the Arch warp (bottom).

You can change the warp at any time by opening the Warp Text dialog box again, or—faster—by choosing Edit > Transform > Warp, which puts warp options on the Options bar and displays one or more handles on the warp envelope.

However, our colleagues Steve Werner and Sandee Cohen (authors of *Real World Creative Suite*) pointed out a way to warp some text in ways the Warp Text dialog box won't (this only works in CS2): While you can't use the cool Edit > Transform > Warp feature on normal text layers, you can on Smart Objects. So select one or more text layers and convert them into a smart object by choosing Layer > Smart Objects > Group Into New Smart Object. Now you can warp to your heart's content.

Improving Word and Letter Spacing

? Where are the options that control letter and word spacing?

☑ Photoshop contains some of the typographical controls also found in sophisticated layout applications like Adobe InDesign, giving you more precision. For example, you can apply letter and word spacing in smaller increments than a space character, and you can apply line spacing in increments smaller than a carriage return. Try these tips to make your type look even more professional.

- To add or remove space between a range of characters, use a Type tool to select them, and then adjust the Tracking value in the Character palette (**Figure 6.9**). Faster, hold down Option/Alt and press the left or right arrows on the keyboard. For larger changes, hold down both Option/Alt and Command/Ctrl.

- To add or remove space between two characters, use a Type tool to click an insertion point between the characters and adjust the Kerning value in the Character palette. The keyboard shortcuts are exactly the same as tracking.

- To adjust line spacing, select lines or a text layer and adjust the Leading value in the Character palette. The keyboard shortcut is Option/Alt and the up or down arrows on the keyboard. For larger changes, add the Command/Ctrl key.

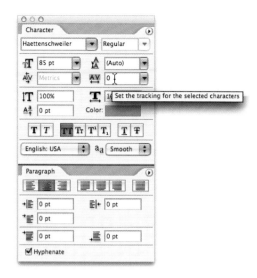

Figure 6.9: The Character and Paragraph palettes contain many options for letter and word spacing.

- To adjust spacing between paragraphs, select paragraphs or an entire text layer, and then adjust the Add Space Before Paragraph value in the Paragraph palette.

- To stop text such as a headline from hyphenating, select the text and disable the Hyphenation checkbox in the Paragraph palette.

- To try different methods for spacing words throughout a paragraph, choose the Justification or Hyphenate controls in the Paragraph palette menu.

TIP: If the Type tool is selected, you can quickly open the Character and Paragraph palette by clicking the "Toggle the Character and Paragraph Palettes" icon in the Options bar. This saves you a trip to the Window menu, and you don't have to memorize any shortcuts.

TIP: By default, the name of a type layer matches the text you enter on the type layer, and it updates if you edit the layer text. However, if you use the Layers palette to rename a type layer, you permanently rename the layer—the layer name no longer updates if you edit the layer text.

Preserving Vector Type in Other Programs

? You say type is vector-based in Photoshop, and I can see that. However, when I save a Photoshop file as a TIFF, I can clearly see that the type is bitmapped. Is there a way to preserve vector type when I use a Photoshop image in another program?

Technically, the vector type is retained in the TIFF (or in a PSD file) as long as you save the layers (as opposed to flattening the file). But unfortunately, every other program—even InDesign CS2—rasterizes the text in these file formats. Therefore, the only way to export a Photoshop file with type layers and preserve the vectors when you import the file into another application is to save the file as Photoshop PDF or an EPS file. Choose File > Save As, select Photoshop PDF or EPS from the Format popup menu. (We prefer PDF to EPS, partly because the text is converted to outlines in an EPS while it remains an embedded font in the PDF.) You can use the resulting PDF document in any program that can import PDF files, such as Adobe InDesign. When you print there, the text will still be vector.

Locating Adobe's Mystery Fonts

? **When I look in the font menu in Photoshop, I see fonts that I don't see in any other applications. When I check Font Book (Mac OS X) or the Fonts control panel (Windows XP), the fonts just aren't there!**

✓ Adobe is sneaky: When you install Photoshop (or the Creative Suite), it adds fonts to your system. However, these fonts aren't placed where you'd expect them. Instead, they show up in a special font folder where only Adobe programs look, and that's why you don't see them in the font menus of other programs.

On Mac OS X, you can find Adobe-installed fonts in the following folder:

`Macintosh HD/Library/Application Support/Adobe/Fonts`

TIP: The more fonts you have, the longer it can take for Photoshop and other programs to start up. You may want to use a font manager—such as FontAgent Pro for Mac OS X—to maximize performance by disabling fonts that you don't always use.

In Windows, you can find Adobe-installed fonts in the following folder:

`C:\Program Files\Common Files\Adobe\Fonts`

If you want to use any of the fonts in other programs, you can move them to the fonts folder for your entire system. On Mac OS X, fonts for the entire system are stored in the following folder:

`Macintosh HD/Library/Fonts`

In Windows, they're here:

`C:\Windows\Fonts`

7

Enhancing Creativity

Enhancing Creativity

*A*LL WORK AND NO PLAY? NO WAY. Photoshop isn't just a production tool—it's also a creative tool. Who doesn't want to get beyond the drudgery of image correction and start playing with brushes and filters? In this chapter you can take advantage of techniques that can put a bit more of your own personality into your Photoshop work. Customize brushes, paint expressively with a graphics tablet, apply filters with abandon, and warp your work in all kinds of ways.

Or maybe you've come from old-school photography, and you simply want to replicate traditional film techniques. Apply a warming or cooling filter, use color to control black-and-white conversions, and simulate the otherwordly look of infrared film. We've got that here too.

We talk about paths at the end of this chapter, because paths give you a way to do an end-run around some of the limitations of image editing. You've already seen how paths can become selections; in this chapter you'll learn how path selection itself works. And while you've always been able to copy and paste paths from Illustrator to Photoshop, in Photoshop CS2 you can paste Illustrator graphics as smart objects—Photoshop's access to all of the creative tools in Illustrator has never been more direct.

So let's get to it. Grab a tool and go wild.

Brushes

Harden or Soften a Brush Edge

? I'd like to paint with a softer edge. How can I adjust the brush to do this?

✓ The Hardness option determines the fuzziness of a brush tip. The Hardness option may not be visible when you open the Brushes palette, because it isn't in the default Brush Presets panel. In the Brushes palette, click Brush Tip Shape to reveal the Hardness option. Or simply Ctrl-click/Right-click a brush on the document and adjust Hardness in the context menu that appears (**Figure 7.1**). If you prefer to use keyboard shortcuts, you can press Shift-] to increase the hardness 25-percent or Shift-[to decrease it. (If you leave off the Shift key, those keys increase or decrease the size of the brush.)

Figure 7.1: A mini version of the Brushes palette appears when you Ctrl-click or Right-click while a brush tool is selected.

Design Your Own Brush

? The brushes that Photoshop provides aren't quite doing it for me; I'd like to design my own brushes. How can I get a brush to do my bidding?

✓ Exploring the Brush tool is like going on a treasure hunt. Useful features are hidden all over the place—on the keyboard, in palettes, and in menus. Here are our favorite brush tips:

- Before you go to the trouble of creating your own brush, make sure that what you want isn't hiding inside the program already. For example, once you open the Brushes palette, you can choose from among a dozen brush sets in the palette's flyout menu—sets such as Dry Media or Wet Media brushes.

- To customize the current brush, use the Brushes palette (**Figure 7.2**), which you can usually find in the palette well in the Options bar.

- If you're looking for a specific brush feature, try looking in every panel in the Brushes palette. Clicking any heading along the left side of the Brushes palette reveals a different options panel.

- You can quickly specify a different diameter, hardness, and preset by Ctrl-clicking/right-clicking on the document with the brush tool and making your changes in the handy context menu that pops up.

- The Options bar contains options specific to the Brush tool, including the blending mode and opacity settings.

- The Airbrush button in the Options bar allows the Brush tool to continue laying down paint as long as the mouse button is pressed, whether or not you're dragging the mouse.

Opacity, Layers, and Brushes

? I have my layer set to 100% opacity, but when I paint, the brush strokes are partially transparent. Why is that?

✓ Layers aren't the only place where you can apply an opacity value. You can also apply an opacity value to the Brush tool and other painting tools. If you're painting or retouching, keep an eye on both the opacity value in the Layers palette and the opacity value in the Options bar, because the two types of opacity are cumulative.

By the way, you can change the opacity setting by typing the value on the keyboard—type 3 for 30 percent, 4 for 40 percent, 55 for 55 percent, and so on. However, if you have any of the painting tools selected, this shortcut changes the value in the Options bar. If you have a selection or the Move tool chosen in the Tools palette, it alters the Opacity in the Layers palette.

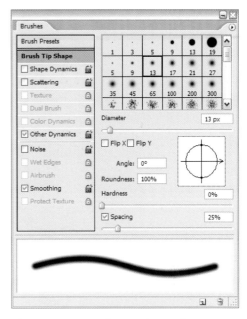

Figure 7.2: Use the Brushes palette to customize every attribute of a brush.

Take a Tablet, You'll Feel Better

? Should I buy a graphic tablet, like a Wacom?

✓ If all you do at work is open files, change them to CMYK, and resave them... well, we send our sympathies, but a graphic tablet won't really help you much. But for virtually everything else—from cropping to retouching—you have far more control over Photoshop with a stylus than if you were using a mere mouse. You'll be able to control your brushstrokes using pressure, just like an actual brush or pencil. Some high-end tablets have a stylus that senses other stylus movements, such as its tilt angle or the rotation of a scroll wheel or of the pen itself.

You control all Photoshop tablet support in the Brushes palette. If some options are visible but dimmed, it means your input device doesn't support that option. For example, the Tilt Scale option is only available if you're using a graphics tablet and stylus that senses tilt angle.

To change how a tablet controls a tool, click on the pane on the left side of the Brushes palette. On the right side of the Brushes palette, look for the Control popup menu. The Control popup menu contains properties that a tablet can control, such as the Pen Pressure, Pen Tilt, Stylus Wheel, and Rotation options.

Filter Fun

Add a Drop Shadow

? I can't find a drop shadow filter anywhere on the Filters menu. Where's it hiding?

✓ Although the Filter menu contains all sorts of goodies, drop shadows are an entirely different kind of thing. Drop shadows are considered a *layer effect*, so they live with the other layer controls. The easiest way to add a drop shadow is to click the Add a Layer Style button in the Layers palette and choose Drop Shadow from the popup menu (**Figure 7.3**). The Layer Style dialog box opens with the Drop Shadow effect selected, and you can adjust the settings from there. After you apply a drop shadow, you can see it attached to the layer in the Layers palette, and you can edit the drop shadow by double-clicking it in the Layers palette.

Because a drop shadow is a layer effect, it applies to an entire layer. If you can't see a drop shadow that you applied, make sure you applied it to a layer that's smaller than the size of the document.

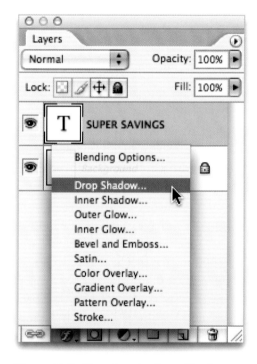

Figure 7.3: Choosing the Drop Shadow layer style in the Layers palette

TIP: The fastest way to position a drop shadow is to drag it around (in the image window) while the Layer Styles dialog box is open. That's typically much easier than dialing in the values in the dialog box controls.

Apply a Filter Again

? After some experimentation, I finally arrived at the filter settings I want. Now I want to apply the same filter to other selections and layers in the same document. Is there a shortcut for this?

☑ There's a shortcut for just about everything! To apply the most recently used filter and settings again, choose Filter > Last Filter (or, much faster, press Command/Ctrl-F). When you use Last Filter, you won't see the Filter dialog box at all; Photoshop simply applies the last settings you used for that filter.

You can also open the dialog box of the last-used filter so that you can adjust its settings. Just press Command-Option-F/Ctrl-Alt-F. For instance, if you didn't get the filter settings exactly right, just Undo it and then use this shortcut to reapply the same filter but with different settings.

Create a Halftone Screen Effect

? How can I create a big-halftone look like you see in pop-art paintings?

☑ Images are normally converted to halftone dots to make them print-

TIP: If you want to apply a layer effect (like a Drop Shadow or Outer Glow) to other layers, you can't use Last Filter to apply that effect again. However, you can use the Layer Styles palette, which is even better. Right-click (or Control-click if you only have a one-button mouse) on the layer style icon and choose Copy Layer Style from the context menu. Now right-click on another layer and choose Paste Layer Style.

able on a press, and they aren't supposed to be large enough to be visible. However, radically enlarged halftones do make a pretty cool graphic effect, and with Photoshop you don't have to paint every dot individually like Roy Lichtenstein did.

To create a halftone dot effect, choose Filter > Pixelate > Color Halftone. In the Color Halftone dialog box (**Figure 7.4**), Max. Radius refers to the size of the halftone dot in pixels. The default screen angles correspond to the traditional angles for color separations, but if you're using Color Halftone as a purely graphic effect you don't need to stick to those angles.

If the image is hard to recognize after applying the Color Halftone filter, select Undo, and use the Image > Image

Figure 7.4: The Color Halftone dialog box (left) and the resulting effect (above).

Size command to upsample the image (increase the pixel dimensions with the Resample Image option on). Then apply the filter again.

Here's one more way to create this effect. It's more time consuming, but you get more options:

1. Start with a CMYK image (choose Image > Mode > CMYK).

2. In the Channels palette flyout menu, choose Split Channels. You'll end up with four separate grayscale images.

3. In the first of these images, choose Image > Mode > Bitmap.

4. From the Method popup menu of the Bitmap dialog box, choose Halftone Screen and click OK.

5. Specify the halftone settings you want (line screen, angle, spot shape) and click OK.

6. Next, choose Image > Mode > Grayscale.

7. Now repeat steps 3 to 6 for the other three files.

8. In the Channels palette menu, choose Merge Channels. Make sure the correct grayscale image is assigned to the proper color (it should be obvious by the file's name).

TIP: If you want to apply the Color Halftone filter to an image destined for CMYK output, convert the image to CMYK before applying the Color Halftone filter so that the cyan, magenta, yellow, and black dots are on the correct channels from the start.

Create an Adjustable Texture

? I'm creating a texture by applying a filter to a layer. How can I have a little more control over the texture than I have in the filter's dialog box?

☑ Textures can add character and interest to a document, but once you apply a texture to an image, it permanently alters the image pixels, making it difficult or impossible to adjust or redo the texture at a later time. Instead, create your texture as a separate layer, so you can manipulate it independently of the image layer.

This solution is based on how the Overlay blending mode works. On a layer with Overlay applied, 50-percent gray is a neutral color that doesn't change underlying layers, colors lighter then 50-percent gray lighten underlying colors as if the Screen mode was applied, and colors darker than 50 percent darken underlying colors as if the Multiply blending mode was applied. Here's how to do it:

1. In the Layers palette, Option/Alt-click the Create a New Layer button.

2. In the Layer Options dialog box, choose Overlay from the Mode popup menu, and turn on the Fill with Overlay-Neutral Color (50% Gray) checkbox. Click OK.

3. Click the eye icon for the image layer to hide it, so that you see only the gray layer.

4. Select the new, gray layer in the Layers palette, and apply a texture from the Filter menu such as

Filter > Artistic > Sponge. If you apply a filter to the gray layer and it appears solid black, gray, or white, try another filter. Some filters act on the edges present in a layer, and the solid gray layer has no edges. Other filters generate their own textures; those filters do produce visible results on a solid-color layer.

5. Click the eye icon for the image layer to make it visible. The texture should now be visible over the image layer (**Figure 7.5**).

As needed, edit the texture layer by manipulating the gray levels or painting on it. For example:

- To reduce the overall intensity of the texture, make an adjustment to the layer's opacity.

- To control the contrast of the texture, Option/Alt-click the Create New Fill or Adjustment Layer button in the Layers palette, choose Levels or Curves, enable the Use Previous Layer to Create Clipping Mask button, and click OK to edit the contrast of the layer. Using the image layer as a clipping mask ensures that the adjustment layer affects only the texture layer.

- To erase the texture from parts of the image, use the Erase tool or paint an area with 50-percent gray. Don't paint the gray layer with black or white.

- To remove the texture from parts of the image in a way that's reversible, use a layer mask filled with white, and paint black in areas where you want to suppress the texture. See the topic "Create Transparency with a Layer Mask" in Chapter 5, *Working with Layers*.

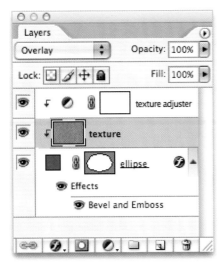

Figure 7.5: From left to right above: The original ellipse layer with the Bevel and Emboss effect; the texture layer with the Overlay blending mode applied, all layers combined, and the texture partially removed by painting on the "texture" layer with a brush set to 50-percent gray. The ellipse and texture layers are also set up as a clipping mask, so that the texture stays inside the ellipse. The "texture adjuster" layer is a Curves adjustment layer that refines the contrast of the texture.

Perspective and Distortion

Rectilinear Distortions

? ■ How do I distort a layer in sort of a trapezoidal way? You know, like the opening credits in *Star Wars*.

✓ Check out the Free Transform command. The Free Transform command is known as a one-stop command for moving, scaling, and rotating layers, but you need to use modifier keys for the wacky effects.

With a non-background layer selected, choose Edit > Free Transform (or press Command/Ctrl-T) and do any of the following:

- To stretch the layer without maintaining its original proportions, drag any handle without pressing any modifier keys. Or, to maintain the proportions, hold down the Shift key while dragging.

- To skew the layer, Command/Ctrl-drag a side handle or Command-Option-drag/Ctrl-Alt-drag a corner handle (**Figure 7.6**).

- To distort the image without maintaining parallel lines for each dimension, Command/Ctrl-drag a corner handle.

If you want more powerful distortion of this kind, or you want to simulate true linear perspective, use the Vanishing Point feature instead. See the topic "Have a Little Perspective," later in the section.

Add Curved or Custom Distortions

? ■ How can I apply curved distortions like fisheye views or waving flags?

✓ Photoshop has always been capable of applying a basic level of nonlinear distortion such as through the Spherize filter, but Photoshop CS2 adds powerful new warping features that are much more useful. With any layer selected, do any of the following:

- To apply a basic distortion, choose one of the filters on the Filter > Distort submenu. Most of these tend to be predefined and don't offer much in the way of customization. The one exception is the Lens Correction filter. While Lens Correction is designed to remove distortion, you can also use it to introduce different types of intentional distortion.

 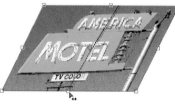

Figure 7.6: Command/Ctrl-dragging a Free Transform side handle to skew an image

- To apply a warp effect, choose Edit > Transform > Warp and then adjust the warp by dragging the lines or points around the image, or by changing the settings in the Options bar (**Figure 7.7**).

- To apply freeform distortion to specific areas of the document, use the Liquify effect (Filter > Liquify). You'll likely want to make a feathered selection around the area you want to affect before opening this filter.

- To use a grayscale image as a bump (displacement) map, choose Filter > Distort > Displace, use the default settings in the Displace dialog box as a starting point (just click OK), and choose a grayscale Photoshop file from disk (**Figure 7.8**). A bump map is a grayscale file where each pixel's level of gray describes how far to displace (move) the same pixel on the layer it's applied to. 50-percent gray pixels don't move, pixels darker than 50-percent gray move in a negative direction (up and to the left), and pixels lighter than 50-percent gray move in a positive direction (down and to the right).

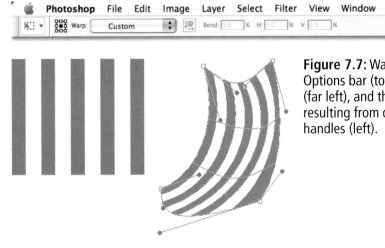

Figure 7.7: Warp settings on the Options bar (top), original image (far left), and the warped image resulting from dragging the warp handles (left).

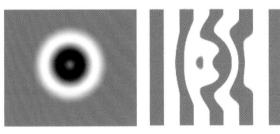

Figure 7.8: A grayscale image (left); the effect of applying the grayscale file to the image as a bump map (center), and the Displace dialog box used to apply the bump map (right).

Have a Little Perspective

? **I need to show a client how their home is going to look after they install a new window. I've got a photo of the house, but it seems like it'll be a lot of work to get the window to match the perspective of the exterior walls in the photo. What's the trick to working in linear perspective in Photoshop?**

✔️ You could illustrate the siding without any perspective and then use the Free Transform command to fit it to the side of the house, as we described in the earlier tip, "Rectilinear Distortions." But if you have Photoshop CS2, there's a way that's both easier and more fun: The new Vanishing Point feature. With Vanishing Point, you can actually work in perspective—including painting, moving, scaling, and rotating. Here's how to get started:

1. Set up any layers and masks you want to use. For instance, if you want to keep the results of Vanishing Point separate from the original image (we usually do), duplicate its layer before continuing.

2. Choose File > Save to save your changes up to this point, because you can't save while you're working with the Vanishing Point feature.

3. Select a layer (an image layer, not an adjustment layer or type layer), and choose Filter > Vanishing Point.

4. When you open Vanishing Point, the Create Plane tool is selected for you. Click four corners to define a perspective plane that exists in the image.

5. Paint, clone, or manipulate selections over that perspective plane, and they'll follow the grid (**Figure 7.9**). You can also paste an image from the clipboard (such as the image of your siding), but see the next solution for tips on images pasted into Vanishing Point.

6. Click OK, then—if you like what you did—save the document again. That way, Vanishing Point will remember the perspective planes you defined so you can exit and enter Vanishing Point repeatedly and continue your work as needed.

7. By the way, while you are creating and editing perspective planes, you can use the following tips:

   - Press the X key to zoom in so that you can precisely line up each corner of the plane.

TIP: Make sure you've selected an image layer before opening Vanishing Point. Vanishing Point can't write changes to a non-image layer, such as an adjustment layer or type layer. Unfortunately, Photoshop doesn't warn you about this, so if you select the layer mask of an adjustment layer and then work in Vanishing Point, all of your Vanishing Point work is discarded without notice when you close Vanishing Point (even if you clicked OK), and there's no way to get it back.

Vanishing Point

Show Edges Diameter: 70 Hardness: 50 Opacity: 100 Heal: Off Aligned OK

Opt+click in a plane, to set a source point for the clone. Once source point is set, click+drag to paint or clone. Shift+click to extend the stoke to last click. Reset

59.3%

Figure 7.9: Cloning a new window using the Clone Stamp tool within a Vanishing Point perspective grid.

- Command/Ctrl-drag a side handle to pull an additional plane out perpendicularly (the surface goes around a corner).

- Drag a side handle to resize any plane (it won't affect other planes). Scaling up a perspective plane is a good way to double-check its alignment to the perspective lines in the image.

- Make sure the perspective planes you create are blue. If a perspective plane is yellow or red, you've drawn a plane that isn't mathematically valid for perspective and not all Vanishing Point features will work. In your blue plane, typically the larger the squares the better.

Help New Arrivals Fit In

? Now that I've pasted an image into Vanishing Point, I can see that it doesn't fit quite right. Do I have to close Vanishing Point and start over again, adjusting the image before I copy it?

☑ Vanishing Point does include a few ways to adjust selections you paste or drag-copy in the Vanishing Point dialog box. Use these tips to help quickly blend changes in with the base image:

- After pasting an image into the Vanishing Point dialog box, you probably need to drag it on top of the perspective plane before the pasted pixels take on the new perspective (**Figure 7.10**).

- When using the Transform tool, use the Flip or Flop options in the Vanishing Point Options bar to reverse the orientation of the selection across the horizontal or vertical axis of the selection, in perspective. This is useful when moving a selection to another perspective plane, where the light may be coming from a different direction than the plane from which the selection was originally made.

- When using the Clone Stamp, Marquee, or Brush tools, try the Opacity option in the Vanishing Point Options bar.

- When using the Clone Stamp, Marquee, or Brush tools, try one of the Heal options in the Vanishing Point Options bar. The On option attempts to match the brightness and color of the surroundings, while Luminance only tries to match the surrounding brightness.

- If you want to use a blending mode that isn't available in Vanishing Point, before you open Vanishing Point put your selection on a higher layer and run Vanishing Point from there. You can then apply the blending mode to that layer.

Figure 7.10: If you paste type or an image into Vanishing Point (top), it snaps into perspective as you and drag it over the perspective grid (bottom). In this example, Vanishing Point was applied to a higher layer so that the pasted type could use the Multiply blending mode.

TIP: When you move, copy, or clone one part of an image to another, set the source to a "nearer" area and the destination to a "farther" area whenever possible, so that your source has more resolution than the destination. If you start from a far area and clone to a near area, you may see pixelization or blockiness.

Darkroom Adventures

Create a Sepia Tone

? **What's a quick way to turn a color image into a sepia-tone image?**

☑ It's easy to apply a sepia-tone effect to a color image. You can use the same principles in this tip to colorize an image using any other hue in the rainbow.

1. In the Layers palette, click the Create New Fill or Adjustment Layer button and choose Hue/Saturation. (If Hue/Saturation isn't available, you may be working with an image that isn't in a color mode that can use Hue/Saturation. Choose a command on the Image > Mode submenu to convert it to RGB, CMYK, or another color mode that can use Hue/Saturation.)

2. In the Hue/Saturation dialog box, enable the Colorize checkbox.

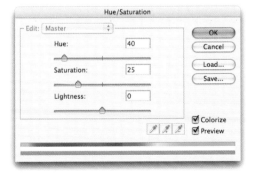

3. As a starting point, set the Hue value to 40 degrees. If you want a slightly different sepia hue, or if you just feel like going wild today, adjust the Hue value (**Figure 7.11**).

Here's another way to accomplish much the same thing: Choose Solid Color from the Create New Fill or Adjustment Layer button (popup menu) in the Layers palette, then pick any color, click OK, and set the new adjustment layer's blending mode to either Hue or Color.

Figure 7.11: Creating a sepia-tone look (above) with a single Hue/Saturation adjustment layer (left).

Create a Duotone

❓ My printer suggested that I set up my images as duotones to make my images look better on my two-color print job. I made an image that looks like a duotone, but it's not separating onto two plates properly!

☑ Duotones are a great way to make images look a little richer when your budget limits the number of inks you can afford to print on a press. To create a duotone, you have to start with a grayscale image and choose Image > Mode > Duotone. If it's grayed out, the image probably isn't in Grayscale mode.

When the Duotone Options dialog box appears, choose Duotone from the Type menu (or Tritone to use three inks), click Load, select one of the files in the Duotones folder (it's one of the preset folders inside the Photoshop folder), and click OK (**Figure 7.12**). Pick a file that matches up with the inks used on the press for your job, so if you're not sure which inks to use or how to customize the duotone curves, ask your commercial printer for advice or read over the chapter on Spot Colors and Duotones in *Real World Photoshop*.

If your printer specifically asks for a duotone, use the Duotone command—don't use another method to colorize your image. For example, colorizing an image by adding a Hue/Saturation layer is not the right way to make a duotone for a press, because it doesn't break the colors down into the inks you're actually using on press. Colorizing with Hue/Saturation is okay if your image is only for on-screen viewing, or if you're printing CMYK. To save your Duotone-mode image, save it as a PSD or PDF file (if you're printing from InDesign) or an EPS file (for QuarkXPress).

Solid Colors in Duotones

❓ I have a duotone image, but I want one area to be printed in a solid color. It doesn't seem like there's any way to do this.

☑ You're right: There's virtually no way to create an area of your image in a single solid ink when you're in Duotone mode. But it's easy if you convert the file from Duotone mode to Multichannel mode. In Multichannel

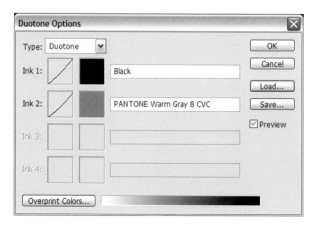

Figure 7.12: The Duotone Options dialog box

mode, each spot color appears as its own channel in the Channels palette. You can then edit the channels individually, placing solid color on one, knocking it out of another, and so on. When you're done, save the file as a DCS 2.0 file (or PSD file for InDesign).

Outsource Your Color

? I love using the Eyedropper tool to sample colors in my image, but how do I get a color from outside the Photoshop document window? If I click outside Photoshop, I switch to the desktop or whatever program I clicked on.

✓ Ah, grasshopper, there is always a way, though the path is not always a clear one. First, select the Eyedropper tool. Now, instead of simply clicking, press and hold the Eyedropper tool anywhere inside a Photoshop window, and then, without letting go, drag the Eyedropper tool past the edge of the Photoshop document window to the color you want to sample. When the foreground color swatch indicates that you've sampled the color you want, release the mouse button. Wax on, wax off!

TIP: It's a good idea to keep the Histogram palette open and visible as you work in the Channel Mixer dialog box, or when performing any tone or color adjustment. Keeping an eye on the Histogram palette can help you notice when you're clipping highlights or shadows.

Apply a Traditional Photo Filter

? Back when I shot on film, I would stick warming or cooling filters on the end of my lens when the lighting conditions called for it. But in this digital age, I can't figure out how to simulate those filters. Is there a way?

✓ Photoshop comes to the rescue again, because traditional photo filters are included. But you can stop looking under the Filter menu for them! You apply a photo filter from the Layers palette. Click the Create New Fill or Adjustment Layer button and choose Photo Filter. In the Photo Filter dialog box (**Figure 7.13**), choose the filter type from the Filter popup menu. You'll find that you can customize the filter by clicking the swatch to pick a custom color, or by adjusting the density. Much more fun than the old glass filters, isn't it?

You can apply the Photo Filter from the Image > Adjustment submenu, too, but we prefer to make it an adjustment layer so we can edit the effect later, simply by double-clicking the adjustment layer in the Layers palette.

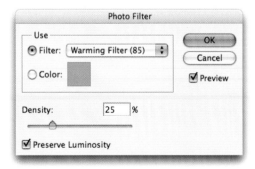

Figure 7.13: The Photo Filter dialog box

Simulate Infrared Film Images

? **Infrared images look really cool. How can I simulate that effect in Photoshop?**

✓ Infrared photography has an ethereal, ghostly quality that's naturally fascinating. Infrared images record how objects absorb or reflect infrared light, which is not visible to the human eye. Traditionally, infrared images are recorded using black and white film sensitized to the invisible infrared wavelengths of light, just below red in the spectrum. In infrared images, objects absorbing more infrared light appear darker, and objects absorbing less appear lighter. An image shot on infrared film can take on a range of appearances depending on whether the photographer used filters during the shot; this tip describes just one interpretation. Here are the steps:

1. Start with a full-color RGB image.

2. In the Layers palette, click the Create New Fill or Adjustment Layer button and choose Channel Mixer.

3. In the Channel Mixer dialog box, enable the Monochrome checkbox (**Figure 7.14**).

4. Increase the Red and Green values; use +100 as a starting point. Decrease the Blue value, use -100 as a starting point. If your image has green foliage or human skin tones, those subjects should now appear noticeably lighter than normal. If your image has a blue sky, that should now appear noticeably darker. If parts of the image start to lose detail as you adjust, back off and move the slider value back towards zero. Click OK.

5. Choose the underlying image layer again and choose Filter > Distort

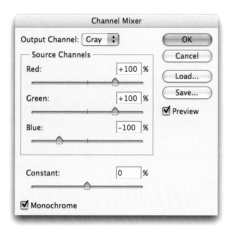  

Figure 7.14: The Channel Mixer dialog box set to Monochrome and with black and white conversion values set (left), the original image (center), and the image after applying the Channel Mixer adjustment layer and the Diffuse Glow filter (right).

> Diffuse Glow. You can use this filter to add some of the glow and grain associated with many infrared images. In the Diffuse Glow dialog box, start by setting Graininess and Glow Amount to low value. For Clear Amount, start with a high value such as 18, and click OK.

6. Or, to enhance the infrared effect, undo the filter, choose Layer > Flatten Image, and then reapply the filter (Command/Ctrl-F).

Note that this tip can only simulate infrared images by exaggerating the red portion of the spectrum that's visible to us humans. It doesn't accurately represent what the scene would look like if it were actually shot with infrared film.

From Color to Grayscale

? **What's the best way to turn a color image into a black-and-white image?**

✓ There are at least three ways to remove color from an image. There isn't really one best way; it depends on the effect you're trying to create.

- To convert an entire image, choose Image > Mode > Grayscale. Photoshop removes the color from the image and also converts the image to grayscale mode. If the document contains layers, they may need to be flattened. The advantage of this method is that it reduces the file size, because a grayscale image requires only one channel. A disadvantage is that the image loses its color forever.

- To remove color from just one layer, choose Image > Adjust > Desaturate. Photoshop removes the color from the current layer, but doesn't convert the whole image to grayscale mode. Desaturating can be helpful if you want to create a grayscale layer in the middle of a color document. Once you desaturate a layer you can't restore its color, except by using the History palette.

If you don't like the way the Grayscale command converts color to grayscale (we rarely do), you can customize the conversion with the Channel Mixer. Colors have different densities; for example, the most vivid yellow can never be darker than the least vivid blue. If you alter the mix of an image's channels (red, green, and blue channels for an RGB image), you'll alter the contrast of an image. That's why the Channel Mixer is a popular color-

TIP: In the Channel Mixer, it's okay for the total percentage to be lower or higher than 100%. However, keep an eye on the highlights, shadows, and Histogram palette to watch for clipping.

TIP: When you convert a color image to grayscale using a Channel Mixer conversion, you can fine-tune the tonal quality of the image by adding a Curves or Levels adjustment layer above the Channel Mixer adjustment layer.

to-grayscale conversion tool with photographers, many of whom are used to altering the contrast of black-and-white film images by putting colored filters in front of the lens.

1. In the Layers palette, click the Create New Fill or Adjustment Layer button and choose Channel Mixer.

2. At the bottom of the Channel Mixer dialog box, turn on the Monochrome checkbox.

3. As a starting point, set each of the Red, Green, and Blue values to 33 percent. This builds the black-and-white image from equal parts of all colors.

4. Adjust the Red, Green, and Blue values until the contrast across the image appears the way you want. To maintain the overall brightness of the image, keep the total percentage close to 100 percent.

5. When you're happy with the appearance of the image, click OK.

> **TIP:** If you come up with a favorite color-to-grayscale conversion using the Channel Mixer or Hue/Saturation methods, click the Save button in the adjustment layer dialog box or record the conversion as an action. Either way makes it easier to apply the same conversion to other images in the future.

Grayscale via Hue/Saturation

? I find the Channel Mixer hard to understand and control. Is there another, easier grayscale conversion method?

✓ Sure. If you're not used to thinking about black-and-white like a photographer, this method is quite simple. It's easier to experiment with this method than it is with the Channel Mixer method, because you drag only one slider instead of three. We learned this technique from world-famous Photoshop guru Russell Brown:

1. In the Layers palette, hold down the Option/Alt key when you choose Hue/Saturation from the Create New Fill or Adjustment Layer button (popup menu).

2. In the New Layer dialog box that appears, choose Color from the Mode menu, and then click OK.

3. In the Hue/Saturation dialog box that appears, make no changes and click OK.

4. In the Layers palette, click the Create New Fill or Adjustment Layer button and choose Hue/Saturation. Set Saturation to -100 (the minimum), and click OK (**Figure 7.15**).

5. In the Layers palette, double-click the thumbnail for the Hue/Saturation 1 layer (the first one you created, with the Color blending mode applied) and drag the Saturation slider until the contrast across the image appears the way you want, then click OK.

Crunch Down Converted Images

? I converted a color image to grayscale, but it's still taking up the same amount of space on my hard disk. Should I compress it or something?

✓ If you use a custom method to remove all color from an image and you don't plan to add back any color, convert the image to grayscale mode by choosing Image > Mode > Grayscale (and flatten the document if asked by Photoshop). The more advanced methods keep the image in RGB mode so that you can edit the conversion later. Converting permanently to grayscale saves disk space and RAM usage because a grayscale image stores data in just one channel, whereas a color image requires at least three channels (red, blue, and green). In addition, if you started from a 16-bit color image, you may want to choose Image > Mode > 8 Bits/Channel. The file size difference between a layered 16-bit color image and a flattened 8-bit grayscale image is huge!

Camera Raw Image for Color and Grayscale

? I shoot weddings, and black-and-white versions of my photos are popular. As I learn more about Adobe Camera Raw, I'm able to do more of my basic corrections in Camera Raw. Can I generate good black-and-white images straight from Camera Raw?

✓ Yes. If you have a camera raw image that doesn't need further tweaking in Photoshop itself, you can use Camera Raw to create a black-and-white version. This tip has a couple of twists and turns because you can't keep two sets of Camera Raw settings active at the same time.

First, open a Camera Raw image and color-correct it to your liking. Click the triangle button next to the Settings popup menu (**Figure 7.16**), choose Save Settings, and name and save an .xmp file. This backs up the current color settings of the image.

Then, in the Adjust tab, drag Saturation to -100, the lowest value. Click

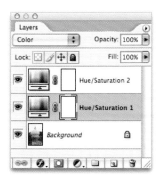

Figure 7.15: Left to right: Adjustment layers applied for the Hue/Saturation method of grayscale conversion, the original image, the default conversion, and the conversion after adjusting the Saturation slider on the lower Hue/Sat layer.

the Calibrate tab and adjust the sliders to produce the black-and-white contrast you want across the image.

When you're happy with the black-and-white version, click the triangle button next to the Settings popup menu, choose Save Settings, and name and save a different .xmp file. This backs up your black-and-white settings for the image.

At any time in the future, you can choose Load Settings from the popup menu under the triangle button and load the color or black-and-white settings for this raw image.

Note: If you altered the Calibrate tab to improve the black-and-white conversion, make sure you reset all Calibrate values before working on the image in color again. The Calibrate tab is normally intended for correcting overall color and tonal balance, not for image effects. To reset the values, Option/Alt-click the Cancel button in the Camera Raw dialog box.

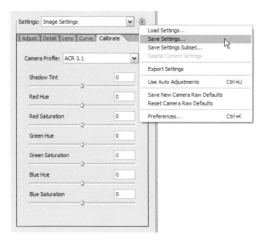

Figure 7.16: The Camera Raw popup menu containing the Load Settings and Save Settings commands, and behind it, the Calibrate tab ready to be adjusted.

Paths and the Pen

Drawing the Path or Shape You Want

 I have trouble drawing with the Pen tool sometimes—and I'm an Illustrator veteran! Photoshop seems to have a few extra modes for the Pen tool. Can you clue me in?

☑ Sure. You're right, the Pen tool in Photoshop does have a few options that aren't the same as in Illustrator. If you pick up the pen tool and it doesn't do what you want, use these tips to find your way

- If the Pen tool doesn't do what you expect, check the Options bar (**Figure 7.17**). You may have selected a button that changes the behavior of the Pen tool.

- By default, when you draw with the Pen tool, each path you draw cre-

Figure 7.17: The Pen tool can behave quite differently depending on which options you select in the Options bar.

ates a new shape layer. (Technically, shape layers are just solid color fill adjustment layers with a clipping path—or "vector mask"—attached to them.) If you want to draw paths as a starting point for selections instead of making shape layers, select the Paths button in the Options bar when the Pen tool is selected.

- To deselect a path you're drawing, press the Esc key.

- If you're about to draw a common shape, like a heart, check to see if Photoshop already provides a preset shape for it. In the Options bar, click the Custom Shape button and then choose a shape from the Shape popup menu on the Options bar. To see the interesting shapes, click on the shape that looks like a blob. That displays the Shape popup menu. For even more shapes, click on the little fly-

TIP: Confused about how the Pen tool works? You're not alone—the pen tool isn't the most intuitive tool to use. The most thorough descriptions and tutorials for the Pen tool exist not in books about Photoshop, but rather in books about Adobe Illustrator, such as Mordy Golding's *Real World Adobe Illustrator CS2*.

out menu at the top of that Shape popup menu. There's a lot of artwork hiding in there.

- If you find the Pen tool too challenging, click the Freeform Pen button in the Options bar when the Pen tool is selected. With the Freeform Pen button turned on, you can drag the Pen tool like a real pen—you don't have to figure out how to click and drag to get corners and curves.

Select Shapes and Paths

? When it comes to paths, I have a heck of a time selecting just what I want to select. I'm never sure if I should be using the Pen tool, the Path Selection tool, the Move tool, or something else.

☑ When you work with shapes and paths, you enter a strange and sometimes confusing world of selection methods, where you need to pay attention to what you're trying to select and which tool you need to use. You select shapes in the Layers palette, and paths in the Paths palette (**Figure 7.18**). Once they're selected, you can move shapes with the Move tool, but you move paths with the Path Selection tool. Fortunately, you can edit both shapes and paths in the same way: by using the Direct Selection tool. With the Direct Selection tool, you can select and edit individual points and segments on a path.

Save and Name Paths

? When I draw paths (not shapes), they tend to pile up in the document window. Can I name them separately or something, like I can with layers?

☑ You can use the Paths palette (Window > Paths) to manage your paths like you do with layers, whether they're basic paths or shape layers. The Paths palette is empty until you draw a path, or when you select a shape layer. When you draw a path with the Pen tool, it appears in the Paths palette as a Work Path—an unnamed path. When you select or draw on a shape layer, the Paths palette displays the path that's being used as a mask on that layer.

As you draw more and more paths (not shape layers), they'll pile up as part of the Work Path. You can maintain different paths by naming them separately in the Paths palette:

- To create a new path name for the next path you draw, click the New Path button at the bottom of the Paths palette.

- To save and name a path, Option/ Alt-click the New Path button.

- To name an existing path (or save the Work Path), double-click it in the Paths palette.

- To move a path to a different named path, select the path with the Path Selection tool, choose Edit > Cut, select another path name, and choose Edit > Paste.

Figure 7.18: The Paths palette displays named paths you've saved, the work path, and the vector paths of shape layers.

Hide or Deselect Paths

? I drew a path and converted it to a selection, but the path is still hanging around. How can I hide the path without deleting it? Select > Deselect All makes no difference.

☑ After you've finished working with a path, such as converting it to a selection, the path typically remains visible. This doesn't indicate that anything is wrong, it just means the path is still selected in the Paths palette. To make sure all paths are deselected, either press Esc or click in an empty area at the bottom of the Paths palette list. You can also choose View > Show > Target Path if you want to control the visibility of the path independently of the path's selection state in the Paths palette.

Paint with Shapes and Paths

? I love that I can create vector objects in Photoshop using shape layers. Can I apply filters to vector shapes or paths?

✓ You wish! If it's a shape layer, you need to convert it to a bitmapped image layer by rasterizing it. Photoshop may offer to rasterize the layer for you when you apply certain effects, or you can rasterize a shape layer at any time by choosing from the Layer > Rasterize submenu.

You can use a path to paint a fill or stroke on a layer, which is useful when you want to keep lots of shapes in your document without having them be visible shape layers. Just select a path in the Paths palette, select an image layer where you want the fill or stroke to appear, and then click the Fill Path with Foreground Color or Stroke Path with Brush buttons (**Figure 7.19**). Here's a shortcut for stroking a path: Select it in the Paths palette, make sure any of the painting tools are selected (such as the Brush tool), and then press Enter.

TIP: Need to select all the points on a path with the Direct Selection tool? Just Option/Alt-click on the path!

TIP: When you select a path that contains sub-paths, all of the sub-paths are selected. To move just one of those sub-paths, use the Path Selection tool. To edit just one of those paths, use the Direct Selection tool.

Figure 7.19: The Paths palette with the pentagon path about to be stroked with the brush and current foreground color.

Paste Paths from Illustrator

? I am more comfortable drawing paths in Illustrator. Can I draw them there and use them in Photoshop?

✓ They don't call it the Creative Suite for nothing! Moving vector objects among the applications is one of the things this Suite does best. However, the way this works depends in large part in how you set up your preferences in Illustrator.

In Illustrator, open the Preferences dialog box and then open the File Handling & Clipboard pane. You'll see a group of options called Clipboard on Quit. What you choose here determines how an Illustrator path shows up in Photoshop.

If you enable the PDF option, the path pastes into Photoshop as a Vector

Smart Object that also appears in the Layers palette. This is quite cool, because it means you can paste a sophisticated Illustrator graphic into Photoshop and later edit it in Illustrator by double-clicking the Vector Smart Object in the Layers palette.

If you enable AICB, when you paste an Illustrator path into Photoshop you'll see choices for pasting: Smart Object, Pixels, Path, or Shape Layer (**Figure 7.20**). As we described above, Smart Object gives you the most flexibility. However, if you just want the path itself, you can select Path or Shape Layer depending on how you want to use it.

TIP: If you change the dimensions of a Vector Smart Object when you edit it in Illustrator, it may appear distorted when you return to Photoshop because it's become different than the size of the Vector Smart Object when it was originally imported. To fix this, choose Edit > Free Transform, and in the Options bar, click the link icon between the dimensions to make the graphic's dimensions proportional again.

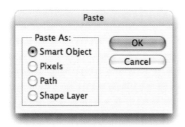

Figure 7.20: The Paste dialog box appears when you paste an Illustrator path, and PDF is disabled and AICB is enabled in the Illustrator File Handling & Clipboard Preferences.

Keeping Color Consistent

Keeping Color Consistent

COLOR SCARES PEOPLE. Deep down inside, we all feel that color is a natural concept that should be intuitive, but somehow computers have a way of making color go awry at every point in the image-making process.

Color would be easier if images came from one kind of input and went out to one kind of output. But that's not the way it is in real life. Part of the complexity of consistent color comes from the fact that Photoshop isn't a point on a line between Point A and Point B; Photoshop is more like an airport hub sitting between 50 different arrival and departure destinations—different cameras and scanners, different monitors to view images on, different printers. How can you simplify this mess? First, by becoming familiar enough with the color input and output requirements of your own images, so that you aren't distracted by the settings related to workflows that don't apply to you. And second, with a little thing called "color management."

With each version of Photoshop, color management has become a little bit clearer, as the folks at Adobe continue to find simpler ways to represent the choices that have to be made. The color management dialog boxes in Photoshop are highly simplified, extremely distilled versions of the stupendous color calculations you never see behind the scenes. In this chapter, we try to orient you within the diverse color options in Photoshop so that you can quickly get set up and pointed in the right direction.

Setting Up Color

Your Monitor, Your Profile

? I have two computers, but the same image looks different on each of them. Do I need to calibrate my monitor?

✓ Calibrating your monitor (making it display colors a certain way) is nowhere near as important as profiling it (making a profile that describes how it *does* display color). As we mentioned back in Chapter 4, *Correcting Images*, the best option is to use a hardware device such as the GretagMacbeth Eye-One. Let us be clear: There is virtually no point in even pretending to trust the color on your screen if you don't create a custom monitor profile. If you have two different screens on which you look at color, each one needs its own profile. Once you have custom profiles and set up Color Settings consistently (see the next solution), you'll see virtually identical color on all your computers.

Set Up Color Settings

? When I first launched Photoshop, it directed me to the Color Settings dialog box. But it might as well have shown me an airplane cockpit, it's so full of controls. How do I know what to choose?

✓ Color Settings sure is an intimidating dialog box (**Figure 8.1**). The good news is that Adobe worked very hard to concoct combinations of color settings that result in good color for

most print and online workflows. With just a little work, you can get much better color. All you have to do is choose the most appropriate preset from the Settings popup menu at the top of the Color Settings dialog box. Once you do that, Photoshop automatically fills in all of the other options for you.

- If you prepare any images for a printing press, choose North American Prepress 2 (or Europe Prepress 2 or Japan Prepress 2). This uses Adobe RGB for the default RGB space, which is a far better space for print output than sRGB (which is the default setting for some silly reason).

- If virtually all your images are destined for the Web, choose North American Web/Internet. But avoid this preset if you ever edit images for high-quality printing because it does standardize on sRGB and even automatically converts non-sRGB images when you open them. (This has ruined many a Photoshop users' day.)

- If you're making images for digital video, choose Monitor Color. But don't use this preset if you ever use CMYK or produce color-managed output!

There is one problem with the Prepress 2 setting: You'll probably see the Profile Mismatch and Profile Missing dialog boxes a lot when opening files. We don't think that's so bad, because it keeps us on our toes, reminding us that we

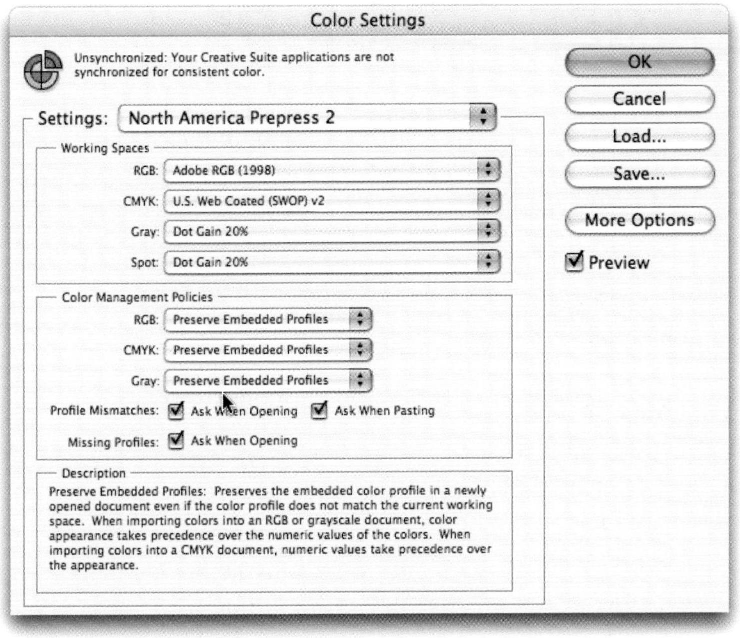

Figure 8.1: In the Color Settings dialog box, choose a preset from the Settings popup menu. The rest of the dialog box updates for you.

need to think about where color is coming from and where it's going. But if it's annoying to you, you might want to turn off the Ask When Opening checkboxes in the Color Settings dialog box. Note that while choosing a preset like North American Prepress 2 will help achieve better color; it's just a start, and it's just setting up the default ("in case nothing else is specified") settings. Your images may use different RGB or CMYK spaces than these defaults. For example, if you're working with a camera raw file, you may want to open it into the ProPhoto RGB working space for editing in Photoshop. But you can do that for one image (in the Camera Raw dialog box) without changing the Color Settings dialog box!

Similarly, when you convert to CMYK using Image > Mode > CMYK Color,

you'll get the default CMYK settings you chose in Color Settings (in this case, SWOP, which we consider "middle of the road" CMYK). But if you have a custom CMYK profile for your printer or output device, then you can use that instead by using Edit > Convert to Profile. (See "Convert from RGB to CMYK," later in this chapter, for more on this process.)

TIP: In most cases, you want the Color Management Policies popup menus to be set to Preserve Embedded Profiles. That way, you can be sure that if you open an image that doesn't match the working space, its own colors will be preserved. If the Policies are set to Convert to Working Space instead, your files may be degraded beyond repair just by opening them. (For example, if you open a ProPhoto RGB image and it gets converted to sRGB behind your back.)

Create a Color-Neutral Work Area

Mac OS X and Windows XP use quite a bit of color to dress up their user interfaces, but when you're trying to color-correct your Photoshop documents, color outside of the document window can be noticeably distracting. If you spend a great deal of time working on projects where color is critical, you may want to remove all distracting color elements from Mac OS X or Windows XP.

Setting Up a Gray User Interface in Mac OS X

Apple kindly provides an alternate Graphite color scheme that draws all controls in grayscale, to minimize the amount of color distraction as you work with color graphics.

1. Choose System Preferences from the Apple menu.

2. Click the Appearance system preference.

3. Choose Graphite from the Appearance popup menu.

4. Choose Graphite or Silver from the Highlight popup menu.

Setting Up a Gray User Interface in Windows XP

Microsoft provides an alternate Silver color scheme that displays most controls in grayscale. The buttons in the title bar are still in color, but the Silver color scheme is still better for image editing than the garish blues and greens of the default Windows XP color scheme.

1. Right-click on the desktop and choose Properties.

2. In the Display Properties dialog box, click the Appearance tab.

3. Choose Silver from the Color Scheme popup menu.

Neutralizing Your Desktop

When you set up a color-neutral work area, don't forget about removing all color from your desktop background picture. On Mac OS X, choose System Preferences from the Apple menu, click the Desktop tab, select Desktop Pictures in the list, and select a grayscale image. In Windows, right-click the desktop, choose Properties from the context menu, click the Desktop tab, and apply a grayscale image or pick a shade of gray from the Color popup menu.

Of course, for best results, this neutral color scheme should extend past the edge of your monitor to your room and perhaps even your clothing (to minimize color reflections). Trying to correct a color cast isn't easy if you're wearing a Hawaiian shirt in a brightly-lit pineapple-yellow room!

Synchronize Color Across the CS2 Suite

? I keep getting a message saying my color settings aren't synchronized. What's that all about?

☑ If you own the entire Adobe Creative Suite (CS2), Adobe makes it easy to set all your Creative Suite applications to the same Color Settings values. It helps maintain consistent color and it's usually worth your while to do so. You can do this in one step from Adobe Bridge by choosing Edit > Creative Suite Color Settings. Just select a Color Settings preset, and click Apply. However, if you later open Color Settings in Photoshop and change it, you'll see that "Applications Aren't Synchronized" message. We just ignore it.

> **TIP:** The preset Color Settings are just starting points. If you have more precise profiles for your workflow, you should select them as working spaces and save your own preset by clicking the Save button in the Color Settings dialog box. Then you can use Bridge to synchronize all the applications to that same preset.

Previewing Color Output

Simulate Printed Color On Screen

? My prints don't match my monitor. How can I set up my monitor so that it shows what will print?

☑ Previewing a color conversion on screen is called soft-proofing. Soft-proofing lets you adjust an image for the best quality final output while you still have access to all the colors in the larger original color space.

To soft-proof an image, choose a color space from the View > Proof Setup submenu. If the color space you want to preview isn't listed on that submenu, choose View > Proof Setup > Custom (**Figure 8.2**), and choose your device's profile from the Device to Simulate pop-up menu.

Then, before you click OK, you'll probably want to leave Preserve RGB Numbers turned off, and turn *on* Black Point Compensation, Simulate Paper Color, and Simulate Black Ink (when available). This tells Photoshop to make your screen look like the final printed output (including the white of the paper stock). If you click the Save button, you can save this new proof setup preset in the default location and Photoshop adds its name to your View > Proof Setup submenu so you can instantly choose it next time you need it.

To toggle between the original and soft-proofed versions, choose View > Proof Colors or press Command/Ctrl-Y. CMYK can't reproduce all the colors

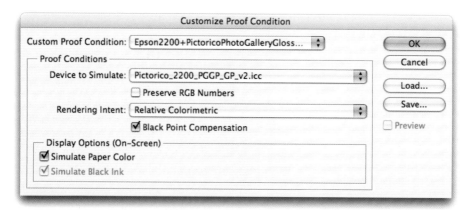

Figure 8.2: The Customize Proof Condition dialog box

available in RGB, and paper can't display as wide a range of tones as the screen, so don't be surprised if an image loses saturation and contrast when you soft-proof in CMYK.

> **TIP:** Close your eyes before you turn on Proof Colors. If your eyes are open, you'll be shocked at how much the colors dim in the soft proof. If you close your eyes during the conversion, your eyes will adapt to the new "white" better.

> **TIP:** All of the features that help you preview color conversions and indicate conversion problems, like Proof Colors and Gamut Warning, are accurate only when you also select the correct profile for your output device in the View > Proof Setup sub-menu. And of course, Proof Colors is only effective when your monitor is precisely profiled.

Check for Out of Gamut Colors

When I print, the details in my highly-saturated colors all merge into a blob of color! How can I tell which colors aren't going to print, or which colors I'll lose when converting to another color space?

Clipping happens when colors in your image exist outside of the color space you're converting to, and it's usually only a problem when the destination color space is smaller (such as when converting from ProPhoto RGB to SWOP CMYK). While Proof Setup should give you a pretty good indication of how colors will change, if you want to see exactly which image colors are clipped (lose detail) when converted to the color space of your output device, you can use the Gamut Warning feature.

Choose View > Gamut Warning to view out-of-gamut colors (**Figure 8.3**). Out-of-gamut colors are marked in gray by default, but you can change the gamut warning color in the Transparency & Gamut panel of the Preferences dialog box. We prefer to use a color not found in nature—like a day-glo green or magenta.

Figure 8.3: Original image (left) and the Gamut Warning command turned on (right). Using a bright green color we chose in Preferences, Gamut Warning indicates that the printer we're soft-proofing can't reproduce all of the blues in the image.

Before and After, Side by Side

? Can I see a side-by-side view of an image and its Proof Colors preview?

☑ No problem! Choose Window > Arrange > New Window to get another view of the same document (**Figure 8.4**). You can turn on the Proof Colors command in one window and off in the other, so that you can compare the original and soft-proofed versions side-by-side. You can see exactly how colors are constrained in the destination color space.

> **TIP:** To change the default Proof Setup preset, close all documents and then choose a Proof Setup preset. When no documents are open, the preset you choose becomes the default.

Figure 8.4: The same document shown in two windows simultaneously: Normal view (top), and Proof Colors view to preview the image on the more limited printer gamut (bottom).

Color Space Conversions

Convert from RGB to CMYK

? **What's the best way to convert RGB to CMYK?**

☑ The best way to convert to CMYK is: Consciously. We're serious; most people just choose Image > Mode > CMYK Color without even thinking. The problem is that you probably don't know *which* CMYK. Is it SWOP or Fogra or the CMYK inks your desktop inkjet uses? There are lots of CMYKs, and you can't get great color unless you tell Photoshop which to use. The most accurate method relies on your obtaining specific printing information in the form of either an ICC profile or custom CMYK specifications.

If you choose Image > Mode > CMYK Color, you're telling Photoshop to use the default CMYK space as defined in the Color Settings dialog box. Instead, consider choosing Edit > Convert to Profile (**Figure 8.5**), which lets you specify a custom CMYK profile as well as control other aspects of the CMYK conversion. For example, while you probably want to leave the Use Black Point Compensation and Use Dither options turned on, you might want to compare the results you get with the Perceptual rendering intent (from the Intent popup menu) versus using the Relative Colorimetric intent (or the Saturation intent). Turn on the Preview checkbox to see how the results differ before clicking OK.

If your printer didn't provide a profile of the final output device, they might be able to give you CMYK specifications instead. If they did, you can enter them manually. Choose Edit > Convert to Profile, then choose Custom CMYK from the Destination Space popup menu, and enter values as directed by your printer.

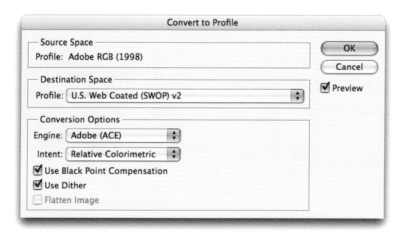

Figure 8.5: In the Convert to Profile dialog box, you can see and change the settings that determine how colors convert between color spaces.

Boost Shadows
for Print

? **When I look at my photos on screen, they look wonderful. When I use Proof Colors to preview them for my printer, the colors—especially the shadows—become muddy.**

☑ Assuming you're using accurate profiles for your printer and your monitor, Proof Colors may simply be telling you the truth. Your camera and monitor can typically reproduce a wider range of tones and colors than your printer or a press, so when you use Proof Colors to preview a printer, it's very likely that you'll see a reduction in contrast, and details in the shadows may mush together—which is exactly what's going to happen on the printer.

How can you adjust an image for output? You don't want to alter the original image data, because you want to preserve all the tones in colors in case you print to a nicer output device someday. If you want to attack the problem using Levels or Curves, we suggest applying these edits with a Levels or Curves adjustment layer named for the printer you're adjusting for. That way, you can turn off the adjustment layer when you aren't printing to that printer, or you can create different adjustment layers that you turn on only for specific output devices.

However, our favorite way of instantly enhancing shadow detail is a feature added in Photoshop: the Shadow/Highlight command (Image > Adjustments > Shadow/Highlight). In the Shadow/Highlight command, increasing the Amount slider for Shadows pulls shadow detail up into a range that narrower color spaces can show more clearly (**Figure 8.6**). You may want to leave the Highlights Amount at 0 unless you also want to darken the highlights. Because Shadow/Highlight isn't currently available as an adjustment layer, we apply it to a copy of the image.

Figure 8.6: Original image (left), loss of shadow detail observed when soft-proofing output on the final medium (center), and shadow detail boosted by applying Shadow/Highlight (right).

Convert Colors
for the Web

? Everybody gives me different advice for how to convert a color photo for the Web. Some say use sRGB, others say monitor color, and others say use Web-safe colors. They also argue about whether or not to embed a profile. What's the straight story?

✓ We tend to think that the wild, untamed days of the Web are largely behind us, but that's not true in the case of color. When you publish images on the Web, you have no control over how people might see the image colors. There are three main problems with color on the Web:

- Only profiled monitors show colors accurately, but a very low percentage of monitors are properly calibrated or profiled.

- With the emergence of color management, images now exist in all kinds of color spaces. But few Web browsers and systems are set up to properly display images with embedded profiles. If you spend all day scanning images in Adobe RGB for later output on a press, and you make Web versions without converting the color space, their colors will look washed out on the Web.

- Images will often look lighter on a Mac than on Windows computers. It has to do with the assumed gamma of the operating system.

Therefore, you can only expect that your images will appear with some variation on the monitors of the world, and take some comfort in the idea that this problem affects everyone else's images, too. However, here are a few tricks you can try to create more consistent color.

- Make sure your images are in the sRGB color space before you upload them for viewing in Web browsers. We generally work in Adobe RGB or Pro Photo RGB, so when we want a Web version, we duplicate the image, use Edit > Convert to Profile to shift it into sRGB space, and then use Save for Web to export the GIF, PNG, or JPEG file.

- You can preview your images using both the View > Proof Setup > Macintosh RGB and View > Proof Setup > Windows RGB commands. These commands simulate how an image looks on Mac OS X and Windows, respectively, if you use the image on the Web without converting its color space.

- If you're on a Mac, consider using your calibration software to profile your monitor at gamma 2.2. This isn't necessary for your work inside Photoshop, which automatically compensates for any monitor gamma you use. However, at gamma 2.2 you'll see Web pages approximately the same way Windows users do. And we actually like the increased contrast from using gamma 2.2 on our Macs.

- For the Web, don't bother embedding an ICC profile when you save or export the file. Almost no Web browsers know what to do with an embedded profile, so all the profile does is add to the file size and transmission time of the file.

TIP: Unfortunately, there isn't a convert-to-sRGB option in the Save for Web dialog box (though it would be a good idea for Adobe to include that). Instead of having to remember to convert to sRGB and export without a profile every time you make Web graphics, make a Photoshop action designed for Web exporting. When you build the action, include the sRGB conversion step (using Edit > Convert to Profile) and then include a Save for Web or Save As (JPEG) step where the Embed Color Profile checkbox is disabled.

Assign Versus Convert to a Profile

? **What's the difference between Convert to Profile and Assign Profile? They seem so similar.**

✓ This is one of the perennial areas of confusion in Photoshop... so it's not just you. When you *assign* a profile, you're telling Photoshop what the numbers behind the colors *mean*. For example, you're saying "fully saturated red looks like *this*." Therefore, when you assign a different profile to an image, the colors change—sometimes dramatically. Open an image from a digital camera, choose Edit > Assign Profile, turn on the

Preview checkbox, and choose different RGB profiles. You'll quickly see that changing the profile changes the meaning behind the image's RGB numbers.

On the other hand, *converting* attempts to maintain the look of the colors by changing the numbers. Don't be puzzled if image colors look the same after converting between profiles. This is exactly how it's supposed to work—the more the converted version looks like the original, the more successful the conversion. However, color shifts can be hard to avoid when converting to a color space of a smaller size or different shape (for example, when you convert from an RGB space to a CMYK space). If the gamut you convert to is smaller than the original gamut, you permanently limit the image to the smaller gamut.

Embedding Profiles

? **Should I embed profiles when I'm saving my documents?**

✓ In general, the only good way to ensure color consistency when moving a file from one computer to the next or from Photoshop to some other application is to turn on Embed Color Profile in the Save As dialog box. However, CMYK profiles are large (they often add between 700 K and 3 MB to your file size), so if you're saving a CMYK image that you know will not need any more editing or repurposing, you might consider turning off this checkbox. RGB profiles are pretty tiny, so we always embed those—well, except for Web images, as we just pointed out.

Locate and Install Profiles

? **I see color profiles in my Proof Setup and Print with Preview dialog boxes that I don't see in the profile folder on my hard disk. Are some profiles built into Photoshop or stored somewhere else? Do I have to install new profiles in a certain folder?**

✓ There aren't any profiles stored inside Photoshop. Profiles installed by Adobe or other installers generally ends up in the right place, but if you download or create custom profiles, you need to drop them in the right folder yourself.

In Mac OS X, Photoshop sees profiles in several places:

- `Computer/Hard Drive/Library/ColorSync/Profiles` (This Profiles folder is at the root level of the computer, so profiles stored here are seen by all users. This is where we tend to put profiles.)

- `Computer/Hard Drive/Users/<your username>/Library/ColorSync/Profiles` (This Profiles folder is inside your account's home folder, so you're the only user who has access to the profiles stored here. If other people use your Mac when logged into other user accounts, they won't be able to use these profiles.)

- `Computer/Hard Drive/Library/Application Support/Adobe/Color/Profiles` (This Profiles folder is in a special Adobe folder in the Mac's main Library folder. Profiles stored here are seen by all users. You should leave this folder alone.)

In Windows XP, Photoshop sees profiles in two places:

- `C:\Windows\system32\spool\drivers\color` (This folder is at the root level of the computer, so profiles stored here are seen by all users.)

- `C:\Program Files\Common Files\Adobe\Color\Profiles` (This Profiles folder is in a special Adobe folder in the shared Program Files folder. Profiles stored here are seen by all users. You should leave this folder alone.)

TIP: To install a profile in Windows for the first time, you don't actually have to drag a profile to the Color folder. There's an easier way: Right-click on the profile and choose Install Profile from the context menu that pops up. It copies the profile to the correct location. To replace an existing profile, the right-click method won't work; you must copy the profile over the old one.

TIP: In Photoshop CS, the Assign Profile and Convert to Profile commands were under the Image > Mode submenu. But in all Creative Suite 2 applications, Adobe moved the color profile commands to the Edit menu so that you can find them in the same place in other Adobe programs.

Organizing and
Finding Images

Organizing and Finding Images

BACK IN THE LATE 1980s, David had the chance to see a computer set up with an unbelievable amount of hard drive space: Two 20 MB hard drives and a 40 MB hard drive, all daisy chained together, using SCSI. He was floored. After all, what on Earth would anyone do with that much storage? Obviously, it didn't take long for us all to find out.

Today, most of us have hundreds or thousands of digital images filling up our hard drives, CDs, DVDs, and pretty much any other storage medium we can get our hands on. It's a double-edged sword: As you get rolling with Photoshop, you can become quite good at processing large numbers of images. The downside to this, of course, is that it's downright painful to organize all these puppies! You may face the challenge of finding a particular image months later, knowing that it's buried somewhere in the hundreds of images you've taken with your digital camera since then.

Some good news comes with Adobe Photoshop CS2 in the form of the new Adobe Bridge application. Bridge ships with all the Adobe Creative Suite applications, whether you buy them separately or together. Don't underestimate the power of Bridge—once you start to discover its annotation, file-finding, and batch-processing capabilities, you'll probably wonder how you ever got along without it. This chapter is dedicated to solutions and techniques to help you with your new best friend.

Building Your Bridge

Getting Up to Speed

? I just started using Bridge, and it's so slow! It doesn't matter which folder I go to—it sits there and builds thumbnail after thumbnail. Is this the way it's always going to be?

✓ Bridge won't always be that slow. The first time you view a folder with Bridge it needs to build and cache thumbnails previews of the images in the folder. We recommend just letting it build the thumbnails while you go get another cuppa. Once Bridge completes building the thumbnails, viewing the same folder the next time should be much faster.

In fact, if you're new to Bridge, you might just consider selecting your hard drive in the Folders palette (in the upper-left corner of the Bridge window), choosing Tools > Cache > Build Cache for Subfolders, and then go away for a long while (we suggest taking a nap). This forces Bridge to systematically build thumbnails for each and every image it finds on your hard drive.

By the way, there's a reason Bridge can seem slow. Bridge opts for quality over speed, building high-quality thumbnails and previews which are often more accurate than the previews generated by other image organizers. Once the previews are built, you can enjoy fast browsing of accurate thumbnails which no longer need to be updated unless you edit an image. Thanks to this emphasis on quality, you may decide that the initial wait was worth it.

Express Document Delivery

? It takes forever to dig down to a folder through the popup menu at the top of an Adobe Bridge window. Isn't there a faster way?

✓ There certainly are a few faster ways to cross the vast distances of your hard drive. Here are a few ideas:

- Use the Folders panel instead of that silly popup menu (**Figure 9.1**). Many folks don't even notice that there is a Folders panel because it's normally hiding behind the Favorites panel. Just click on the Folders tab or choose View > Folders Panel. The Folders panel displays disks using a tree-style view much like the List view in Mac OS X or the Folders view in Windows Explorer. Click a triangle to flip open a folder, and you can reveal its contents while keeping visible the "big picture" of the rest of the disk. If you go back and forth between two or more folders, you can keep them visible simultaneously in the Folders panel; click any folder's icon to view its contents in the main panel (what Adobe calls the content area).

- If you've opened a folder recently, you can revisit it by choosing its name from the popup menu at the top of a Bridge window.

- If the file or folder you want to view in Bridge is already open on

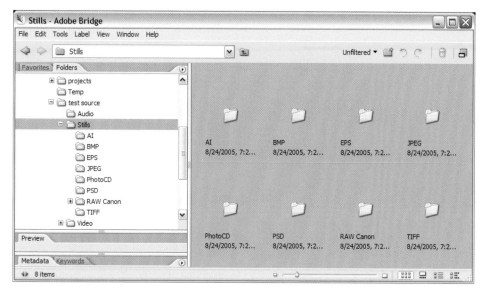

Figure 9.1: The Folders panel displays your files and the file structure.

the desktop, don't bother navigating there in Bridge. Instead, just drag the file or folder onto the Adobe Bridge application or dock icon (Mac OS X) or its application window (Windows). Bridge opens it in its own new window. (In fact, on Mac OS X, you can drag the title bar icon of a file or folder to the Bridge icon. This saves a step when the file or folder window is already open.)

- Take the time to save favorite locations in Bridge. With a folder or file selected in the content area, choose File > Add to Favorites. Now the file or folder is available as a shortcut in the Favorites panel. If the favorite is a folder, it also appears in the popup menu at the top of the Bridge window.

Bridge Crossings

? What's the easiest way to switch between Bridge and Photoshop?

✓ Because Adobe Bridge is meant to be a close companion to Photoshop, Adobe added all kinds of ways to switch between Bridge and Photoshop:

- Both applications have a File menu command that jumps to the other application. In Photoshop, it's File > Browse. In Bridge, it's File > Return to Adobe Photoshop CS2.

- The Options bar in Photoshop contains a Go to Bridge button that switches to Bridge. That's the

TIP: When you're looking at a file in Bridge and you want to know where it is on your hard disk, choose File > Reveal in Finder/Reveal in Explorer (or right-click on the file and choose this from the context menu).

button with the little shell and magnifying glass icon.

- In Bridge, selecting an image and choosing the Open command opens the image in Photoshop by default. If the image is a raw camera file, it opens in Camera Raw in Photoshop.

- Of course, you can use the built-in application switching shortcuts to flip between Photoshop and Bridge. On Mac OS X, the shortcut is Command-Tab. In Windows, it's Alt-Tab.

Use Multiple Bridge Windows

? **I have images in several different places on my hard disk. Why can't I split the Bridge window to show me more than one location at a time?**

☑ You can't always get what you want, but in this case, you'll get what you need. Bridge lets you open multiple windows. It's not immediately obvious to most users, but all you have to do is choose File > New Window (or press Command/Ctrl-N), and another window opens (**Figure 9.2**). Or, you can Command/Ctrl-double-click on a folder inside of Bridge to open it in a new window. You can then arrange the windows any way you like, and you can drag and drop files between them.

Figure 9.2: Multiple Bridge windows viewing different folders, and with each window using different view settings.

Tile Windows Semi-Automatically

? **Is there a way to tile or cascade multiple Bridge windows?**

☑ Well, you know, that's one area of Bridge that we find puzzling. While you can have multiple windows open in Bridge, Bridge doesn't have any specialized window arrangement commands like Photoshop does. Unlike Photoshop, window names aren't even listed on the Windows menu! Fortunately, you can use the Workspace feature in Bridge to set up your own semi-automatic window arrangements. In this example, we'll tile two windows so that one takes up the left half of the screen and the other takes up the right half (**Figure 9.3**).

1. Open two windows in Bridge. If needed, choose File > New Window to open the second window.

2. Arrange the two windows the way you want them.

3. Click the left window to activate it.

4. Choose Window > Workspace > Save Workspace.

5. Name the workspace (such as "Window Left"), give it a keyboard shortcut, and enable the Save Window Location as Part of Workspace checkbox. Click OK.

Figure 9.3: We instantly positioned and sized the left window using a saved workspace. The right window uses a similar workspace that positions it on the right side of the screen. Both workspaces are set to display thumbnails only.

6. Click the right window to activate it, and repeat steps 4 and 5.

7. Press the first workspace keyboard shortcut you made to resize the current Bridge window to fit the left side of the screen, and the second keyboard shortcut you made to resize a window to the right half.

The fact that you can save workspaces for a Bridge window is extremely handy in a number of situations. For example, you might make a workspace that reshapes a Bridge window to be a narrow column of thumbnails off to the side, and another that maximizes the Bridge window on your second monitor. Note that workspaces don't just remember where the window should be on screen, but also the layout of the panels within the Bridge window. For example, you can drag the panel dividers into different configurations—one with a really big Preview panel and no Metadata panel, another split evenly between the Folder panel and the thumbnail panel, or whatever—and then save workspaces for each of these.

Annotating and Organizing

Organize with Keywords

? I see Bridge has a Keyword panel. Should I go to the time and trouble of adding keywords when I already have images sorted in folders?

☑ There are limitations to using the file system (folders) to organize images. For example, you can name folders after categories, but if a single image belongs in three categories, you can't store that image in three different folders. (Well, you can by saving three copies, but that's probably not helpful.) Using descriptive filenames aren't so great either, because there's a limit to the amount of detail you can have in a filename before it's too long to manage easily.

Professional and serious amateur photographers use a better approach. They don't organize images based on their location on disk. Instead, they use keywords that describe an image in far more detail than file or folder names ever could. For example, you can use Adobe Bridge to add keywords like "beach," "driftwood," and "sand" to an image, and later on you can use Bridge to find all images that contain any combination of those keywords—no matter where they're stored on the disk. Here's a quick guide to adding keywords.

1. Make sure the Keywords panel is visible (View > Keywords Panel).

2. Select one or more images.

3. In the Keywords panel, enable the checkbox for any keywords you want to attach to the image (**Figure 9.4**). If the keyword you want to use doesn't already exist in the list, click the New Keyword button to add it.

Figure 9.4: Adding keywords is easy with the Keywords panel in Bridge.

Remove Keywords for Multiple Images

? **How can I remove keywords from more than one image at a time? When I tried this, the keyword checkbox didn't clear. Instead, there was a dash in the box.**

✓ Yeah, that one threw us for a loop for a while, too. If you want to remove a keyword from multiple selected images, you may need to click the keyword checkbox twice. The first time you click, the checkbox may appear with a dash (–), indicating that the keyword is still applied to some of the selected images. If you want to remove the keyword from all selected images but you see the dash, click the box again to clear it completely.

Metadata vs. Keywords

? **Keywords are metadata, right? Why can't I manage my keywords in the Metadata panel?**

✓ Adobe split these into two different panels for a very important reason: They're concerned you're not getting enough exercise and they want to encourage you to move your mouse and click more. Seriously, the distinction between the two is kind of fuzzy. They're

> **TIP:** You can organize keywords in the Keywords panel by creating keyword sets. Adobe Bridge already contains a few keyword sets the first time you open it, but you're free to add, delete, or rearrange keyword sets any way you like. Keyword sets exist only to help you organize photos within Adobe Bridge; they aren't stored with the documents themselves. You create a keyword set by clicking the folder icon at the bottom of the Keywords panel.

probably in two different panels because the keyword list can become very long.

Watch out for redundancy between the Metadata and Keywords panels. Before you add new keywords, check to see if they already exist as an IPTC metadata field. For example, you might not want to bother adding keywords or keyword sets for countries, because Country already exists as an IPTC Core metadata field (**Figure 9.5**).

Annotating IPTC Core Metadata

? **What's up with the IPTC Core section of the Metadata panel?**

☑ Large organizations like news bureaus and stock photo houses want their files to have highly standardized metadata, so that the images coming

Figure 9.5: The IPTC Core segment of the Metadata panel is most useful for organizations cataloging their documents using IPTC standards.

from thousands of sources are filed in a reasonably consistent way. That makes images much easier to find later. Many organizations follow the image identification standards worked out by the International Press Telecommunications Council (IPTC), and Adobe Bridge supports that standard in the IPTC Core section of the Metadata panel (View > Metadata). If you want to learn more about the proper use of the fields in the IPTC Core section, visit *newscodes.org*.

Note that the first fields in the IPTC Core section—the ones that begin with the word Creator—have to do with the person who created the image. From the Headline field on down, the fields have to do with the image content itself. So if you shot a photo in London but you live in Boston, you'd enter "Boston" in the Creator: City field, and "London" in the "City" field.

> **TIP:** When you enter metadata, you can commit the entry by pressing the Enter key on the numeric keypad—not the Return key above the Shift key, which starts a new line.

Apply Metadata in Bulk

? I think I see the value of entering all this metadata, but is it ever tedious! Surely there's a shortcut to filling in these fields for every one of my images? I'm adding hundreds of images a week.

☑ That's a legitimate concern. If you're entering 30 fields of information for 200 photos you just took on a trip or assignment… let's see… 30 times

200… you need a better solution! Use a metadata *template* to fill in multiple fields at once.

Metadata templates let you complete the most repetitive parts of metadata entry just about instantly. For example, you can select multiple images and apply a metadata template containing the metadata that all selected images have in common, such as your contact and copyright information or the location of a shoot. All of those fields are then applied to all selected images. The only metadata left for you to enter manually would be the details that differ among individual photos. Let's take a look at how this works:

1. In Adobe Bridge, select one image to use as an example for the template you're creating.

2. Using the IPTC Core and Keywords panels, enter the metadata you want in the template you're creating, and delete any metadata you don't want in the template.

3. With the image still selected, choose File > File Info. Click the triangle button in the top right corner of the File Info dialog box, and choose Save Metadata Template (**Figure 9.6**).

4. Name the template, and click OK. The template is now added to the menu you just used.

To apply the template, select one or more images and do one of the following:

- To have the template fill in fields that are currently empty, choose Tools > Append Metadata, and choose the name of the template from the Append Metadata sub-menu.

- To have the template replace the data in fields that are also have data in the template, choose Tools > Replace Metadata, and choose the name of the template from the Replace Metadata submenu.

- Choose File > File Info, click the triangle button in the top right corner of the File Info dialog box, and choose the name of the template from the popup menu. This works like the Replace Metadata command.

Streamline Metadata Templates

? I took a look inside one of the metadata templates I created, and it seems to have information that's specific to one image. Is that going to cause problems? If so, is it easy to clean up the template?

☑️ If you're comfortable with editing HTML-like text code (it's actually XML), you can open a metadata template in a text editor, you can remove all of the metadata that's image-specific, to keep the templates clean and avoid unex-pected results. This solution assumes you've already saved at least one metadata template, and it will make sense only if you already have some experience editing XML, HTML, or a similar language.

1. In Adobe Bridge, select an image and choose File > File Info. For this step, it doesn't matter which image you select; you won't be making any changes.

2. Click the triangle button in the top right corner of the File Info dialog box, and choose Show Templates. Open the XMP folder (it should be selected automatically), then open the Metadata Templates folder.

3. In the Metadata Templates folder, make a backup copy of the metadata template you want to edit, just in case something goes terribly wrong while editing.

4. Use a text editor to open the metadata template you want to edit.

5. Edit any values or delete sections as needed (**Figure 9.7**). Keep the first and last three lines in the file. As with XML or HTML, if you remove a section, you need to make sure you remove it entirely, from its opening bracket to its closing bracket.

Figure 9.6: Saving a metadata template from the File Info dialog box

6. Save the template in the same Metadata Templates folder, making sure it's saved as a text file with a .XMP filename extension. If it doesn't work right, throw it out and start over from a copy of the backup you made in step 3.

If you're interested in more in-depth information about customizing metadata templates and using them efficiently, read our friend Bruce Fraser's book, *Real World Camera Raw*, published by Peachpit Press.

Annotate Now, Relax Later

? I added a bunch of keywords to some JPEG images, but when I went to find the camera raw files that I used to generate the JPEGs, I realized that the keywords aren't in the original camera raw files. Is there an easy way to sync those up?

✓ We're sorry to have to break it to you, but: No, not really. You'd have to add the keywords to the raw files manually. This is one reason we recommend that you make a habit of using Adobe Bridge to annotate your original images with necessary metadata *as soon as you copy them onto your computer*. If you do this, any versions or duplicates of those images will have the correct metadata. It's not fun or sexy to enter metadata, but it's one of those times when taking a little time now can save a huge amount of time in the future.

An increasing number of photo-related applications, services, and even operating systems can view, search for, and perform actions on images based on their metadata. If you enter metadata information in Bridge, you reduce the chance that you'll have to enter the same information all over again before you send copies of the images to other places. Some online photo-sharing services like *smugmug.com* also recognize metadata, preserving and using the captions, keywords, camera info, and other metadata embedded in the images you upload to that service. Depending on the functions supported by such services, you and your users may be able to see captions and take advantage of the embedded metadata in your online gallery, such as searching on keywords, with no additional work on your part other than entering the data into Bridge.

Figure 9.7: Editing metadata templates is powerful, but not for the faint of heart.

Fast File Finding

Find Files with Bridge

? Now that I've entered all that meta-data... how do I use it?

✓ Entering metadata can be a long, discouraging chore until you actually need to take advantage of it—and that usually happens when you need to find images. If you've added good keywords and other metadata to your images, finding them is a snap.

In Adobe Bridge, choose Edit > Find (or press Command/Ctrl-F). Specify the search source and criteria. If you want to

TIP: When using the Find command in Bridge, we recommend enabling the Show Find Results in a New Browser Window checkbox so that if you want to try more or different searches, the original window is still around to use as the source.

add more criteria, click the + button in the Criteria section (**Figure 9.8**).

Click Find. The window containing the results is labeled Find Results in the title bar so that you know you're not looking at a folder.

Save Searches as Collections

? I need to find all the files pertaining to one of my clients... and I need to do this search at least once each day. Can't I save my search criteria?

✓ You need to create a collection. A collection is essentially a saved search, not a group of actual files. Because a collection is a saved search, a collection can keep itself up to date as your files change. For example, if you wanted quick access to all images of trees, you'd use the Find command to locate all images using

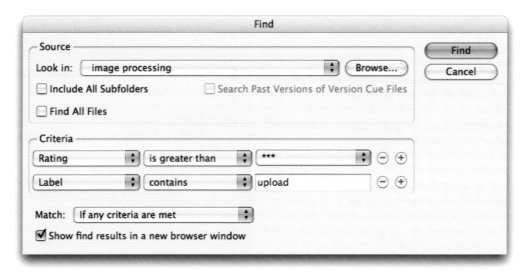

Figure 9.8: Bridge lets you find files using a wide variety of search options.

the keyword "tree," and save the search as a collection. When you annotate more images with the "tree" keyword, they'll automatically be added the next time you open the collection. Even better, you can tell a collection to always search in such-and-such folder, or you can tell it to perform the search in whatever folder you happen to be in. Here's how you do it:

1. In Adobe Bridge, choose Edit > Find.

2. Specify the search source and criteria. If you want to add more criteria, click the + button in the Criteria section.

3. Click Find. The title bar of the window containing the results is labeled Find Results so that you know you're not viewing the contents of a folder.

4. Click the Save As Collection button at the top right corner of the Find Results window (**Figure 9.9**).

5. Name the collection. If you always want this collection's search to start from the same folder you used for the current search, enable the Start Search from Current Folder checkbox.

6. Click Save.

The next time you want to perform that same search, display the Favorites panel, and click the Collections icon. In the content area, double-click the collection you want to use.

Figure 9.9: After you perform a search, you can click the Save as Collection button at the top right corner of the Find Results window. Click the Collections icon in the Favorites panel to see your saved collections.

Find Photos with Spotlight (Mac OS X)

? I love using the Spotlight search feature in Mac OS X (10.4 or later). Does Bridge work with Spotlight at all?

☑ Bridge and Spotlight do work together. This is great, because you can find a photo by its metadata without even opening Bridge. Just click the Spotlight icon at the right end of the menu bar, enter any keywords or metadata you've added to files using Bridge, and press Return or Enter. Spotlight lists all files that contain the terms.

But wait, there's more: In the Spotlight menu, click Show All. In the Spotlight window that appears, flip up all the header triangles except for Images. Click the "(x) more…" at the bottom of the Images section, to display all Images results (**Figure 9.10**).

And that's not all: Click the icon view button and you'll see thumbnails of all the images that Spotlight found. (Click the slideshow button and you'll get a slideshow right away.) Select an thumbnail and choose File > Get Info, and in the More Info section of the Get Into button you'll see the file's metadata, including metadata you entered in Bridge.

However, when looking for images with Spotlight, you may run into a snag with camera raw files: Because raw files can't be modified, your adjustments and metadata are stored in the Adobe Bridge cache or in XMP metadata files, not in the images themselves. If you search for metadata you entered for raw files, the search may turn up their associated XMP files instead of the images.

Figure 9.10: You can use Mac OS X's Spotlight feature (above) for finding images, and then use Get Info to peek at the metadata for a selected image (right).

Production Practices

Batch Process Images from Adobe Bridge

? Bridge seems to be made for processing lots of images at once. What are some of the ways I might be able to do that?

✓ Batch processing is certainly part of the idea behind Bridge. Here's an overview of the wide range of things you can do once you've selected multiple images in the Bridge window:

- You can upload selected images to share them with other people online or order prints, books, calendars, and greeting cards. To do this, choose from among the Tools > Photoshop Services submenu.

- You can process your selected images using features from Photoshop or Illustrator, by choosing from the Photoshop or Illustrator submenu (under the Tools menu). Of particular interest here to us is the Tools > Photoshop > Batch command, which you can use to process selected images using any action in Photoshop. We talk more about actions and batch processing in Chapter 4, *Correcting Images*.

- If you can write or download a script, you can add it to the Tools menu. You can read information about interapplication scripting in the Bridge JavaScript Scripting Reference, which is installed with Adobe Creative Suite 2. You can find scripts at *studio.adobe.com*.

- A great example of a custom script is Dr. Brown's Services, a set of scripts created by Photoshop master Russell Brown. Dr. Brown's Services include Merge-A-Matic, which combines selected image frames into an animation; Place-A-Matic, which creates a high-dynamic-range image from a camera raw file; and Caption Maker, which generates captions from file metadata. After you install Dr. Brown's Services, they appear on the Tools menu. You can download Dr. Brown's services and other useful tools and tutorials from *www.russellbrown.com*.

Archive Camera Raw Images

? My camera raw files are filling up my hard disk, so I'm going to archive them to DVD. Anything I should know before I start burning the discs?

✓ You might think that you can archive camera raw files the way you archive everything else—just throw them on a disk and stick it on the shelf. However, it's not that straightforward. First of all, because camera raw image data is read-only, your edits and annotations are saved by Bridge and Camera Raw to another file (either the Camera Raw database or XMP "sidecar" files, depending on how you set up your preferences). You need to archive that information along with the images (we'll tell you how in a moment). Second, camera raw files differ for each camera and often for each camera model, creating the possibility that older raw formats may eventually cease to be supported.

Adobe has come up with a way to solve both of these problems, through the open Digital Negative (DNG) format. A DNG file contains all the same information as a camera raw file and the edits you've applied, without permanently altering the image data itself. If you want, you can also embed the original raw file in the DNG file. It's a very straightforward operation, because all you're doing is putting raw files into one end and watching DNG files come out the other end.

It's best if you make sure your raw images are corrected and annotated as completely as possible before you archive them, so that they're in good shape and easy to search. Let's get going:

1. Download the Adobe DNG Converter for your platform. You'll find it at the following URL: *www.adobe.com/support/downloads/*

2. Start Adobe DNG Converter and follow the numbered steps in the Digital Negative Converter dialog box (**Figure 9.11**); they're straightforward but we do have some suggestions:

- In step 1, only camera raw files are processed in the folder you select.

- In step 2, we recommend saving to a different folder to ensure you don't overwrite your original raw files.

- You can use step 3 to rename your files.

- In step 4, the preference defaults are usually appropriate. If you want to keep your raw file inside the DNG copy, you can click Preferences and enable the Embed Original Raw File checkbox here.

3. When you're ready, click Convert.

After the conversion, use Adobe Bridge to examine the folder containing the DNG files you just generated. You can open them in Camera Raw to see if they converted properly. When you're satisfied with the conversion, you can keep the DNG files for your archives and delete the original raw files.

Preserve Bridge Settings for Posterity

? I burned some of my images to a CD. Now when I view the CD in Bridge, the images are missing the ratings and sort order I applied in Bridge before burning the images to CD. Did I miss something?

☑ You have to remember that Bridge saves a lot of your work (rating, rotating, and so on) in a cache file. By default, Bridge uses a centralized cache (one huge file on your hard drive). If you move the images to any other disk using a program other than Bridge (such as burning a disc), you will likely lose your prebuilt thumbnails, ratings, labels, sort order, and other information you've

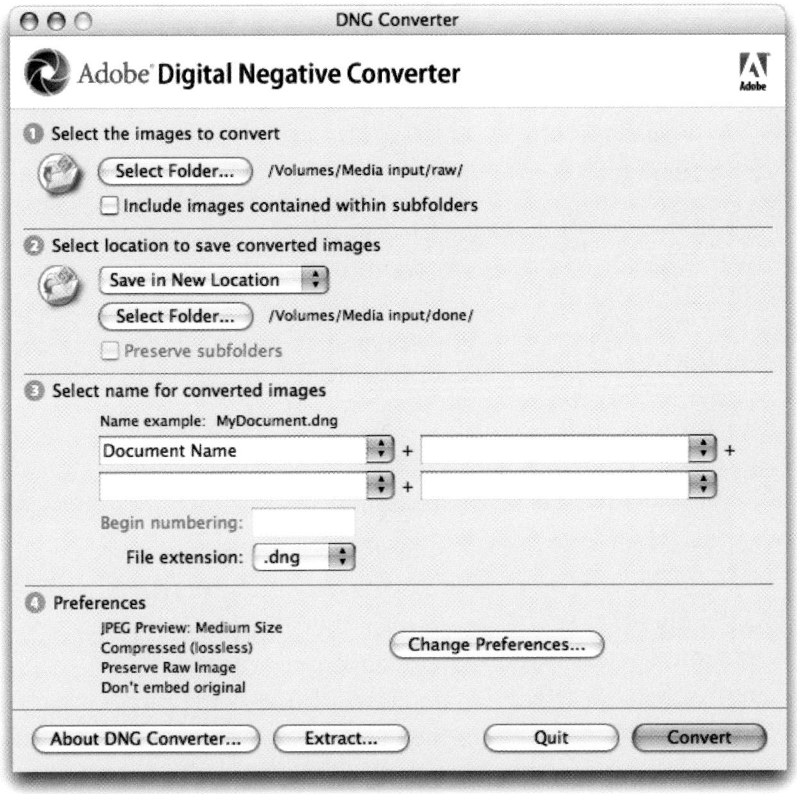

Figure 9.11: The DNG Converter makes easy work of turning raw files into easy-to-archive DNG.

applied in Bridge. You can get around this in two ways. First, when your cache is centralized, choose Tools > Cache > Export Cache to generate portable cache files that you can send or burn along with the images. Alternately, you can open Bridge's Preferences (Command/Ctrl-K), open the Advanced panel, and choose Use Distributed Cache Files When Possible. This way, you'll get lots of little cache files in each of your image folders. Just make sure you copy those files from place to place and disk to disk.

TIP: You don't have to open Bridge just to work with a file's metadata. Just open the file and choose File > File Info in Photoshop to open the File Info dialog box. However, Bridge offers the Metadata and Keywords panel as well as the File Info dialog box (it's on the File menu there, too). Bridge's greatest contribution, though, is that you can edit metadata for more than one image by selecting more than one image before you choose the File Info command.

10

Printing, Saving, and Exporting

Printing, Saving, and Exporting

*I*MAGES RARELY BEGIN AND END THEIR LITTLE LIVES IN PHOTOSHOP. Rather, the images you capture from digital cameras, scanners, or other programs—and even those you do build using Photoshop's tools—are typically edited in Photoshop and then head off toward some greater calling. An inkjet printer, perhaps, or a printing press. Maybe a Web page (not to be confused with a Web press) or a—shudder—PowerPoint presentation.

Wherever your images will land, you need to make sure they're properly prepared for the journey and the destination. A photograph to be printed on newsprint needs very different handling than one to be published on the Web or shown on a DVD. A graphic designed for archival-quality fine art printing surely requires a different workflow than a snapshot you want to place in a company newsletter.

In this chapter we offer lots of solutions for making sure you send your images down just the right path, as well as tips for how to ensure you get optimal quality once they're ready to be imaged.

Printing

Preview a Print Job

? I seem to waste a lot of paper with my print jobs. Sometimes an image prints at a very different size than what I see on screen; other times I get unexpected margins. How can I head off these problems before I waste another sheet?

☑ We feel your pain. Paper and ink aren't cheap, particularly if you use an inkjet printer. The Print with Preview feature can help you avoid expensive, preventable output mistakes.

Choose File > Print with Preview (**Figure 10.1**), and you'll see a dialog box with a thumbnail view of the image on the paper. The most useful thing to know about the Print with Preview dialog box is that the thumbnail preview you see is based on the settings in the Page Setup dialog box. Everything you see in the thumbnail—paper size, outer margins, and orientation—are taken from the printer manufacturer's print driver, not from Photoshop. For example, if the image is tall but the page in Print with Preview is wide, click the Page Setup button and change the paper orientation to be wide.

Any time the preview doesn't look right, click the Page Setup button and make absolutely sure that the current printer settings are correct for your printer and job. If they aren't, you might send the wrong data to your printer, and strange things can happen.

Here are a few other useful tidbits about Print with Preview:

- The thumbnail isn't color-managed, so don't freak out if the color doesn't look right. To preview output colors, use the View > Proof Setup command instead. (We discuss color management issues more in Chapter 8, *Keeping Color Consistent* and in the topic "Color-Managed Printing," later in this section.)

- You can position the image on the page by disabling the Center Image checkbox, then dragging the image or adjusting the Position values. You can drag the image only when the Show Bounding Box checkbox is enabled.

- Click More Options for complete control over output appearance. When you display the additional options, the Output panel contains page marks and adjustments that are mostly useful for prepress output, and the Color Management

> **TIP:** One factor that affects print quality is the resolution of the image. You need to know the resolution that works best with your final output device—check your printer manual; or when preparing images for a press, check with your prepress service provider. You also need to know whether the image you're printing has enough resolution to meet the resolution requirement without resampling; we cover how to do this in Chapter 3, *Image Editing Basics*.

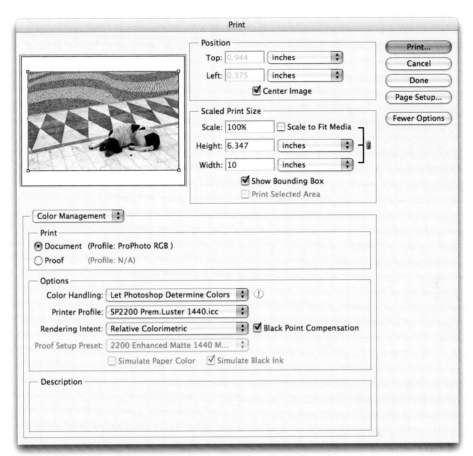

Figure 10.1: The Print with Preview dialog box (which is unfortunately just titled "Print") can help you minimize output measurement problems.

panel provides advanced control over printed color.

- Print with Preview is such a useful reality check that you might want to see it every time you print. Just press Command-Option-P/Ctrl-Alt-P. Or, if you're in the habit of choosing the Print command by pressing Command-P/Ctrl-P, you can use the Edit > Keyboard Shortcuts command to reassign the Print command to the Print with Preview command. That way, when you press Command-P/ Ctrl-P, you'll see the Print with Preview dialog box.

TIP: If your black-and-white prints aren't as neutral as you would like, try a printer that uses cartridges containing actual gray inks, such as the Epson 2400. Third-party grayscale inksets are also available for some inkjet printers, though they can be more difficult to use. See *www. piezography.com* or *www.inksupply. com/bwpage.cfm*

Centering a Print on Paper

? My prints aren't centered on the page, even if I enable the Center Image checkbox in the Print with Preview dialog box. Why doesn't centering work, and how can I get it to work?

✓ Remember that in the Print with Preview dialog box, the page size, orientation, and margins Photoshop uses are obtained from the manufacturer's printer driver. When you enable the Center Image checkbox, Photoshop starts measuring from the margins the printer driver provides. Photoshop can't see beyond that; it has to believe what the driver says. If the printer driver sends Photoshop uneven margins, the page won't be centered. You'll be able to see this in the Print with Preview thumbnail. Some printers, such as many in the Epson line, have default paper sizes that create a larger margin along the trailing edge of the paper to maintain a good grip on the paper (**Figure 10.2**); this can prevent centered printing.

> **TIP:** The printer driver tells Photoshop what options are available, such as paper sizes, inks, and resolution. If you haven't set up your printer properly, you might not see the right options for your printer, or your jobs may not print as expected. When you have a printing problem, the first thing you should check is the Page Setup dialog box.

> **TIP:** Need crop marks? The Print with Preview dialog box contains a panel that adds various printer marks to an image, including crop marks. Choose File > Print with Preview, click More Options, and choose Output from the popup menu under the preview. You can now select the Corner Crop Marks and Center Crop Marks options.

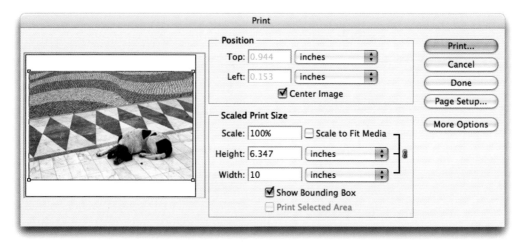

Figure 10.2: The preview thumbnail shows that the print won't be centered—it will be shifted to the left due to a wide margin on the trailing edge, dictated by the driver and Page Setup settings.

If you see uneven margins in the Print with Preview thumbnail, try looking in the File > Page Setup command to see if there's another paper size that has even margins on all sides. If such a paper size is available and you select it in Page Setup, the page centers properly and you'll see this in Print with Preview.

If no page size gives you even margins all around, you can try using the Image > Canvas Size command to add a bit of extra canvas to one side of the image to balance out the uneven side.

Save Paper on Test Prints

? It usually takes me a few tries before I perfect a print. How can I use as little paper as possible when making test prints?

There's certainly no need to use up an entire sheet of paper for each print when you're making quick test prints. Use Print with Preview to scale and position your test prints so that they only take up part of the page (**Figure 10.3**). For example, by using Print with Preview, you can shrink a test print so that it uses up the top half of a page, and you can make your second test print use up the bottom half of the same page. The great thing about sizing test prints this way is that it doesn't affect the actual image size and resolution saved with the document.

Printing Two Or More Per Page

? I want to print three images on the same page. Do I really have to print three times?

No, no, no. Photoshop can print two or more images at the same time, though it's not immediately obvious how because it has nothing to do with the Print or Print with Preview

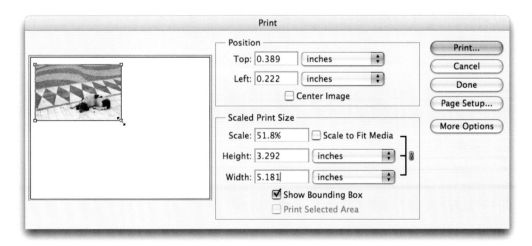

Figure 10.3: By changing the Postion and Scaled Print Size options, you can control the size and position of a document on the print medium.

Figure 10.4: Picture Package lets you print two or more of the same (or different) images.

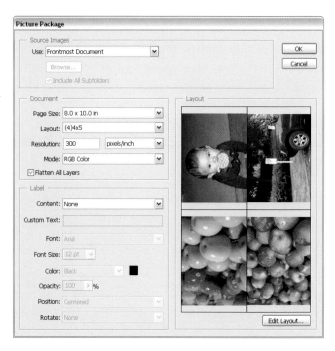

features. Rather, you choose File > Automate > Picture Package (**Figure 10.4**).

Picture Package lets you lay out different versions of the same picture (like school photos, where you want so many wallet-sized, and so on). Or you can use it to lay out different images on one page. Choose from among the options in the Use popup menu, then choose the number and size of the image from the Layout popup menu. To change an image, click the preview picture (Photoshop asks you to choose an image from disk). When you click OK, Photoshop does all the work compiling the image for you; when it's done, go ahead and choose Print with Preview to print it.

Preparing Screen Shots for a Press

? **What's the best way to convert a screen shot for CMYK printing? I'm told that the usual conversion methods don't really work for screen shots.**

☑ Screen shots can be a challenge to print well, because the nature of a screen shot is inherently opposite to the nature of a print. Screen shots are low-resolution RGB files, while printed images are ideally high-resolution CMYK files. When you need to print screen shots—for example, in a manual or tutorial book—use these tips.

- Print screen shots much smaller than the original size. A screen shot consists of a fixed number of pixels at the resolution of the screen, such as 800×600 pixels at 100 dpi or so on today's displays. In print, that looks both too large and coarse. Screen shots often look good at 50 percent of their original size. Not only do screen shots fit better on a page this way, scaling to 50 percent doubles their effective resolution so they look sharper too.

- You typically do *not* want to increase the resolution of a screen capture using Image Size. That usually just makes it blurry.

TIP: If you make significant changes to a document when you make test prints, such as resizing or cropping, and you don't want to risk saving those test changes with the original document, make a quick duplicate document for your test prints. With the original document open, choose Image > Duplicate. If you enable "Duplicate Merged Layers Only," your test duplicate is flattened, which can save RAM. If you decide to edit the original, close the duplicate without saving and make another one before your next test print.

- Rather than use a format like GIF or PNG, you should save in a high-quality file format. For prepress, use CMYK TIFF. For photocopiers or quick printing, JPG may be acceptable if you use a high-quality level of compression.

- When converting from RGB to CMYK, consider maximizing Gray Component Replacement (GCR)

so that as many areas of the screen shot as possible (without altering the color balance) are printed on the black (K) plate. This makes your screen shots appear more solid and neutral gray when they come off of the press. If your service bureau has an ICC profile for their press, specify that when converting from RGB to CMYK (using Edit > Convert to Profile) and GCR happens automatically. Otherwise, when you're in the Convert to Profile dialog box, choose Custom CMYK from the Destination Space popup menu, and enter values you can get from your service bureau, making sure that GCR is set to Maximum (**Figure 10.5**). Then use this Custom CMYK setting when converting RGB screen shots to CMYK with the Convert to Profile command.

If you use the GCR conversion method or an ICC profile with GCR built into it, apply it only to screen shots and similar synthetic images. Do not apply

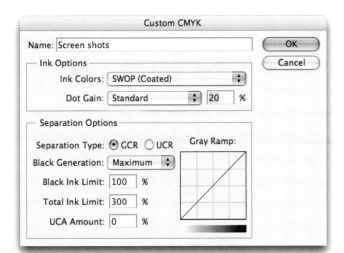

Figure 10.5: One example of Custom CMYK settings that convert screen shots for a press using maximum GCR. The actual values depend on the press your printer uses.

this Maximum Black Generation to photographs unless directed by your service bureau—convert those using conventional RGB-to-CMYK techniques.

Color-Managed Printing

? **I'm trying to print from Photoshop to a good color printer (not separations), and I'm completely confused by the color management options in Photoshop. First of all, the terminology reads like technical gobbledygook. Second, some options show up in more than one place. Ultimately, my prints don't look right. Can you help make sense of all of this?**

✔ Sure. If your printer driver supports color management properly and you have accurate printer profiles, you can achieve better color than the out-of-the-box settings for a printer. Here's how:

1. Choose File > Print with Preview. If you only see the top half of the dialog box, click More Options (**Figure 10.6**).

2. Choose Color Management from the popup menu under the preview.

3. In the Print section, select Document.

4. In the Options section, choose Let Photoshop Determine Colors to have Photoshop convert the image colors to the printer's color space.

5. In the Options section, choose a profile that matches the printer, inkset, and paper you're using. (In a worse-case scenario, if you can't identify the right profile or you know you don't have one, you may want to choose Let Printer Determine Colors from the Color Handling popup menu. Then tell the printer driver to use sRGB—or your image's native RGB working space—in step 8.)

6. In the Options section, choose Relative Colorimetric from the Rendering Intent popup menu, and also enable the Black Point Compensation checkbox. (In a few cases, Perceptual may look better, but start with Relative Colorimetric.)

7. Click Print.

8. In the Print dialog box, make sure the correct printer is selected as the target printer. Unless you chose Let Printer Determine Colors in step 5, you should now find your printer driver's options for printer color management and turn it *off* (otherwise, you'll get double color management which is—in a word—bad). The location for turning this off in the driver varies for different printer models. (If you did choose Let Printer Determine Colors in step 5, then leave the printer color management turned on.)

9. Click Print.

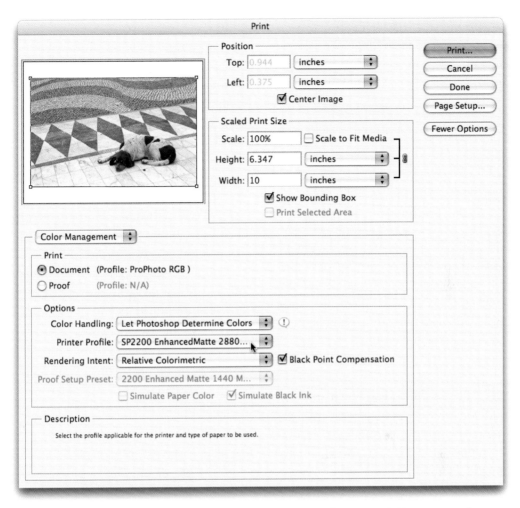

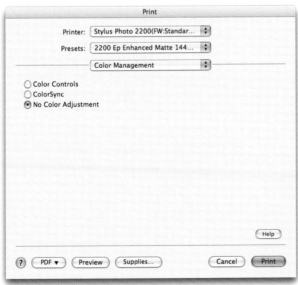

Figure 10.6: You can use the Color Management section of the Print with Preview dialog box (above) to control the color conversion on the way to the printer. After you click Print, the printer driver may provide options for turning off color management on the printer side, to avoid a conflict with Photoshop color management (shown at left for an Epson 2200 printer).

Where Do Printer Profiles Come From?

? I'd like to print better color, but I don't see profiles for my printer in the Options section of the Print with Preview dialog box. Where do I find printer profiles?

✓ First of all, it's important for us to mention that output profiles don't just describe a printer. They describe a specific combination of a printer, ink, and paper. For some printers, the printer driver installer also installs profiles for that printer. If printer profiles are installed by the driver installer, you'll see them in the Color Management options of the Print with Preview dialog box, and in the View > Proof Setup > Custom dialog box.

If the printer driver doesn't install printer profiles, you can make custom profiles. Most people have custom profiles made through a service (available in larger cities or online). You can also buy profiling products, but those usually aren't cheap and they can require a bit of expertise to operate properly.

Custom profiles are useful even if you have manufacturer profiles, because the profiles you get from a printer manufacturer are generic in nature—they don't account for the actual variations between individual printers coming off a production line. You can also use custom profiles for soft-proofing to your monitor (using the Proof Colors command), letting you use your monitor to preview how colors print on your printer. We talk about soft-proofing in Chapter 8, *Keeping Color Consistent*.

Images for Other Programs

Import Photoshop Documents Directly

? I want to use Photoshop images in Adobe InDesign and Illustrator. What's the best format to use to save Photoshop files for these other programs?

✓ While many grizzled veterans of digital media are used to converting Photoshop documents to formats like TIFF, EPS, or JPEG before using them in other applications, that step is much less necessary these days. Today, more

applications—particularly those from Adobe—can import Photoshop files with no conversion needed. Not only that, but you often have more flexibility when you stay with the Photoshop format. For example, if you import a Photoshop file into InDesign, you can make individual layers in the imported Photoshop document visible or invisible. When planning a workflow involving Photoshop documents, it's worth your while to look into whether you can simply use your original Photoshop document in the other application. If you can, you won't have to generate and track as many files.

Control Photoshop Layers from InDesign

You can control a Photoshop document's layer visibility from within InDesign CS2. In fact, if you place the same Photoshop file in an InDesign document multiple times, you can have different layers visible in each instance of the placed file, while the layer settings in the original Photoshop file remain unchanged. This can be very useful when you've used Photoshop layers to create different versions of an image in one file, cutting down on the number of files you have to manage.

You can turn on and off layer visibility either when you place the PSD file, or after it's already on your page. To control Photoshop layer visibility from an InDesign layout, select the placed Photoshop document and choose Object > Object Layer Options (**Figure 10.7**). In the Show Layers area, click any eye icon to show or hide that layer. Alternatively, you can choose a layer comp from the Layer Comp popup menu (as long as you have saved some layer comps in Photoshop's Layer Comp palette).

Next, choose an option from the When Updating Link popup menu. To preserve the visibility settings applied in InDesign even if they change in the original Photoshop document, choose Keep Layer Visibility Overrides. When you place the same file multiple times in InDesign and vary the layer visibility settings, you definitely want to choose Keep Layer Visibility Overrides.

To always maintain the visibility settings you set in Photoshop, choose Use Photoshop's Layer Visibility. But this means the visibility settings you make will be wiped out as soon as you update a modified link.

To control layer visibility when you place the document in InDesign, turn on the Show Import Options checkbox in InDesign's Place dialog box. This tells InDesign to display the Image Import Options dialog box. Then click the Layers tab, where you have the same controls as the Object Layer Options dialog box.

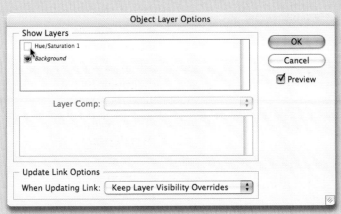

Figure 10.7: In InDesign CS2, the Object Layer Options dialog box gives you control over which layers of a Photoshop file are visible in the InDesign layout.

Adobe InDesign, Illustrator, GoLive, Acrobat, After Effects, and Premiere Pro can all directly import a PSD file. In Adobe GoLive, an imported Photoshop file becomes a Smart Object, which means you can optimize the image for the Web from within GoLive without having to make any changes in Photoshop and without altering the original Photoshop document.

If you're using a program that can't import a Photoshop document directly, you can use the File > Save As command to save a Photoshop document into another format. For high-quality printing, use TIFF. For general-purpose desktop printing, TIFF, JPEG, and PNG typically work well. For on-screen viewing, JPEG, PNG, and GIF are often used.

Import Photoshop Images into Illustrator

? **Is there a best way to import a Photoshop image into Illustrator?**

☑ There are a bunch of ways to get a Photoshop image into Illustrator. You can open a Photoshop document in Illustrator by any of the following:

- On the desktop or from Bridge, drag one or more

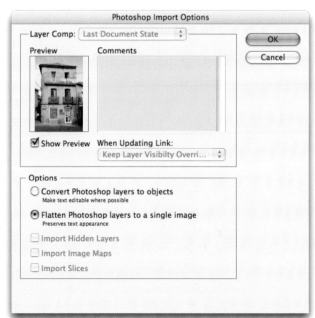

Figure 10.8: In Illustrator CS2, the Photoshop Import Options dialog box gives you control over how a Photoshop file imports into Illustrator.

Photoshop documents onto the Illustrator program icon (Mac OS or Windows) or application window (Windows).

- From Illustrator, choose File > Open, locate and select one or more Photoshop documents, and click Open.

- From Bridge, select one or more files documents and choose File > Open With > Adobe Illustrator.

- When Illustrator opens the file, it displays the Photoshop Import Options dialog box (**Figure 10.8**), where you can control how layer comps, layers, and text import. If you added Web features to the Photoshop document, you can also control how image maps and slices import. When you've selected the options you want, click OK.

The Photoshop Import Options dialog box opens once for each document you selected to be opened.

Trace Photoshop Documents in Illustrator

? Does Photoshop have an auto-trace feature?

No, but if you have Adobe Illustrator CS2, you can automatically trace a Photoshop image using the Live Trace feature included in it. Live Trace comes with a number of useful presets that produce different "looks." To apply Illustrator Live Trace to an image:

1. Select one or more Photoshop documents in Bridge, and choose Tools > Illustrator > Live Trace.

2. Bridge switches to Illustrator and displays the Live Trace dialog box (**Figure 10.9**). Most of the options, like Presets, are the same as the ones you'll find when applying Live Trace from within Illustrator, but we should explain the options that are different:

- The Vectorize to Layers in Single Document option is available if you selected multiple images in Bridge. If you enable this option, Illustrator creates just one new document with each image traced as a separate layer in the document. If you don't enable this option, Illustrator traces each image to its own document.

- The Save and Close Results option results in new Illustrator documents saved to disk. If you don't enable this option, each new trace document remains open.

- The Source area simply lists the documents you selected in Bridge.

- The Destination option provides options for naming documents saved as a result of tracing.

3. Click OK.

Compress Images Down to Size

? There are so many ways to compress images. When should I compress, and how?

Compress copies of your original images only when storage space or transmission time are limited. The most common example is when you want to include images in e-mail messages or Web pages.

There are two kinds of compression: lossless and lossy. Lossless compression

Figure 10.9: When you select a Photoshop document imported into Adobe Illustrator CS2 (color image at left), you can click the Live Trace button in the Illustrator Control Palette (top), to create a customizable vector tracing (top right). If you select multiple Photoshop images in Bridge and choose Tools > Illustrator > Live Trace, you can trace multiple images using the dialog box at right.

preserves the exact appearance of the original image, and lossy compression makes a few compromises in visual quality. You might think that lossless compression would always be preferable, but unfortunately, lossless compression can reduce an image's file size only so far before it can't compress any further—and at that point, the file is usually still too large for purposes such as posting on a Web page. TIFF is an example of a format that supports lossless compression.

You can save a TIFF file with no compression, LZW compression, or Zip compression. Both LZW and Zip are lossless; Zip takes a little longer but is usually much better at compressing images than LZW.

Like MP3 compression for music, lossy compression removes data that you are less likely to notice, such as colors or tones that our eyes don't see very well. Lossy compression also lets you control the trade-off between quality and file size. You can save more space by increasing the amount of compression, but the more space you save, the more image data is thrown out and the worse the image looks. JPEG is a common example of a format that applies lossy compression.

If you're going to save a file with JPEG compression, it's best to keep an original uncompressed version in case you need to edit again later. To save the JPEG file, turn on the Save As a Copy checkbox in the Save As dialog box (to avoid overwriting your original), and for additional savings, disable all of the other checkboxes in the Save section.

If you want to apply lossy compression or you're preparing Web graphics, you can choose File > Save for Web (**Figure 10.10**), which has several features that can help you evaluate the file's size-vs.-quality tradeoff.

Enable Previews for Other Programs

? When I try to use Photoshop files in other programs that say they support Photoshop files, I sometimes don't see the image—I just get a blank placeholder. Is there a switch I need to flip somewhere?

You're on the right track. Just because an application says it supports the Photoshop format doesn't mean it knows how to read all of Photoshop's features—otherwise, they'd be Photoshop too. Some other applications only know how to read a flat (unlayered), 8-bit RGB Photoshop file, so if you try to open or import a more sophisticated Photoshop file, the document may come up blank.

Fortunately, there is an answer. Photoshop offers an option called Maximize PSD and PSB File Compatibility. If you import a Photoshop file into another application and the Photoshop document appears blank, go back to Photoshop and enable this preference in the Preferences dialog box. This feature adds a flattened version of the file to

Figure 10.10: In the Save for Web dialog box, you can quickly determine the optimal compression settings for JPEG, TIF, and PNG files by comparing different settings side by side.

Store Multiple Variations in One File

The adjustment layers in Photoshop are now so powerful and flexible that you can change images in radical ways without ever actually degrading your original image data. That means you can backtrack all the way to the beginning of your work in many cases. If you like being able to keep your options open, using adjustment layers is for you, and you can adapt the ideas in this tip for any time you want to define different variations of an image with adjustment layers.

Making Variations

One use for adjustment layers is to store more than one variation of an image inside the same file. For example, you might need both a grayscale and a color version of the same image. You can do this with adjustment layers, and if you later find you need to touch up the original image, doing so updates *both* the color and black-and-white variations of the image. If you later discover a red eye, scratch, or other defect in the image, you only have to edit the master, and the other variations update automatically.

The trick is to keep the master and each set of adjustment layers in distinct groups in the Layers palette. In our example (see the facing page), we keep the black-and-white adjustment layers in a separate group. To use the color variation of the image, hide the Black & White layer group. To use the black-and-white variation of the image, show the Black & White layer group.

We often use this technique for repurposing the same image to different outputs. For instance, we might have one set of adjustment layers that correct an image for a particular printer, and another set that optimize the image for Web output. When you want to use one of these, simply make that group visible and hide the other layer groups. You can easily manage any number of layer visibility combinations using the layer comp feature.

Flattening Them Out

To create a flattened copy of any variation of the image, turn on and off the appropriate layer sets, choose Image > Duplicate, turn on the Duplicate Merged Layers Only checkbox, and click OK. If you are creating a black-and-white copy, choose Image > Mode > Grayscale after the duplication. The reason we recommend creating flattened duplicates of the color and black-and-white documents for final use is so you don't accidentally flatten or alter the many layers that make up the color and black-and-white variations.

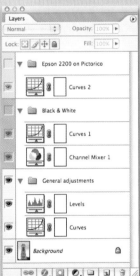

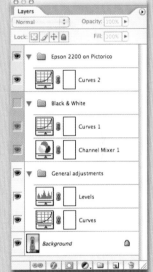

The "General Adjustments" layer group contains color and tone adjustments that apply to all variations.

The "Black & White" layer group contains adjustment layers that convert the color image to black & white, and a Curves adjustment layer fine-tunes tones only within that layer group.

The "Epson 2200 on Pictorico" layer group adds adjustments we'll turn on only when printing to that printer and paper combination, after using Proof Colors to preview the output. The Black & White layer group is turned off, because its adjustments don't apply to this printer and paper combination.

the Photoshop document. When other applications read the Photoshop file and aren't able to decode all of the features in the document, they can at least read the flattened version. This is more than enough when you only need to view or print a Photoshop file and you don't need to edit it.

The only downside to the Maximize PSD and PSB File Compatibility preference is that adding the flattened version increases the file size. If you don't frequently use Photoshop documents in other applications, consider disabling this preference. Let's set it up:

1. Choose Photoshop > Preferences > File Handling (Mac OS X) or Edit > Preferences > File Handling (Windows).

2. Choose Always or Ask from the Maximize PSD and PSB File Compatibility popup menu. Choosing Always is more convenient, because Photoshop will always embed a flattened version when you save a Photoshop document. Ask is less convenient because you'll always see an extra Maximize Compatibility dialog box when you use the Save As command.

3. Click OK.

Save to Unavailable File Formats

? I'm trying to save a file in the JPEG format, but in the Save As dialog box, JPEG is dimmed. Why would Photoshop be unable to save a file as JPEG?

✔ When a Photoshop document uses features that aren't available in the format you're trying to use, the format or specific feature checkboxes may not be available in the Save As dialog box. Try each of the following until the format you want becomes available in the Save As dialog box:

- Choose Image > Duplicate. This creates a copy of the document that won't affect the original, because we're about to change a few things.

- Choose Image > Mode > RGB Color, and then choose Save As and see if the format you want is now available. If it is, then your original document uses a color mode that isn't supported in the format you want. Many file formats support only RGB, not CMYK, LAB, or indexed color.

- Choose Image > Mode > 8 Bits/ Channel, and then as in the previous step, see if the format becomes available in the Save As dialog box.

TIP: If you need to convert a Photoshop document to another format, don't overwrite or throw out your original Photoshop file, because other formats may not support all of the features you can save in a genuine Photoshop file. For example, JPEG files can't have layers or editable type. A quick way to create a copy from your original Photoshop document is to choose the File > Save a Copy command. Just remember that after you save a copy, your original document remains open.

Many file formats support only 8-bit files. They might not support 16-bit or 32-bit images.

- Choose Layer > Flatten Image before choosing Save As. Some file formats can't store layers.

In short, you can usually save to any format you want if your file is a flattened 8-bit RGB or grayscale image—the lowest common denominator for file formats.

Saving a Copy of a Document

? **I'm in the Save As dialog box. Photoshop has enabled the As a Copy checkbox and added the word "copy" to the end of my filename. Why does this keep happening?**

✓ You've chosen Save As options that will create a file with less data than the document you're saving, and Photoshop wants to make sure you don't

TIP: To prepare images to be used in Microsoft Office, choose the PNG option in the Save As dialog box, or just copy and paste. Also, images you use in Office don't need to be the highest resolution. An 8-bit RGB image at 150 dpi or lower should be fine for most uses in Microsoft Office. For PowerPoint, ignore dpi and simply set the image size (Image > Image Size) to fit the pixel dimensions of the presentation monitor or projector, such as 800×600 pixels or 1024×768 pixels.

wipe out your original data. For instance, if you're working in a layered document and you choose Save As and disable the Layers checkbox, Photoshop enables the As a Copy checkbox (**Figure 10.11**).

Adobe added this feature because in earlier versions of Photoshop, too many people accidentally replaced their lovingly crafted layered documents with a flattened version, because they disabled

Figure 10.11: The As a Copy option at the bottom of the Save As dialog box turns on automatically when you choose a Save option that may result in data loss if you were to save to the same filename as the currently open document.

the Layers checkbox and saved to the same file name without realizing the consequences.

The other reason you'll see As a Copy enabled is when you're saving to a format like GIF, PNG, or JPEG that simply can't store all of the information in the original file. For example, JPEG can't store layers, so if you save a layered document as a JPEG, Photoshop enables the As a Copy checkbox.

There's one more important difference between having As a Copy enabled or disabled. When As a Copy is enabled, the document you return to after the Save As dialog box goes away is the same document you saved. The copy you saved is stored as a separate file on disk that isn't opened. In this way, if you saved a document using As a Copy and turned off layers or other features in the Save As dialog box, you can continue to work on the full-featured version with layers.

Make Photoshop Backgrounds Easy to Remove

? **I placed a Photoshop document in Adobe InDesign, but the background is white. I was hoping the background would be transparent. What went wrong?**

☑ When you know in advance that the background of a Photoshop document will need to be removed later, it's best to set up the Photoshop document so that the background is ready to remove. There's more than one way to do this, and the way you do it depends on where the image is going:

- If you're going to use the Photoshop document in Adobe InDesign, put the subject on a non-background layer. Better yet, remove the background layer. InDesign can read layer transparency, so if you make areas of a layer transparent in Photoshop (so you can see the checkerboard pattern), it will be transparent in InDesign.

- If you want a soft edge, feather or blur the edge of the layer, layer mask, or alpha channel that defines the transparency. Applications like Adobe InDesign and Adobe After Effects can read the alpha channels and layer masks in a Photoshop document. We talked about layer masks in Chapter 5, *Working with Layers*.

- If you're importing the Photoshop document into an application that doesn't support layer masks or alpha channels, check and see if the application supports clipping paths—vector paths that define a background. To make a clipping path, outline the subject with the pen tool (set to Paths mode in the Options bar), double-click the path in the Paths palette to name it, then choose Clipping Path from the Paths palette menu in Photoshop to define that path as a clipping path (**Figure 10.12**). Applications like Adobe InDesign and QuarkXPress can read Photoshop clipping paths. A clipping path can only create a hard edge, not a soft one.

Figure 10.12: Telling Photoshop this path should be a clipping path.

Around the Office

? **What's the best way to prepare a photo for laser printing, faxing, or a copy machine?**

✓ Laser printers, faxes, and most copy machines don't reproduce images as well as a good printer, so you don't have to provide the same quality that you would for a press. An 8-bit image at 150 dpi or below should be a good starting point; you can test it on your office equipment and tweak it from there. It's more important to adjust the image so that the subject is easy to see after being degraded by office equipment. For example, you might want to crop the image to enlarge the subject, and adjust the image so that the subject has higher than normal contrast.

Make a Multiple-Page Document

? **Is there a way to make a multiple-page document from Photoshop images?**

✓ You can use the PDF Presentation feature to make one document out of many Photoshop documents. Let's say you scanned all of the receipts for a project, and they currently exist as multiple images. You can use the PDF Presentation command to combine all of those scanned receipts into a single PDF document of project receipts. The most convenient way to do this is to open Adobe Bridge, select all the files you want to combine, and choose Tools > Photoshop > PDF Presentation. In the PDF Presentation dialog box, select the Multi-Page Document button and click Save.

Using an Online Service

Prefer photographic prints to inkjet output? Want a poster-sized print? No problem! You can use an online service to print your photographs by choosing File > Print Online. Photoshop launches Adobe Bridge, selects current image, and automatically chooses Tools > Photoshop Services > Photo Prints. The Photo Print service uses Kodak's EasyShare Gallery (also known as Ofoto.com; in Photoshop CS, it uses Shutterfly).

Note that Kodak assumes that your JPEG images are in the sRGB color space and automatically applies brightness and contrast adjustments to your images unless you turn off their Kodak Perfect Touch feature.

Images for the Internet

Prepare Graphics for the Web or E-Mail

? **I created some graphics for my Web page, but the edges aren't sharp—they look smudged. What am I doing wrong?**

☑ You might be using the wrong compression method. Solid colors don't compress well with JPEG, which is designed for photos and graphics with continuous tones. Solid colors compress much better using PNG or GIF. However, while PNG is better than GIF, PNG isn't properly supported in a certain #1 Web browser which will remain nameless, so many Web designers still use GIF.

Again, the Save for Web dialog box gives you quite a bit of control over the trade-off between image quality and file size. Unlike JPEG, you can reduce the number of colors in a GIF file to try and lower the file size further.

Web-Safe Colors: Safe, or Out?

? **Do I need to use Web-safe colors for all Web graphics?**

☑ A few years ago, we all made a big deal out of Web-safe color palette—the 216 color common to all browsers and operating systems. The theory was that if you used colors from this palette, they wouldn't shift. But the Web-safe palette was designed for a world where most computers displayed 256 colors on the monitor. But it's the twenty-first century now, and the world has changed: Computers sold today display thousands or millions of colors out of the box, so you shouldn't limit yourself to a 216-color palette. And that's a good thing—those Web-safe colors were ugly!

Create Animations for the Web

? **How can I make an animated Web graphic?**

☑ Photoshop CS2's Animation palette makes it pretty easy! You create animation by changing the content of each frame based on your document layers. Here are the basic steps:

1. Organize your art so that the parts you want to animate are on their own layers, and move them to their initial positions.

2. Choose Window > Animation to display the Animation palette (**Figure 10.13**).

3. Click the Duplicates Selected Frames button to copy the initial frame, and edit the layers to take it to the next major step in the animation.

4. Select the two frames in the Animation palette, and click the Tweens Animation Frames button. Set options and click OK.

5. Click the Plays Animation button to preview the animation.

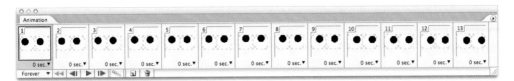

Figure 10.13: All of these frames in the Animation palette started out as a single Photoshop file, with a layer of black circles and a layer of white circles. The only three manually animated frames are of the eyeballs looking left, up, and right; the rest were tweened by Photoshop.

TIP: You can create more sophisticated Web animations in Adobe ImageReady. ImageReady is installed in the same folder as Photoshop.

TIP: When animating a layer, you aren't limited to moving layers around. You can also animate attributes like layer styles, blending modes, opacity, and visibility. For instance, to fade a layer, duplicate a frame in the Animation palette, set that layer's opacity in the new frame to 0%, and tween between that frame and the previous frame.

Create Slices for the Web

? How can I use Photoshop to create a Web image with slices?

The easiest and most flexible way is to use layer slices. A layer slice is based on the area of a layer, and its great advantage is that when you edit the layer, the slice updates to match the new shape so that you don't have to re-draw the slice. To make a layer slice, select a layer in the Layers palette and choose Layer > New Layer Based Slice (**Figure 10.14**).

You can also use the Slice tool to create slices over areas of a Photoshop document. Or you can create slices from guides: First, drag ruler guides out of the rulers and arrange them. Select the Slice tool and in the Options bar, click the Slices from Guides button.

Any slices you draw appear in color and are called user slices. Because all slices must be rectangular, Photoshop automatically creates additional slices for any non-rectangular areas left over by your slices—these are called auto slices, and have gray borders. To edit slices, use the Slice Select tool.

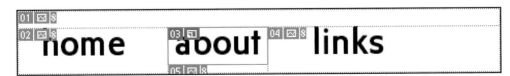

Figure 10.14: No need to draw a slice manually: The About layer has just been turned into a layer slice by selecting it and choosing Layer > New Layer Based Slice.

When you create the final Web output, the Save for Web dialog box includes the Slice Select tool so that you can optimized slices differently, if you want. After you click Save, the Save Optimized As dialog box provides options for which slices to export. Because a sliced image results in multiple files, the final output consists of files collected in a folder. It's a pretty darn good idea to ask Photoshop to export the HTML, too. That way, an HTML file describes how the slices fit together is exported along with the images.

Create Web Galleries

? How can I make an HTML gallery that I can upload to my Web server?

You can do it very quickly and easily. Just choose File > Automate > Web Photo Gallery (**Figure 10.15**), specify the options, and click OK. When it's done, your Web gallery pops open in your Web browser so you can check it out right away (**Figure 10.16**). You can take the resulting folder and upload it to the Web using an FTP utility or a Web authoring program such as Adobe GoLive.

You can choose from a number of gallery styles. The style names starting with the word "Flash" use some pretty slick Flash transitions, and are definitely worth a try.

As with other Automate commands, you might find it more convenient to select images in Adobe Bridge and then choose Web Photo Gallery from the Tools > Photoshop submenu.

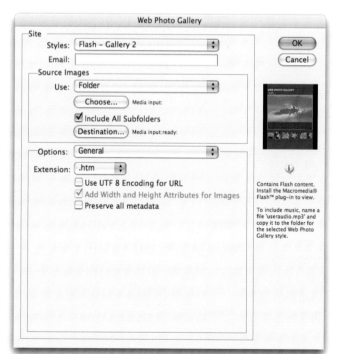

Figure 10.15: The Web Photo Gallery dialog box makes quick work of stylish online galleries for friends, family, and clients—just add your own Web server space.

Figure 10.16: An sample (and simple) Web Photo Gallery

TIP: It's worth exploring the other useful packaging options on the File > Automate submenu, including Contact Sheet II and Picture Package.

Preserve EXIF and Other Metadata in JPEG Files

? I uploaded some photos to a photo-hosting site that lets viewers see EXIF metadata for an image and search on image keywords. But when I create JPEGs from my Photoshop files, all of that information is gone. Where'd it go?

✓ You probably used the Save for Web dialog box to generate the JPEG files. Normally, there's nothing wrong with that; Save for Web does a great job of creating small JPEGs that show up fast on a Web site. However, in

TIP: The File > Automate > Web Photo Gallery dialog box contains an checkbox that lets you preserve all image metadata, which you can enable or disable.

order to create such small files, Save for Web strips out all non-image data from a file, including EXIF shot information added by a digital camera, and any keywords or other metadata you've added. It's the better option when you only want to display the image on a Web page.

The solution is to use the JPEG option in the Save As dialog box instead. The JPEG option in the Save As dialog box is more concerned with saving complete files rather than minimal files. When you create a JPEG file using the Save As dialog box, the thumbnail, EXIF data, and other metadata are preserved with the image file. It's the better option when you want other people to know everything about the image. Just make sure you haven't included any embarrassing or confidential data with the image!

TIP: If you want to control the image metadata people see on the Web, open the Web versions of your images in Adobe Bridge and use the Metadata and Keyword panels to edit the metadata in just those versions.

It's Showtime!

Make Images Look Good on TV

? I put some of my photos on a DVD, but they are kind of fuzzy and hard to see. The colors look a little washed-out too. How can I get it right?

✓ Standard-definition video (not HDTV) is a very low-resolution medium. When you prepare images for television, you can follow many of the same rules that you would for Web graphics. For example:

- Crop images to make the subjects more prominent, and to make details easier to see. You might also want to crop to the 4:3 horizontal aspect ratio of a standard television screen, or to the 16:9 aspect ratio of HDTV. Consider cropping vertical images too, to reduce or eliminate the big empty black areas that would normally appear on both sides of a vertical photo on TV.

- Choose Image > Image Size or File > Automate > Fit Image to size the images to 640×480 pixels, which is a typical resolution for standard-definition video. If you plan to use your video or DVD software to zoom in on the image, use proportionally larger pixel dimensions. For example, if you want to be able to magnify images by 2× in your video software while

preserving detail, you might resize images to 1280×960 pixels instead of 640×480.

- If you add graphics to your images, use lines at least several pixels thick. Because of the way television draws frames, lines that are too thin flicker annoyingly.

- Convert the images to sRGB color. If you use images in a larger color space such as Adobe RGB, colors may not look right on television.

Present a Live Slide Show

? Where in Photoshop can I present a slide show of my photos?

✓ You need to look in a slightly different place. Not in Photoshop, but in Adobe Bridge, which has a nifty slide show built right into the program. While Bridge isn't intended to be a full-blown presentation program (for example, it lacks transitions), it's more than

TIP: For the best image quality and display performance when creating a PDF slide show, use images already sized for the typical pixel dimensions of the monitor or projector on which you expect to display the presentation, such as 1024×768 pixels. Images that are too large will make the PDF file too large on disk.

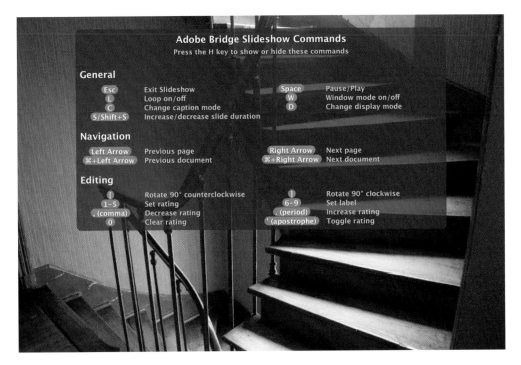

Figure 10.17: In Adobe Bridge, the View > Slide Show command displays documents in a full-screen view. If you press H, you see this helpful cheat sheet describing everything you can do in the slide show.

adequate for viewing your images in a distraction-free environment.

The slide show feature is largely self-explanatory. When you start a slide show, Adobe Bridge briefly displays a message telling you the number of files to be shown and the shortcut keys for playback and the help screen; the help screen lists all of the shortcut keys that operate only when the slide show is running. To start the show:

1. Open Adobe Bridge and select the files you want to display. If you want to display all of the files in a folder, select one file or no files. To begin the slide show at a specific file, select that file before you start the slide show.

2. Choose View > Slide Show.

3. When you're ready to start playback, press the spacebar. If you want to change slide show options, press H at any time (**Figure 10.17**).

4. To exit the slide show, press Esc.

Showing off your images is not the only purpose of the slide show in Adobe Bridge. If you open the help screen in Adobe Bridge (press H while a slide show is playing), you'll find shortcuts for rotating, ranking, and labeling. You can even delete images while the slide show is running by pressing the Delete key. (Be careful!) These reasons make the slide show an excellent tool for your first pass through a new set of images, because the slide show gives you a nice full-screen view of your images as you rank, rotate, and delete them as needed.

In fact, the Bridge slide show is more of a quick aid to sorting and culling than a presentation tool. You can tell by the attention paid to the ranking and labeling options, compared to the lack of transitions and random playback.

Create a Slide Show to Send Out

? **Is there a way to send a slide show to a client or family member?**

✓ You can create self-contained slide shows straight from Adobe Bridge or Photoshop. The PDF Presentation command lets you create an interactive slide show as a file you can give to others, who can run the slide show by themselves. A PDF slide show works on any computer that has Adobe Reader or Adobe Acrobat installed. (However, it won't work in non-Adobe PDF viewers such as Apple Preview.) You can even add transitions to a Photoshop slide show.

1. In Adobe Bridge, select the files you want to display. If you want to display all of the files in a window, select all files (Edit > Select All) or no files (Edit > Deselect All).

2. In Adobe Bridge, choose Tools > Photoshop > PDF Presentation.

3. In the PDF Presentation dialog box, select Presentation from the Output Options group. If needed, use the Source Files options to delete files from or add files to the list. Specify other options as needed, and click OK.

4. To start the slide show, open the PDF presentation document. Pressing the spacebar starts the slide show. Pressing Esc exits the slide show. To restart the presentation, close and reopen the PDF presentation in Adobe Reader or Acrobat.

Alternately, to make one of these from within Photoshop, choose File > Automate > PDF Presentation.

Index

C

Cache file information, 211–212
Calendars, 211
Calibrating monitors, 97, 184
Camera Raw
    archiving images, 211–212
    Auto checkboxes, 41–42
    batch converting, 39–40
    Brightness, 37
    Cancel button, 40–41
    Contrast, 37–38
    converting files, 38
    correction copying, 112–113
    cropping, 61
    Curves tab, 38
    Done button, 40
    duplicate features, 36
    Esc key, 40
    Exposure, 36–37
    grayscale, 175–176
    keywords, 207
    Open button, 40
    opening images, 35
    overview, 34–35
    Reset button, 41
    rotating, 80–81
    Saturation, 38
    Save button, 40–41
    Shadows, 37
    sharpening images, 119
    Spotlight, 210
    straightening, 80–81
    supported cameras, 35
    Update button, 41
Cameras
    Camera Raw supported, 35
    dust spots, 91
    noise, 109–110, 118–119
    opening photos, 32–33
    panorama mode, 139
    resolution, 54–55
Cancel button, Camera Raw, 40–41
Canvas Size, 57, 61
Caption Maker, 211
Capture
    sharpening, 119
    video, 63
Card readers, 33
Card, shortcut, 11
Cascading windows, 15, 201–202
Cataloging. *See* Organizing
CDs, 212–213
Centering prints, 220–221
Channels
    Channel Mixer, 173–174
    Curves dialog box, 98–99
    Duotones, 170–171
    halftone dots, 161–162
    histograms, 92
    masking, 70–73
    selecting by, 67–68
    viewing, 69

Choking selections, 74
Choosing layers, 128–129
Cleaning
    Metadata templates, 206–207
    screen shots, 34
Clear blending mode, 103
Clipboard, 179–180
Clipping, 91–92, 93, 133, 135, 150, 188–189
Clone Stamp tool, 104
Cloning image parts, 168
Closing
    documents, 16
    image windows, 15
CMYK, converting from RGB, 190–191
Cohen, Sandee, 152
Collages, 137
Collapsing palettes, 13
Collections, file, 208–209
Color
    artifacts, 109
    Assign Profile, 193
    background, 17
    blending mode, 103
    blending modes, 103
    calibrating monitors, 184
    comparing proof, 189
    Convert to Profile, 193
    converting to grayscale, 173–174
    correction, 90, 96–99
    Curves dialog box, 98–99
    distortion, 109
    dodge blending mode, 102
    Duotones, 170–171
    embedding profiles, 193
    eyedropper, 171
    halftone dots, 161–162
    installing profiles, 194
    locating profiles, 194
    management, print, 224–226
    multiple monitors, 20–21
    negative film, scanning, 44–45
    neutral work area, 186
    out of gamut, 188–189
    palette, 17
    print, 184–185, 187–191
    profiling monitors, 184
    sampling, 171
    selecting by, 65–66
    separating, 170–171
    sepia tone, 169
    shadows, 191
    soft-proofing, 187–189
    space conversions, 190–194
    synchronizing, 187
    text, 148–149
    video, 184–185
    Web-safe, 238
    websites, 184–185, 192–193

Color Burn blending mode, 102
Color Management Policies, 185
Combining images, 137–139
Commands. *See* individual commands
Committing
    Metadata entries, 205
    text changes, 146–147
Comparing proof colors, 189
Composite images, 137
Compressing images, 175, 229–231, 238
Comps, layer, 130, 131
Contact Sheet II, 241
Context menus, 24–25
Contract selections, 74
Contrast
    Camera Raw, 37–38
    Curves dialog box, 98–99
    histograms, 92
    textures, 163
Convert to Profile, 193
Converting
    color spaces, 190–194
    DNG, 211–213
    files, Camera Raw, 38
    guides, 25
    images, Camera Raw, 39–40
    screen shots for printing, 222–224
    selections, 71–73
Copy machines, 237
Copying
    corrections, 112–113
    document settings, 32
    documents, 83–86, 235–236
    image parts, 168
    layer styles, 160–161
    text, 145, 146
Correcting
    actions, 120–124
    adjustment layers, 111–113
    batches, 120–124
    blending filtered areas, 105
    blending modes, 101–103
    Burn tool, 105–106
    color, 96–99
    darkening, 105–106
    digital camera noise, 118–119
    Dodge tool, 105–106
    evaluating images, 90–94
    filters, 94–95
    globally, 94–103
    Healing tools, 104–105
    highlights, 100–101
    History, 108
    images, Camera Raw, 39–40
    layer masks, 106–107
    lightening, 105–106
    locally, 104–108
    low-resolution, 114

Picture Package, 221–222
Pictures. *See* Images; Photos
Piezography.com, 219
Pin Light blending mode, 103
Pixels
　aspect ratio, 62–63
　duplicating, 85
　halftone dots, 161–162
　locking, layers, 129–130
　per inch (ppi), 56
　print size, 19–20
　textures, 162–163
　viewing actual, 90–91
Plug-ins, migrating, 7
Point type, 144
Points, selecting, 177
Policies, color, 185
Polygon Lasso, 65
Pop-up tools, keyboard
　　shortcuts, 21–22
Ppi (pixels per inch), 56
Preferences
　file, backing up, 27
　font previewing, 147
　migrating, 8–9
　UI font size, 10
Premiere Pro, 228
Prepress color, 184–185
Preserving windows, 16
Presets
　color settings, 187
　document, 32
　Proof Setup, 189
　shapes, 177
　tool, 22–23
　type formatting, 146
Preventing errors
　action, 122–123
　batch, 123–124
　locking layers, 129–130
Preview
　color output, 187–189,
　　192–193
　documents, 18
　enabling, other programs,
　　231–234
　fonts, 147
　printing, 218–222
Print
　black-and-white, 219
　centering, 220–221
　color management,
　　224–226
　converting color spaces,
　　190–191
　crop marks, 220
　Duotones, 170–171
　multiple on page, 221–222
　Online services, 237
　orientation, 218
　page setup, 218
　preparing color, 184–185,
　　187–191
　previewing, 218–222
　profiles, printer, 226
　screen shots, 222–224
　shadows, 191

sharpening for, 119
size, 19–20
test, 221, 223
Printers
　black-and-white, 219
　drivers, 220, 226
　laser, 237
　profiles, 226
　resolution, 53, 218
Productivity, image correction,
　　111–116
Profiles
　converting to, 193
　embedding, 193
　installing color, 194
　locating color, 194
　printer, 226
Profiling monitors, 97, 184
Proofing, soft, 187–189
PSB File Compatibility,
　　231–234
PSD files, 153
Pulling in selections, 74
Punctuation, 151, 153
Puppies, organizing, 197

Q

Quality, image, maintaining,
　　109–110
QuarkXPress, 236
Quick Mask, 70–72, 133, 150
Quick Reference card, 11
Quotation marks, 151

R

RAM, 28, 139
Ranges, text, selecting, 146
Rasterizing
　shapes, 179
　text, 144, 153
Ratio, aspect, 62–63
Readers, card, 33
Real World
　Adobe Illustrator CS2, 177
　Creative Suite, 152
　Photoshop, 6
Red images, 70
Reduce Noise filter, 95, 109–
　　110, 119
Reducing file size, 25–26. *See
　　also* Compressing images
Relative image size, 57
Removing
　backgrounds, 68–69,
　　236–237
　keywords, 203
Renaming
　files, 26–27
　type layers, 153
Resampling, resolution, 55–56
Reselecting, 71

Reset button, Camera Raw, 41
Resizing
　image batches, 121–122
　images, 57
　type, 145
　windows, 16
Resolution
　Bicubic, 56
　Camera Raw, 38
　Canvas Size, 57
　correcting low, 114
　cropping, 60–61
　DVDs, 242
　effective, 52–53, 54–55
　files, 52, 53–54
　Fit Image, 57
　image, 218
　image batches, 57
　Image Size, 57
　images, 52–57
　monitor, 10, 53
　print size, 19–20
　resampling, 55–56
　sampling, 52
　screen shots, 222–224
Restoration, scanning, 43
Restoring cropped images, 58
Reusing filters, 161
RGB, converting to CMYK,
　　190–191
Roman Hanging Punctuation,
　　151
Rotating selection marquee, 74
Rules, layers, 132
Russellbrown.com, 211

S

Samples per inch (spi), 56
Sampling colors, 171
Sampling resolution, 52, 55–56
Saturation, 38, 103
Save As option, 235, 241
Save button, Camera Raw,
　　40–41
Saving
　adjustment layers, 113
　Bridge locations, 199
　Bridge workspaces,
　　201–202
　color-to-grayscale
　　conversion, 174
　document copies, 235–236
　embedding profiles, 193
　file searches, 208–209
　history, 114–115
　multiple crops, 78
　multiple variations,
　　232–233
　palette arrangements, 13
　paths, 178
　Quick Masks, 71–72
　tool settings, 22–23
　unavailable file formats,
　　234–235

Scaling selection marquee, 74
Scanning
    batch, 42–44
    defect-removal during,
        94–95
    descreening, 47–48
    line art, 45–46
    negatives, 44–45, 48
    overview, 42
    sampling resolution, 52
Scratch Sizes, 28
Scratches, 90–91, 94–95
Screen. *See also* Monitor
    blending mode, 102
    display, type, 149–150
    halftone, 161–162
    modes, 16–17
    shots, 34
    shots, printing, 222–224
Scripts, 211
Scroll bars, 14
Scrolling, laptops, 91
Sculpting selections, 70
Searching files, 208–210
Selecting
    area, 75
    backgrounds, 68–69
    blurring, 75–76
    border, 76
    channels, 67–68, 69, 70–73
    color, 65–66
    converting paths, 77
    distorting, 74
    feathering, 75–76
    Lasso, 64
    layer masks, 72–73
    layers, 128–129
    line, 75
    Magnetic Lasso, 64–65
    masking, 70–73
    paths, 177
    Pen tool, 77
    Polygon Lasso, 65
    pulling in, 74
    Quick Mask, 70–72
    rotating, 74
    saving multiple crops, 78
    scaling, 74
    smoothing, 67
    spreading out, 74
    text ranges, 146
    text shapes, 150
    Threshold, 66–67
    tone, 65–66
    transferring between
        documents, 76
Sending slide shows, 244
Separating colors, 170–171
Sepia tone, 169
Sets
    brushes, 158
    keyword, 203
Settings, monitor, color,
    184–188

Shadows
    adjustment layers, 112
    Camera Raw, 37
    Curves dialog box, 98–99
    drop, 160
    enhancing, 100–101
    print, 191
Shapes
    duplicating, 84
    Pen tool, 176–177
    selecting, 177
    text, selecting, 150
Sharpening
    Camera Raw, 36
    digital camera noise,
        118–119
    Smart Sharpen, 117–119
    Unsharp Mask, 116–117
Shifts, color, 109
Shortcuts
    adding, 123
    adjusting numbers, 23–24
    Batch command, 122
    blending modes, 101
    commiting text changes,
        146–147
    editing, 123
    function keys, 123
    last-used filter, 161
    modifier keys, 123
    overview, 10–11
    tools, 21–22
    view, 90
Showing
    layers, 130
    palettes, 13
    tool tips, 5–6
Shrinking test prints, 221
Shutterfly, 237
Silver-based black-and-white
    film, 48
Simulating
    infrared, 172–173
    photo filters, 171
Size
    Camera Raw images, 38
    Canvas Size, 57, 61
    cursors, 23
    document, 14
    Fit Image, 57
    Image Size, 57
    print, 19–20
    resampling resolution,
        55–56
Slices, 239–240
Slide shows, 242–244
Slow computer, 28. *See also*
    Disk space
Smart
    Guides, 132
    Objects, 84–86, 152,
        179–180
    Sharpen, 117–119
Smoothing
    selections, 67
    type, 149

Snapping
    crop tool, 58
    layer guides, 133
    palettes, 15
Soft edge, brushes, 158
Soft Light blending mode, 103
Soft-proofing, 187–189
Softening mask edges, 136
Software, scanning, 42–44
Space menu, 38
Spacing
    paragraphs, 153
    type, 149–150
Speed
    Bridge, 198
    computer, 28
Spherize, 164
Spi (samples per inch), 56
Spot Healing Brush, 104
Spotlight, 210
Spots, dust, 91
Spreading out selections, 74
sRGB, 192–193
Star Wars, 164
Status bar, document window,
    14
Step-and repeat layouts, 84–86
Storing
    adjustment layers, 113
    fonts, 154
    multiple variations,
        232–233
Straightening
    images, 78–82
    Measure tool, 115–116
Stroking type outlines,
    148–149
Styles, text, 148
Stylus, 159
Sub-paths, 179
Swatches palette, 17
Synchronizing
    color, 187
    multiple windows, 18
System Layout, 149–150

T

Tablets, graphic, 159–160
Templates, Metadata, 205–207
Test prints, 221, 223
Text. *See also* Fonts; Type
    color, 148–149
    committing changes,
        146–147
    headlines, 153
    hyphenation, 153
    importing, 145
    justification, 153
    kerning, 152
    leading, 152
    moving between
        documents, 146

paths, 150–151
punctuation, 151, 153
selecting ranges, 146
selecting shapes, 150
spacing, 152–153
styles, 148
tracking, 152
warping, 151–152
wrapping, 151–152
Textures, 162–163
Threshold, selecting by, 66–67
Thumbnails, building speed, 198
TIFFs, 153
Tiling windows, 15, 201–202
Tone
    correction, 90
    Curves dialog box, 98–99
    enhancing, 100–101
    selecting by, 65–66
Tools
    cursors, 23
    options bar, 22
    palette, 4
    Presets palette, 22–23
    saving settings, 22–23
    shortcut keys, 21–22
    showing tips, 5–6
Tracing, 229
Tracking, type, 152
Transferring selections
    between documents, 76
Transforming
    images, 78–83
    selections, 74
Transparent
    brush strokes, 159
    layers, 133–134
Trapezoids, 164
Trimming images, 63
Tritone, 170
Tweens Animation Frames, 238
Type. *See also* Fonts
    anti-aliasing, 149
    area, 144
    bitmaps, 144, 153
    clipping mask, 150
    color, 148–149
    committing changes, 146–147
    defaults, 146
    editing, 144–147
    font folders, 154
    handles, 145
    headlines, 153
    hyphenation, 153
    importing, 145
    justification, 153
    kerning, 152
    leading, 152
    masks, 150
    mass formatting, 148
    moving between
        documents, 146

paths, 150–151
point, 144
previewing, 147
punctuation, 153
resizing, 145
selecting ranges, 146
smoothing, 149
spacing, 149–150, 152–153
stroking outlines, 148–149
tracking, 152
vector, 144, 153
website display, 149–150
wrapping, 151–152
Typefaces. *See* Fonts

U

UI font size, 10
Undo, 71, 111
Ungrouping palettes, 12–13
Units of measure, 56
Unsharp Mask, 116–117
Update button, Camera Raw, 41
Upgrading
    keyboard shortcuts, 10–11
    menus, 11–12
    migrating, 7–9
    monitor resolution, 10
User interface font size, 10

V

Vanishing Point filter, 166–168
Vector
    mask, 133, 134
    objects, 84, 179–180
    Smart Objects, 179–180
    type, 144, 153
Version Cue, 4
Vertical
    guides, 25
    scrolling, 14
    Type Mask, 150
Video
    capture, 63
    color, 184–185
View
    Actual Pixels, 90–91
    channels, 69
    documents, multiple, 18
    histograms, 91–92
    magnification, 4
    print size, 19–20
    shortcuts, 90
    speed, Bridge, 198
Visual Infinity, 95
Vivid Light blending mode, 103

W

Warping
    images, 165
    text, 151–152
Waving flag, 164–165
Websites. *See also* Internet
    Adobe Studio, 6
    animated graphics, 238–239
    color, 184–185
    converting color spaces, 192–193
    graphics edges, 238
    HTML gallery, 240–241
    inksupply.com, 219
    newscodes.org, 205
    ofoto.com, 237
    Photoshop, 6
    piezography.com, 219
    preserving metadata, 241
    russellbrown.com, 211
    sharpening for, 119
    slices, 239–240
    type display, 149–150
    Web-safe color, 238
Werner, Steve, 152
Windows
    background color, 17
    cascading, Bridge, 201–202
    document, 4, 14
    multiple, Bridge, 200–202
    organizing multiple, 15–16
    synchronizing multiple, 18
    tiling, Bridge, 201–202
    zooming, 16
Word spacing, 152–153
Work area overview, 4–5
Workspaces
    Bridge, 201–202
    migrating, 9
    palettle arrangements, 12–13
Wrapping
    text, 151–152
    type, 144

X, Y, Z

XML Metadata templates, 206–207
XMP files, 41
Zooming
    Actual Pixels, 90–91
    documents, multiple views, 18
    windows, 16

Check Out These Other David Blatner Books from Peachpit.com

Colophon

The body of this book is set in in
Adobe Warnock Pro Regular and Frutiger LT Std
Bold Condensed; heads are set in Warnock Pro
Light Display and Frutiger LT Std Black Condensed.

Text was prepared in Microsoft Word and laid
out using Adobe InDesign CS2. We used a Xerox
Phaser 8850 for proofing pages.

The book was printed at Courier Kendallville
on a Lithoman IV, on 60 lb. Influence Matte. The
book cover was printed on 12pt C1S cover with
matte film lamination.